WHY DOES SCHIZOPHRENIA DEVELOP AT LATE ADOLESCENCE?
A Cognitive-Developmental Approach to Psychosis

WHY DOES SCHIZOPHRENIA DEVELOP AT LATE ADOLESCENCE?
A Cognitive-Developmental Approach to Psychosis

Chris Harrop

and

Peter Trower

School of Psychology, University of Birmingham, UK

WILEY

Other Wiley Editorial Offices

John Wiley & Sons Inc., 111 River Street, Hoboken, NJ 07030, USA

Jossey-Bass, 989 Market Street, San Francisco, CA 94103-1741, USA

Wiley-VCH Verlag GmbH, Pappellaee 3, D-69469 Weinheim, Germany

John Wiley & Sons Australia Ltd, 33 Park Road, Milton, Queensland, 4064, Australia

John Wiley & Sons (Asia) Pte Ltd, 2 Clementi Loop #02-01, Jin Xing Distripark,
Singapore 129809

John Wiley & Sons Canada Ltd, 22 Worcester Road, Etobicoke, Ontario, Canada, M9W 1L1

Wiley also publishes its books in a variety of electronic formats. Some content that
appears in print may not be available in electronic books.

Library of Congress Cataloging-in-Publication Data
  Harrop, Chris.
    Why does schizophrenia develop at late adolescence? : a cognitive-
    developmental approach to psychosis / Chris Harrop and Peter Trower.
      p. cm.
    Includes bibliographical references and index.
    ISBN 0-470-84877-4 (alk. paper) – ISBN 0-470-84878-2 (alk. paper)
    1. Schizophrenia–Etiology.   2. Shizophrenia in adolescence.   3. Psychoses in
    adolescence.   4. Developmental disabilities.   I. Trower, Peter, 1938–   II. Title.

    RC514.H334 2003
    616.89′82071–dc21
                                                                        2003057154

British Library Cataloguing in Publication Data
A catalogue record for this book is available from the British Library

ISBN 0-470-84877-4 (hbk)
ISBN 0-470-84878-2 (pbk)

Typeset in 10/12pt Palatino by Dobbie Typesetting Limited, Tavistock, Devon
Printed and bound in Great Britain by TJ International Ltd, Padstow, Cornwall
This book is printed on acid-free paper responsibly manufactured from sustainable
forestry in which at least two trees are planted for each one used for paper production.

DEDICATION

I want to dedicate this book to two of the teachers who inspired me at school: David Dwyer and Randall Lewton; also to Garth, Pat and Sarah Harrop, to Katie and Brenda, and Freeda Sangra.

Chris Harrop

To my daughter Stephanie, and in memory of Doris, my Mother.

Peter Trower

TABLE OF CONTENTS

ABOUT THE AUTHORS

Chris Harrop completed his PhD at the University of Birmingham. Subsequently, he has also completed his Clinical Training Doctorate at the University of Birmingham, and is now a lecturer in the School of Psychology there, as well as a Practising Clinical Psychologist.

Peter Trower completed his clinical training at Leeds University and his PhD by published work at Bristol University, following a programme of research with Michael Argyle on social-skills training in the 1970s. He is a senior lecturer in the School of Psychology, at the University of Birmingham, and a Consultant Clinical Psychologist. He is a Fellow of the British Psychological Society and an Associate Fellow of the Albert Ellis Institute for Rational Emotive Behaviour Therapy in New York. He has published a number of books and articles on social-skills training, cognitive behaviour therapy and self-construction theory.

ACKNOWLEDGEMENTS

Chapter 2 has been adapted from Harrop, C., Trower, P. & Mitchell, I.J. (1996) Does the biology go around the symptoms? A Copernican shift in schizophrenia paradigms. *Clinical Psychology Review* **16**, 641–654. Reproduced by permission of Elsevier Science.

Figure 2.1 has been adapted from H. F. Jackson (1990) Are there biological markers for schizophrenia? In: Bentall, R. P. (Ed) (1990) *Reconstructing schizophrenia*. London: Routledge. Reproduced by permission of Thomson publishing services for Taylor and Francis Group, London.

Chapter 3 has been adapted from Harrop, C. & Trower, P. (2001) Why does schizophrenia develop at late adolescence? *Clinical Psychology Review* 21, 241–265. Reproduced by permission of Elsevier Science.

Figure 3.1 is reproduced from Hafner *et al.* (1993) The influence of age and sex on the onset and cause of schizophrenia. *British Journal of Psychiatry* **162**, 80–87. Reproduced by permission of the Royal College of Psychiatrists.

Table 3.1 is reproduced from McGorry, P.D., McFarlane, C. & Patton, C.G. *et al.* (1995) The prevalence of prodromal features of schizophrenia in adolescence: a preliminary survey. *Acta Psychiatrica Scandinavica* **92**, 241–249. Reproduced by permission of Blackwell Publishing.

The Self and Other Scale in Appendix 1 is reproduced from Dexter-Smith, S., Trower, P., Oyebode, J. & Dagnan, D. (in press) The Self and Other Scale. *Journal of Rational-Emotive and Cognitive-Behavior Therapy*. Reproduced by permission of Kluwer Academic/Plenum Publishers, New York.

Quotes from Jean-Paul Sartre's *Being and Nothingness* reproduced by permission of Thomson publishing services for Taylor and Francis Group, London, for worldwide rights excluding the US and Canada. US and Canada rights by permission The Philosophical Library of New York.

Many thanks to Dr. Paul Patterson for his comments on an earlier draft of this manuscript.

INTRODUCTION

MYTH OR MADNESS?

Schizophrenia, insanity, nervous breakdown – whatever the labels, these are some of the most distressing and dramatic experiences of the human condition. The notion of "madness" has occupied great thinkers throughout history. Shakespeare, for example, wrote often about different forms of "madness". Since the turn of the last century, this "madness", or schizophrenia, has been studied more methodically, and much more is known about it. However, the picture remains confusing and unclear.

In this book we develop an alternative approach to the established models which we believe helps clarify some of the core issues.

WHAT IS SCHIZOPHRENIA?

But first of all, we need to ask what exactly we are talking about. In truth, many of these terms – madness, breakdown, insanity – are lay terms which, if they are referring to a serious condition probably *mean* schizophrenia. But what is schizophrenia? Who are these "mad people"? We are talking about real people, people you probably know.

John

Meet Mr and Mrs Jones. They were worried sick about their 19-year-old son, John. He was a bit of a star – he was really popular with his numerous friends, he got good grades without much apparent effort, he was a natural sportsman. But even before the end of school, his parents had started to notice that he had begun acting quite differently. He seemed to be more withdrawn, often quite touchy, and he looked tired and strained. After he left school and got a job, the changes in his personality began to seem more like a Jekyll and Hyde transformation. One day John got really upset with his Dad and was accusing him of spying on him! This was so out of character and such a worrying development for John that his parents thought it safest to just check with their GP. The GP tried to reassure them it would all blow over; he said it was just adolescence – a hiccough – John would grow out of it. Mr and Mrs Jones weren't particularly happy with that, and would have preferred specialist help, but agreed, uneasily, to sit tight.

Then it all got worse. John was found wandering around in the middle of the night, shouting barely coherent things at passers-by. One of the few themes that could be made out in his rantings was that voices had been telling him that other people were spying on him. Next thing he was brought home by the police, and a psychiatrist visited to interview John. Mr and Mrs Jones were told that John had schizophrenia. They were told he needed to be put into hospital, against his will if necessary. Very reluctantly, Mr and Mrs Jones agreed that he should go. John was absolutely furious. He refused to go, and in the end the police were called and they escorted poor John off to hospital. Once there John got even more angry – to him it was like being put in prison without charge. From the staff point of view, they had no choice but to physically restrain John and give him an injection of a major tranquilizer to calm him down. From John's point of view, several aggressive male nurses jumped him, sat on him and "stabbed" him with a needle; John, the former star, felt he was being treated worse than a criminal. From his point of view, his parents had betrayed him, and the staff and the doctor were in league with them. John felt he had no-one in the world on his side, and it felt like the end of the world. Meanwhile, his parents were in a torment of worry, feeling helpless and hopeless. They could make little sense of what had happened; one doctor came and explained that John had schizophrenia, which was a brain disorder and he would probably need to take medication for the rest of his life (which is by no means the scientific consensus, as we will see later). For the time being staff felt they could do little more than restrain John, keep him under constant observation, and stop him from leaving the ward.

A Global Experience – Interesting Statistics

Such a story is familiar to mental-health service staff throughout the country, and throughout the Western world. The details vary, but a similar scenario seems to repeat itself time and again. The majority are young men [the ratio is usually six male to one female (Häfner et al., 1993a)]. These men are typically in their late teens or early twenties, and are behaving in ways seen as increasingly bizarre and strange. Their behaviour develops into a crisis and ends up with them being admitted into hospital, traumatic for everyone concerned.

This picture isn't just our anecdotal impression gained from working in our local mental-health service. No less an authority than the World Health

Organisation has confirmed that similar cases occur with roughly the same frequency around the world, from rural India to inner-city Australia (Sartorius *et al.*, 1986). There are large numbers of people involved as well: about 45 million people worldwide have been estimated to have a diagnosis of schizophrenia (see Figure 1). Depending on where we live, over the course of our lifetimes, we have (statistically) a 0.4–1.9 per cent risk of having a schizophrenic episode (Jablensky, 1997). For every 1000 people in the country at the moment, between 2 and 7 will have schizophrenia ("prevalence"). The cost of such large numbers of people needing help is huge; it has been estimated that between 0.5 and 1.4 per cent of the Gross National Product of Westernised countries goes on mental-health services. For example, at any one time, around half of all NHS beds in Britain are allocated to those with mental-health problems (McGuire, 1991).

And the problem doesn't end with diagnosis and hospitalisation. The outlook for these young men and women and their families is often a bleak one. After discharge from hospital, a majority of them will become depressed some weeks or months later. A number will attempt suicide, and a proportion will succeed. Many will end up back in hospital, for a second or third time. In some cases, people will have many readmissions. Some people grow into their 30s and 40s dependent on mental-health services, living marginalised lives without employment, without a partner or family of their own, living relatively joyless and impoverished lives.

In John's case, things seemed initially to be looking up. After a while, the staff felt his symptoms had improved and the medication seemed to be "controlling" the illness; John was discharged. From John's view, he was being let out of prison. He felt beaten and humiliated, stigmatised and robbed of his very sense of self-worth. He hated the effect the medication had on him – it made him feel like a zombie – but he felt threatened that he would be sectioned again if he didn't take it. In a rare moment of optimism John tried to get his old job back, but he was turned down – he found his

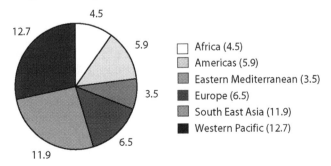

Figure 1 Estimated Numbers of People Worldwide with Schizophrenia (in millions). *Source:* from *World Health Report 2001: Mental Health.* World Health Organisation, Geneva

mental-health record was the reason. He became more withdrawn from his former friends – he felt they saw him as a "nutter" now. He got more and more depressed, and as he got more depressed he became more paranoid. John soon had another crisis, and another compulsory hospital admission . . .

All the evidence indicates that this nightmare scenario is as serious a problem in the 21st century as it was in Shakespeare's day.

We urgently need to ask some questions:

- What is happening to these young people?

- Why such *young* people?

- Why such a devastating condition as *schizophrenia*?

- Is adolescence a time of particular vulnerability to schizophrenia? If so, what is it about adolescence that makes it so?

- What are we doing about it, and perhaps more importantly, what are we *not* doing about it?

- What can the individual do to help him/herself?

- What can the family (and other carers) do?

- What are the mental-health professionals (psychiatrists, social workers, nurses, occupational therapists, psychologists and others), other professionals, lay people, society at large, doing about it?

- Is there anything else that research suggests might help?

This book addresses most of these important questions.

WHO IS THIS BOOK FOR?

Traditionally, books like this are written to be read solely by professionals. We wanted this book to be different. We wanted it to be open and accessible to everyone with a stake in dealing with the condition, the people who experience schizophrenia at a personal and day-to-day level – including those who have had episodes of schizophrenia themselves, and their relatives. This stems from a concern that all the various stakeholders are reading different literature, often with widely differing perspectives. It also comes from a desire to ground the book in the lives of the people involved, which are often discussed in the professional literature in a way that can seem remote and dehumanised to non-professionals. We quite like the idea of the people personally involved being able to read the same books as the professionals, so that what is said and done is kept honest and transparent to everyone. This approach also helped us to keep things relevant, as we tried to imagine what these young people and those closest to them would want to know, given what they might be experiencing.

HOW TO USE THIS BOOK

Approaching the issue from the perspective that young people and their families will also be reading the book, what is the first question they usually want to ask? The first question is always: *What is happening to me/my son/ daughter/friend or partner? What is this "schizophrenia"?*

We address this question in Section One of this book.

Unfortunately the answer varies according to whom we ask, as we see in Chapter 1: we briefly review the differing perspectives on schizophrenia held by various stakeholders, and find that one explanation seems to dominate all others – namely that schizophrenia is a biological illness.

In Chapter 2 we address the next question: *Who is right?*

We show that 100 years of research has failed to satisfactorily explain the mystery of schizophrenia, partly, we argue, because researchers have been looking at the problem from too narrow a perspective. We make our case for an alternative perspective, and one that has been largely dismissed by medical researchers until recently.

We then move on to the main question of the book, which is (of course) closely linked to the "What is it?" question. We ask: *Why does "schizophrenia" develop in late adolescence?*

This is the topic for Chapter 3. Is adolescence a special period of vulnerability, and if so why? We show a remarkable and puzzling finding – that a large minority of adolescents go through an apparently psychotic-like period. We take a close look at the milestones of adolescence and the stresses and turmoil that these milestones can bring. Out of this analysis we draw out the beginning of a psychological, developmental explanation for psychotic breakdown.

In Section Two we take this further to suggest that a psychotic breakdown in adolescence and early adulthood is often, if not usually, a sign that the person has not developed a healthy sense of self. We argue that the self is not something we simply have but rather something we have to construct, and problems in this self-construction process in adolescence contribute to psychosis.

In Section Three we illustrate how this happens using detailed accounts from a number of cases from our own research.

Finally, in Section Four, we ask: *What can be done about it?* Here we outline our own therapeutic approach, both to work on the crucial developmental processes we have mentioned, and also to focus on techniques to help with problems in self-construction.

Where Should I Start?

For the Lay Person

If you are a lay person – perhaps you know or are related to someone experiencing psychosis or who has had a personal experience – you may want to start with an explanation of the psychiatric system; for this you should read Section One first. This section should help you understand the various, often conflicting, attitudes which are held by different professionals can be so confusing. It should also help you decide your own position, because it compares and contrasts the models somewhat. Finally, in Chapter 3, we take a new path, with some original ideas about the adolescence angle.

If you are interested in questions like "What is the self?" and want to try some interesting thought experiments that will give you a working knowledge of a long and venerable debate on the nature of the self, try Section Two. This section focuses on the implications of this debate for psychosis, particularly ways in which it can help us make sense of some of the more seemingly-incomprehensible experiences of psychosis.

If you want a taste of how this intellectual debate works in practice, Section Three contains a lot of case material from the lives of people who have had a psychosis, illustrating these ideas in real life (particularly Chapters 13 and 14). Many of the situations described here will seem very familiar to our readers, we are sure.

Finally, Section Four discusses what these ideas mean in practice for people with a psychosis, and what they can do to help themselves. This section builds on the ideas from the rest of the book, but should be accessible on their own, for those impatient to get to practicalities.

For Professionals

If you are a professional working in the field, Chapter 1 might feel familiar, as it describes for the layperson the viewpoints of the various interested mental-health professionals. If you want to compare and contrast these positions, then Chapter 2 does this. If you would like a new approach that focuses on the adolescence angle, this is given in Chapter 3.

For those professionals who have long thought that there is something about the self that is fundamentally important (and also for those who have never seriously considered this possibility before), Section Two contains a simplified history of this most famous and crucial topic. We argue that the topic of "the self" is vital to a complete understanding of psychosis. Much of this section is written in an experiential way that should make the topic come alive, emphasising its personal relevance.

For those professionals who like to keep things practical, and who want to see how this debate can help us understand the real lives of people who have had a psychosis, Section Three contains a lot of case-study material. Many, if not most, of these situations will feel familiar to mental-health professionals, although the section will offer a fresh perspective and understanding of these. The theoretical themes of the book up to this point really come alive when you read about them in real-life situations. In a sense, these chapters are the heart of the book.

Finally, those professionals who want to see the practical benefit of these ideas can read Section Four; this section focuses on the practical implications for therapy and self-help that follow from the theories in the rest of the book.

Whatever angle or experience you come to this book from, we hope it will provoke fresh thinking and new, more optimistic perspectives/ways of coping – perhaps in your work, or in your life.

SECTION ONE

WHAT *IS* THIS SCHIZOPHRENIA?

People often ask: What *is* this schizophrenia thing? Is it an illness, a split personality, or is it a myth? They would get a different answer depending on whom they ask. In the first chapter (Chapter 1) of this section we paint in the landscape of understandings of schizophrenia, illustrating what the various professionals believe about schizophrenia. To contrast these views, and show how they differ from each other, we also try to give a flavour of the divergences between each group of thought, and the astonished annoyance with which these various groups often regard each other. Most of these views are not views that we hold ourselves – they reflect the more extreme positions that some colleagues take. We also clarify the difference in terminology between "schizophrenia" and "psychosis".

This question, "What is it?", and the questions that follow from it are not just intellectual musings: the answers are extremely important because they have enormous consequences for large groups of people; for example, they have implications for treatment – drugs, hospitalisation, how people involved are regarded by professionals, society. Many people's lives (as we have said, around 1–2% of the population) are played out against this backdrop and affected in enormous ways by the picture painted within these debates.

Having painted this hazy, confusing landscape, we try to produce a clearer picture in the next chapter (Chapter 2), with some of our own arguments. One of the most important issues to be resolved is the relationship between the biological and the psychological/social side of psychosis. If, after all, schizophrenia is primarily biological then any psychological approach is just (to mix a metaphor) bandaging and washing – useful perhaps, but nothing like as important as the right drugs or surgery.

Finally, in Chapter 3 we "start proper" our look at the psychology of schizophrenia, to find a better understanding of it. Our starting point is the fact that schizophrenia generally develops in late adolescence, a fact that has been strikingly overlooked by the literature until very recently. Chapter 4 elaborates on how the link between the themes developed in Chapter 3 and psychosis might come about.

CHAPTER 1

SCHIZOPHRENIA: WHAT IS IT?

What *is* schizophrenia? What causes it?

One hundred years since schizophrenia was supposedly "discovered", many would still argue that we still don't know.

Same Question, Different Answers

We should say straightaway that the question "What is schizophrenia?" is misleading, because what people are usually implicitly asking is "What causes it?" So, for example, a psychiatrist will typically say it is an illness, but what he is really saying is that "the presentation (of symptoms and so on) is caused by an underlying illness (which is not itself seen)".

Our approach to the question is to take the reader on an imaginary walk around an imaginary psychiatric hospital to talk to a number of imaginary people – professionals, patients and relatives. This story will enable us to convey the diversity of views that exist.

As we have said, if you were to walk into a psychiatric hospital near you and ask people you met, "What is schizophrenia?" you would very likely get different answers depending on who you talked to. Many people would probably say "That's a good question, I've often wondered that myself". If you were to ask them whether schizophrenia always develops in late adolescence, some might say: "I'm not sure it does because I've met many people who develop psychotic behaviours later in life, for example, in their fifties." They would be right to point this out. However, as we'll show later (Chapter 3), between 50 and 80 per cent of people who develop schizophrenia do so in late adolescence/early adulthood. (Sartorius *et al.*, 1986). In this book we are generally writing about that 50 to 80 per cent.

Different Perspectives, Different Emphases

A psychiatrist in the hospital gives you a different point of view: "Schizophrenic symptoms are first seen in late adolescence but the critical cause happens much earlier. It is due to complications with pregnancy and birth in people who are vulnerable to that sort of thing anyway. It just happens that these problems aren't seen until late adolescence. Schizophrenic symptoms are due to an imbalance of brain chemicals."

He continues: "As far as I'm concerned, schizophrenia is a brain disease, and generally what is most important for my patients is that they get medication. The newer anti-psychotic medications nowadays are very effective, anyway (as were the old neuroleptics). The newer meds have fewer side-effects, even if they are remarkably expensive."

Perhaps he goes on to assure you . . .

". . . and they do work. Just as well; I'm legally responsible for my patients and if something goes wrong, as they can do very rarely, if they kill themselves or someone else I'm in big trouble. I need something I can rely on. I also need tangible things; medical insurance companies in particular need to know exactly what illness people have, and exactly what treatment will work best. They'll not be very impressed if I say I'm not really sure, they'll go to someone who *is* sure. Medical insurance needs medical precision, medical details, treatments proven to work on huge samples."

If this psychiatrist was one of the more extreme (and out of date) of the profession, he might say:

"One thing that doesn't make a schizophrenic calmer is talking to them about their symptoms. That's the worst thing you can do. Of course you talk to them with some sympathy, about how they feel, how their meds are working, but the more psychotic things patients say are just meaningless speech, they don't mean anything. Listening to them is like listening to the tune a piano makes as you hit its innards with a lump hammer, or douse it with petrol and fry it. There are no patterns there, no hidden meanings. Some mental-health professionals annoy me because they try to collude with patients, talk to them as if people really are out to get them, or they really do hear Jesus's voice, or whatever. And they call this psychological therapy! It just gets patients agitated, makes them worse, and makes them stop taking their medication. You can have someone perfectly stable on their meds, and next thing one of these individuals starts trying to be their best friend. And then as they've found an audience for it, the patient gets more psychotic than ever. So the family gets agitated, and the nurses get agitated and I get agitated because they look like they might do something silly and I have to raise the medication dosage again to control the brain chemicals this individual has stirred up and I have to look like the big bad wolf, sectioning and bullying everyone. And then this 'colleague' gets to look all disapproving of me, and now the patient distrusts me and hates me.

"I would stop some of these so-called 'colleagues' getting near schizophrenics, while they are unwell, they can be a real liability. They stir up emotions and run the risk of making them a lot worse. Some so-called therapists are always looking for hidden meanings, magic that just isn't there. These therapists don't understand about the medical issues involved. Schizophrenia has always been treated by medical people, since it was first recognised at the start of the last century. We know so much more now, all the research we've done since then, that we can finally put to rest any ideas that it isn't biological. Those myths are now completely disproved. What some of these therapists think is utterly irrelevant.

"I'm a medically-trained doctor and the medical approach is the most relevant one for schizophrenia. Fair enough some conditions have grown to be seen as more psychological – depression, anxiety, eating disorders – but schizophrenia is a different beast altogether. People who have it are so fundamentally different; it just has to be biological."

Perhaps this psychiatrist is holding some scientific psychiatry journals, its pages full of glossy adverts from pharmaceutical companies, showing smiling, attractive, healthy and confident-looking people with the tag-line *I'm happy because I'm taking drug X.*

Alongside the psychiatrist happens to be a representative from the drug company . . .

"I'm in the hospital today to put the finishing touches to the free meal and promotional gifts scheduled for this week. We often put on remarkably good lunches (high quality, I'm sure everyone here will agree), and give away a remarkable amount of pens, post-its, mugs, gadgets, clocks and perhaps trips to major sporting events. We also sponsor schizophrenia conferences, at some cost. I don't think we get as much control over the conferences as we should do, considering that we bankroll them. We do sponsor some conferences that are more psychological, but we get to have a few speakers that are more pro-medication if we sponsor. Of course, we are a commercial outfit, so we are keen to sell our product, but I like to think we also provide a public service, helping people in distress. We bend over backwards to provide financial help for new drug-trials, trying to prove these drugs work. And without absolute rigorous proof they work, treatments wouldn't be provided by insurance-based schemes. It is worth our while helping, though; the market for psychiatric drugs is worth many billions worldwide."

The drug rep wanders off, whistling to herself, and you move on.

Another psychiatrist, this one a bit older and wearing sandals, stops you. This person seems to have a very different story to tell, and calls you to one side, into an office, whispering:

"We sussed a lot of this out in the sixties. That was a great time, everyone throwing off their chains and rebelling against the constraints of society. We used to say 'psychosis is just a trip, like acid; you had to let yourself be open to this sort of higher plane. If you went with your psychosis it would take you to where you needed to be'."

The older man pauses, frowns and looks into the middle distance . . .

"Even if where you needed to be was writing mysterious messages on the walls in your own shit . . . (see Barnes & Burke, 1973; Reed, 1977). We used to say 'there's no such thing as mental illness, it's a complete myth, a delusion that society holds.' These are life issues brought on by a society that just doesn't work (see Szasz, 1974, 1987).

"What causes schizophrenia? I'll tell you: the problems are with the pressures society puts on us. In a strange way, people with a psychosis might be seen as very sane. You might even wonder if we are the ones who are mad, putting up with all this rat-race and having these silly pretensions! We all race around like everything is so important, but we forget the important things, the soul, the meaning. And I'll tell you what else: families are generally the problem. Even in the best of families you get all these mixed messages: 'Be successful – but not more successful than me'; 'Be independent – but don't make me feel redundant'. The families of people with schizophrenia are more disturbed than the patients. You should see the way some of my patients' parents act towards them. Families cause schizophrenia."

What About the Family?

The rebelliousness of this older man might appeal to you. Leaving their office, to your horror, you bump into some family members of people with a psychosis who appear to have overheard the man's last comment. They seem to you a varied and interesting group. In fact, a typical cross-section of society's parents, all classes (although perhaps slightly more working-class parents). One of them regards you with a sceptical eye, and referring to the psychiatrist's comments says:

"We're well aware that certain people blame us for our children's problems. Many of us do in fact blame ourselves. I suppose it is only natural for us parents to want to protect our children from harm; I know I just wish there was something I could do to help. By the same token, it is only natural for us to feel it is some sort of failure on our part if our children are chronically unhappy. I do worry that I should be more sympathetic to my son's condition, but he drives me up the wall. He shouts at his mother and me all the time, never washes, his room stinks, he can't keep a job, he talks rubbish, he seems really arrogant and condescending. I'm actually scared of him, my wife doesn't dare be alone with him; she had to give up her job because she couldn't cope with it all. He's always shouting at us to give him lifts, buy him things. Our lives would be so much better if he wasn't living at home. *And that man blames us? Maybe he should try living with our son before pronouncing on us!"*

Another says:

"Our daughter isn't much trouble, but she just looks so unhappy, I just wish there was something we could do to help. She isn't going out, having fun, meeting boys or enjoying herself at all, and it's such a shame. She just stays at home all the time, murmuring to herself in her room. When she does go out I worry about someone taking advantage of her. I also worry what will happen to her after I'm dead when there's no-one to look after her – where will she live? How will she cope? She certainly couldn't look after herself at the moment."

Another one says:

"It can't be our fault because it's a biological condition. My son's brain chemicals are the things going wrong somehow. And that means we can help because the doctors say his medication should help and we can help make sure he takes his medication. If psychosis wasn't biological, it would be our fault."

They argue amongst themselves about whether this is true, and whether these various premises are logically connected.

Can Complementary Skills Mean Different Agendas?

A psychologist is passing by who seems to have yet another story to tell . . .

"People with psychosis are the victims of society. These are the ones who have fallen by the wayside. Most of them just have phenomenally low self-esteem, which they hide by acting as if they think they're really great. You can't help wondering what their lives have been like.

"We call the people we work with 'clients' or 'services users' to get away from the word 'patient' – that word implies too much that they are medically ill in the traditional sense; it also makes people feel quite down-rank and powerless. I work with clients on a weekly basis, usually for around 10–20 sessions or perhaps longer. There isn't anything like enough psychologists, so only a lucky few clients get to meet with one of us. I talk with them, hopefully make them feel valued and listened to, help them understand the way their mind works. I try to build a client's strength up but there are barriers to this – maybe someone in the street hassles them, or perhaps someone in the Jobcentre is a bit too firm with them and they can get really unhappy and paranoid again, be set back for months. Alternatively, the psychiatrist occasionally puts them on a new drug, and then my client is too much of a zombie to speak and they can't remember anything we do.

"On the whole, psychiatrists only see clients for 10 minutes every month, and then tell everyone else who works with them day-in and day-out how that person should be treated. If the client gets better the psychiatrist sees it as due to the medication rather than my psychologising or the nurses' great skill in handling them. If clients get worse it is down to my unsettling them or the nurses' lack of care."

One of the few professionals you haven't yet met is the Community Psychiatric Nurse mentioned by the psychologist. You manage to track one of these down so as to hear her piece. She looks tired:

"I have quite a large caseload of people with a psychosis I look after, more than I feel I can safely manage because we are short-staffed at the moment. It is a round-the-clock job; I end up working a lot of weekends and evenings. I give them their medications and keep an eye on how well they are doing. I also help them with benefits, housing issues, other self-care issues, although these are often things a social worker does for them. Most of my clients are in the community, although from time to time they might become unwell and they might be in hospital.

"For some of them, I am the closest thing to family they have got; many live miles away from their parents, or their parents have died. I feel pretty close to most of them, and I often end up listening to some odd and fantastic stories; you get used to being sympathetic in this job. If something awful happens involving them, I can get into big trouble, so I am keen for them to take their medication. I don't know what I think about whether schizophrenia is biological or not. I'm not sure I really care about the biological/psychological argument. People rarely listen to what I say, anyway. The psychiatrist is my immediate boss."

The Client's View

Finally, you meet some of the clients with a psychosis. How do they look? Most of them look surprisingly normal. Some of them seem slowed up, and their speech sounds a bit slurred. Many of them are quite badly dressed, and don't seem to be looking after themselves. One of them says:

"We are a sorry sight to look at; lots of us chain-smoke and are overweight; that's because of the medication. It makes you put weight on and slows you up. And there's nothing else to do but smoke, hasten yourself towards the end. Some of us who have been here longer have tremors . . ."

He puts out a rather shaky, nicotine-stained hand to show you what he means.

". . . the older medication used to give you tardive dyskinesia, which is like a form of Parkinson's disease. Not to mention the dry mouth, and the eye-rolling you sometimes get."

You interrupt to ask the clients what they think causes schizophrenia. You get a real mixed bag of views. Some of the views are familiar – you've heard them from the other people you've spoken to here: "it's a brain disease", "it's because of society being unjust and putting pressures on people", "it's because my parents never loved me enough". Some are less familiar: "it's because the voices in my head have made me mad", "it's because people have been saying bad things about me", "it's because of something awful I did when I was 17", "it's because of a particular person who has always had it in for me", "it's because the medication they've given me has turned me into a zombie", even "there's nothing wrong with me".

They reason:

"If it's my brain chemistry, does that mean there's nothing I can do to help myself? Does that mean I can never get better, and will have to take this medication for the rest of my life? I may as well kill myself now."

and

"I don't want to tell people about my diagnosis because I feel sure they wouldn't want anything to do with me again . . . I'm not even sure I want to know myself. I keep asking myself: 'Am I this bad person, this danger to society?' I must be if I am a schizophrenic. In previous centuries, they used to chain people with mental illnesses up in dark cells and crowds used to pay to see them and jeer at them."

So What IS the Answer?

Coming away from all these different parties with their different opinions and perspectives, you could be excused for feeling your head was spinning. But this brief fictional drama represents what is really happening, and has been happening for the last 100 years. It's important to be aware of the underlying political issues.

Who is right?

Which explanation is right?

Where can we start to examine these issues?

What, if anything can anyone do to help?

SCHIZOPHRENIA OR PSYCHOSIS?

So far, all the people involved – the stakeholders – have talked in terms of schizophrenia and psychosis, but are the terms interchangeable? Do they mean the same thing? Not quite . . .

Diagnosis

Biological researchers still mostly use the term "schizophrenia". Schizophrenia is the official, legal, diagnostic category. A diagnosis of schizophrenia can be given if two out of five specific types of behaviour and thoughts are seen and have been present for six months or more (see Table 1.1, page 11).

There are two diagnostic systems, one originating in America called the DSM (the Diagnostic and Statistical Manual of Mental Disorders, now in its fourth edition; APA, 1994), and the more global ICD-10 (International Classification of Diseases, now on its tenth revision; WHO, 1992). The various diagnoses are not described by causes, as you might intuitively think, but by outcomes; this is because causes are not known in any exact manner. The diagnostic criteria are agreed on by committees composed of a wide range of the experts of the day, who thrash things out in light of their clinical experience and on the basis of the latest research.

It is useful for a legal definition of schizophrenia to exist because in legal circles things have to be precise. For example, if there is the question of a person being compulsorily locked up, there have to be clear criteria for what sort of behaviours might bring that about. However, the definition is a little bit arbitrary: one sign out of five and you are not officially "a schizophrenic"; two out of five and you are. This is important when you consider the terms "schizophrenia" or "schizophrenic" have accumulated a lot of baggage over the century for which they have existed.

Public Perception – the Myth of the Mad Axeman

The media almost always portrays schizophrenia as something that makes people dangerous, because the media's job is to arouse interest, stir drama. A friend of ours who worked in radio news admitted recently that her editor wouldn't let her do any sort of item on schizophrenia without mentioning the few cases over the last 10 years where someone with a mental illness has murdered a complete stranger. Typically she would be asked to interview a relative of the deceased.

Although such murders are appalling tragedies, the statistics show that in fact only a very small number of people with a diagnosis of schizophrenia have committed murders. Of the 6–700 homicides a year in the UK, 40–50 will be attributable to schizophrenia (Taylor & Gunn, 1999); i.e. around 90 per cent are committed by people who do not have mental-health problems. By comparison, there are 3500–4000 deaths per year from road accidents. Only 13 per cent of the few homicides committed by people with schizophrenia were of strangers, therefore the risk of being murdered by a psychotic stranger is dramatically less real than the man in the street might feel. The proportion of homicides committed by people with a mental illness has been steadily decreasing by three per cent per year since 1957, according to UK statistics; whatever newspaper editors may think, the data clearly shows that on safety alone, services are improving.

The reality is that people with schizophrenia are more likely to be a danger to themselves than to others. Statistics show a 10–13 per cent greater lifetime's risk of suicide in people with schizophrenia than the general public (Baxter & Appleby, 1999; Gunnel *et al.*, 1999). It doesn't seem unreasonable that the disparity between people with a psychosis being seen as dangerous (when the stats show they are not) plays some part in this exceptionally high suicide rate.

Table 1.1   DSM-IV Criteria for Schizophrenia

According to DSM-IV, the diagnostic criteria for schizophrenia are:
A. Characteristic symptoms:
Two (or more) of the following, each present for a significant portion of time during a 1-month period:
1) delusions
2) hallucinations
3) disorganized speech (e.g. frequent derailment or incoherence)
4) grossly disorganized or catatonic behaviour ('catatonic' means 'immobile')
5) negative symptoms, i.e. affective flattening (i.e. appears to have no social emotions, or just grossly inappropriate ones), alogia (no words), or avolition (appears to have no will of own, or volitional force)
Note: Only one criterion A symptom required under some circumstances.

B. Social/occupational dysfunction in one or more major areas for a significant portion of time
C. Duration: continuous signs for at least six months
D. Not suffering from schizoaffective and mood disorder
E. Not suffering from substance abuse or another general medical condition
F. Not suffering from a pervasive developmental disorder (unless prominent delusions or hallucinations are also present)

Source: From *Diagnostic and statistical manual of mental disorders: DSM-IV* (4th edn) (1994): APA.

Labels and Terms

Newspapers often use the term "schizophrenic" to describe a mental state when someone appears to hold two conflicting views. Another popular misconception that "schizophrenic" means a person with split personalities, who can act as completely different people at different times. In fact, that condition is generally known as "dissociative identity disorder" and is a different thing to what is properly considered to be schizophrenia. Thus the term "schizophrenia" has a use in day-to-day life that is different to its technical meaning.

The term "schizophrenia" is necessary in legal situations, because it can be tightly defined. Psychosis is a preferable term otherwise, because it has fewer negative connotations, and also doesn't imply that the person has a brain disease in the way that schizophrenia is traditionally seen. Technically speaking, in DSM-IV the term "psychosis" refers to schizophrenia and, also the "high", "manic" stage of bipolar disorder (formerly referred to as "manic depression"). For our purposes, the most important definition of psychosis is "a gross impairment in reality testing".

It is best described in conjunction with another well-known term, "neurotic", with the old adage that "*neurotic* people build castles in the air, *psychotic* people live in them".

So these are the differences between the terms schizophrenia and psychosis. Modern services try to avoid using the term "schizophrenia" because of the negative associations; they also try to avoid calling people with a psychosis "schizophrenics" as that's such a stigmatising label (and it doesn't even help describe them, as its common usage is so different to the reality). In this book we mainly use the term "psychosis", although we often use "schizophrenia" where we are referring to some of the established literature that has been published using this label.

So, let's get back to the central themes of this book: What is schizophrenia about and what can anyone do to help?

CHAPTER 2

BIOLOGICAL DISEASE OR PSYCHOLOGICAL PROBLEM? WHO IS RIGHT?

Having met the key stakeholders in the previous chapter, you are now aware that there is great controversy over a whole range of issues to do with schizophrenia/psychosis. One of the most fundamental issues is one on which there is quite a lot of agreement: a majority of people agrees that psychosis is, at heart, biological. A small minority reject the importance of the biology altogether, and another minority take an integration-based position. Because the majority sees psychosis as primarily biological, we look carefully at these issues in this chapter, perhaps inviting those who are most convinced of the biological argument to reconsider the basis for this position. After all, if the condition is biological, what's the point of looking at the psychology and social aspects; they would just be side-effects of the biological disease? You wouldn't want to know the "meaning" of symptoms of other diseases like measles or chickenpox.

But *is* schizophrenia a disease with a biological cause that just hasn't been completely worked out yet? As was seen in the previous chapter, schizophrenia's status as a biological disease is such a "given" for many people that for them, to question it is ridiculous.

However, in this chapter we question schizophrenia's disease status quite fundamentally. The chapter continues in two parts. First we look at what biological differences there appear to be between people with a psychosis and "normal" people, and we look at the evidence that such "meat-based" differences cause any psychological differences, a perspective that might seem reasonable at first sight. Then we make the case that the opposite view is equally compelling – that is, a model where the cause is psychological and social. This would suggest that biological differences could be caused by psychological mechanisms. Our aim in this chapter is not to prove that either biological or psychological factors causes schizophrenia – that would be a re-run of some old and tiresome arguments about whether nature is more influential than nurture, genetics more important than environment, or whether "mind" is more important than "brain". Rather we seek to reconcile the two camps: both must be considered to provide an adequate explanation of psychotic symptoms. In the latter part of the chapter, we conclude by revisiting a classic debate, looking at whether or not schizophrenia meets any reasonable criteria for a valid "disease" at all.

OF CHICKENS AND EGGS: HOW DO BIOLOGICAL DIFFERENCES AND SYMPTOMS OF PSYCHOSIS RELATE?

In what ways might the biology be linked to psychological symptoms of psychosis? Figure 2.1 shows a few suggested cause-and-effect relationships that seem to be commonly used.

(1)   It is theoretically possible that there is no cause-and-effect relationship.

(2)   This refers to a direct relationship of biology causing symptoms; for example as levels of brain chemicals vary, then levels of psychotic symptomatology vary.

(3)   This represents the traditional stance of the man who first "invented" schizophrenia at the turn of the last century (Bleuler, 1911). He felt sure that another unknown factor mediated between biological difference and psychological symptom's occurrence. This item can also illustrate vulnerability/stress models (such as those of Nuechterlein, 1987), so that some unknown general "stress" precipitates a psychotic episode in people with biological differences, in the same way that stress might make eczema worse. A small biological difference and a large amount of stress may produce symptoms, or a large biological loading and a small amount of stress.

(4)   In this example, biological differences are not related to the symptoms, and result from another factor (for example, extensive medication or inactivity). This is not that unlikely, given that many people with a psychosis are on high doses of strong medication often for many years. Similarly, many psychosis sufferers lead very inactive lives, stuck in hospitals or staying mostly at home.

Items (5) and (6) are our suggestions. They are novel in that they go against the intuition that problems with the brain cause mental problems. In the mind/brain dichotomy of French philosopher René Descartes, it can seem like only the brain part is particularly scientific (Rose, Kamin & Lewontin, 1984); however, this kind of reductionism has long been too prevalent in this field and we would like to turn the whole thing around.

The first alternative that we propose [item (5) in Figure 2.1] is that *many* (or

Figure 2.1   Diagram Showing how Biology and Psychological Symptoms could Potentially Relate

1. No association: it's a fluke!

2. Physical differences cause the psychological symptoms directly

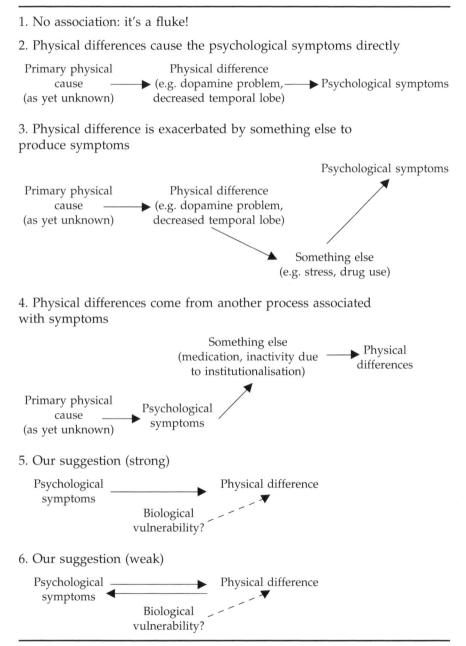

Primary physical
cause ——▶ Physical difference
(as yet unknown)   (e.g. dopamine problem, ——▶ Psychological symptoms
decreased temporal lobe)

3. Physical difference is exacerbated by something else to produce symptoms

Psychological symptoms

Primary physical
cause ——▶ Physical difference
(as yet unknown)   (e.g. dopamine problem,
decreased temporal lobe)

Something else
(e.g. stress, drug use)

4. Physical differences come from another process associated with symptoms

Something else
(medication, inactivity due ——▶ Physical
to institutionalisation)   differences

Primary physical
cause ——▶ Psychological
(as yet unknown)   symptoms

5. Our suggestion (strong)

Psychological ——————————▶ Physical difference
symptoms
Biological
vulnerability?

6. Our suggestion (weak)

Psychological ——————————▶ Physical difference
symptoms ◀——————————
Biological
vulnerability?

Source: Based on Jackson, H. F. (1990). Are There biological markers for schizophrenia? In R. Bentall (Ed) *Reconstructing schizophrenia*. London: Routledge

perhaps *most* or even *all*) *of the biological differences seen in the brains of people suffering from psychosis are produced by the psychotic symptoms.* Thus the biological differences would be the biological response to or implementation of a psychotic mental state. This changes the direction of causality round so that the symptoms of psychosis can be viewed as on a par with the biology in determining the cause of the condition. At its most basic, this is saying that the psychological side has been seen as a "junior partner" to the biology, as if the psychological is an epiphenomenon of the biological (Rose, 1984); i.e. that the psychological is an almost irrelevant side-effect that just happens to emerge from the biological.

Recent neurobiological evidence lends support to this alternative view, by showing that it is possible for long-term changes in the structural make-up of the brain to be produced without any drugs or surgery. For example, some recent work has shown that rats who are given modest but unusual sensory stimuli (for example, glued to a moving record turntable, unhappily enough) for an extended period of time can be shown to have lost a small number of brain cells in highly specific places related to the sensations produced (unfortunately for the rats, these subtle and precise changes in their brain structures are demonstrated at post mortem!). Thus, neural representations of unusual psychological and environmental stimuli alone are enough to induce drastic and permanent changes in brain structure (Mitchell *et al.*, 1995). There is also evidence that stress hormones are particularly toxic to some sets of neurones such as in the hippocampus (to do with memory). Thus, a particularly frightening event can be responsible for the loss of quite a few cells in memory areas; it has been speculated that this is a form of rapid-action learning, so that particularly important, life-threatening episodes can be learnt from as quickly as possible (Mitchell *et al.*, 1998).

Once the conceptual shift towards the psychological has been made, another perhaps more satisfactory proposal is as follows [item (6) in Figure 2.1]: *The biological and psychological work in a reciprocal and iterative fashion.* This would involve changing the straightforward billiard-ball view of causation for a more sophisticated one. Philosophers of science have taken a dislike to the over-use of such strict Hume-ean (after Scottish philosopher David Hume) models of causality in scientific models (Harré & Secord, 1972). Asking "what causes schizophrenia?" has been hindered by not considering that there are different ways in which "causes" can be linked to "effects". It might be that more useful metaphors could be found from disciplines other than mechanics, for example, quantum physics, connectionist modelling or meteorology. In the present context we suggest it could mean that the symptoms produce changes in the brain, and that these in turn shape the form of the symptoms. These would not be discrete actions but ongoing and reciprocal interchanges. Perhaps the psychological and biological differences are best thought of as emergent properties of a myriad of small psychological and biological changes, each affecting the other.

The next step in our argument will be to examine the evidence for a biological difference and assess what sort of differences have been reliably found, and what evidence has been put forward to claim that they come before the symptoms.

THE BIOLOGY-CAUSES-SYMPTOMS CASE

Why is it assumed that schizophrenia is a biologically-caused condition, probably due to some brain problem as yet undiscovered? There are only so many ways to research the brain of a person suffering from schizophrenia; it will be argued that the brain differences found are very closely linked with the techniques used; in many cases it is a case of methodology dictating theory. Historically, animal work has tended to focus on studying behaviour following a piggling (labotomising) of specific areas of the brain, rather than manipulating the environment and observing the effects on the brain. (We really do mean "piggling" here, as the original work involved using the equivalent of a hot soldering iron in the brain!) It is a small step from there to having a multitude of theories, all of which only postulate that damage to particular parts of the brain causes schizophrenia. Other main biological or structural ways to investigate biological factors are post-mortems in humans, brain scanning experiments (PET, CT, MRI) and Input/Output experiments (drugs). A critical question which must be addressed by researchers adopting any of these biological or structural approaches is whether they can tell us anything about whether the biological change came before the symptoms.

VENTRICULAR ENLARGEMENT: ORIGIN OR CONSEQUENCE?

The importance of this issue of whether biological change comes before the symptoms can be seen by considering the case of *ventricular enlargement* in schizophrenia. (Some readers may be put off by the complicated-sounding names used for parts of the brain, when actually many names are far more trivial that their grand latin titles suggest. For example, "substantia nigra" means "black substance"; "striate cortex" means "stripey-looking cortex"; and "globus palladus" means simply "pale globe".) The word "*vent*ricles" comes from the same word as "air *vents*", as it refers to the sizeable fluid-filled spaces within the brain. These spaces, and whether or not they are enlarged, are relatively easy to spot at both post-mortem and (more recently) using live brain-scanning.

Few reliable structural differences in the brains of people with a psychosis have been seen at post-mortem; "schizophrenia was known in the first half of the last century as the 'graveyard of neuropathologists' due to a frustrating and inconsistent search for brain abnormalities associated with the illness" (Kotrla, Sater & Weinberger, 1997, p187). This failure may however reflect the fact that post-mortem studies are difficult to conduct because of the difficulty in getting material (at least in Britain). People with a psychosis often die in old age or else when young from some accident (frequently self-inflicted) such as might cause damage to the brain. The studies that have been done can tell us little about whether or not the structural change came before the symptoms because in every case they use the brains of clients who have suffered from psychosis for a long time, and quite possibly on medication for decades.

As technology has improved, brain-scanning experiments have replaced post-mortem studies. Some studies have shown enlargement of the lateral, or "side", ventricles, especially of the inferior horn in a small number of cases. This enlargement would be interesting because it would mean the temporal lobe (i.e. "the lobe near the temples") was smaller than usual; alternatively a nearby structure, the hippocampus (so named because it is shaped like a sea-horse), could be smaller. The problem would be lateralised, the largest effect usually being seen on the left (e.g. classic studies such as Johnstone et al., 1976, or Shelton & Weinberger, 1986). This is a widely believed finding (although many studies have failed to replicate it; e.g. a paper contemporary to these classics: Jernigan et al., 1982) However, it still falls short of saying that the pathology involved in producing enlarged ventricles produces the symptoms.

Three lines of argument have been followed to claim increased ventricular size and decreased temporal lobe size produces psychological symptoms:

(1)   When we originally published a version of this chapter in 1996, there were a number of studies claiming to investigate at the very onset of psychosis (in other words to demonstrate that the relevant parts of the lateral ventricles were enlarged at the very start of psychosis and therefore predated the symptoms). For instance Weinberger et al. (1982) found that 20 per cent of people with psychosis who were within two weeks of their first admission for psychiatric illness showed ventricles larger than expected for their age. However, until very recently such studies involved subjects being scanned no earlier than at the time of their first admission for treatment (e.g. Weinberger et al., 1982; Nyback et al., 1982; Schultz et al., 1983). There is a well-documented and sizeable delay between first psychotic symptoms and time when an individual accesses treatment. The mean treatment lag is approximately one–two years, with some variability (Beiser et al., 1993; Loebel et al., 1992).

Any comparison of people *with* symptoms to people *without* symptoms can't prove that biological factors are primary. That sort of evidence would have to be obtained from prospective studies in which potential biological differences were assessed prior to the onset of psychiatric symptoms. Some better-designed studies have tried this recently, using "at-risk" adolescents. Phillips *et al.* (2002) were able to scan people before they were more than mildly troubled and not psychotic, and then again 12 months later, when some had become psychotic. Their results were explosive. They found that people who went on to become psychotic actually started with *larger* hippocampus volumes than those who didn't. They concluded their results were

> a different pattern of brain volume changes than is described by the neurodevelopmental model (p153)

i.e. that these results simply did not fit with the idea that brain damage occurred in the first few years of life. In fact, they concluded "these results support more recent suggestions that brain structural changes at a relatively late stage in the development of psychotic illness (such as prodromal and peri-psychotic phase) are necessary" (p153). A similar study found similar results (i.e. that a change in the volume of the temporal lobe was associated with psychotic symptoms, but that there was no evidence the reduction pre-dated symptoms; Lawrie *et al.*, 2002).

Finally, there is evidence that even if there are reductions in the temporal lobe in people who are psychotic, these reductions show every sign of being reversible (Keshavan, Haas & Kahn, 1998). This would suggest it is not brain damage at all, more temporary brain adaptation.

(2)   The death of a large number of brain cells is usually accompanied by the activation of small biological "vacuum cleaners" (called "microglia"). These microglia can easily be seen in brains at post mortem. Evidence of these microglia has not been seen in the brains of people with a psychosis at post-mortem (Roberts & Bruton, 1990). This led people to assume that the small size of the temporal lobe could only have been because that brain had failed to develop properly; if it were due to cell loss any later in life there should have been evidence of microglia. Therefore, the reduced size of the temporal lobes in the brains from people with a psychosis was assumed to arise from a developmental problem very early in life rather than a degenerative process that would occur after the onset of schizophrenic symptoms. This became the established view for many decades, and motivated a lot of research into finding a link between psychosis and birth complications such as difficult deliveries or mothers having flu during critical periods of pregnancy. Such relationships have been claimed and disputed for many years (Crow, 1994), and people are still conscientiously researching the topic today, certain that if they just look carefully enough,

they will find the cause of psychosis, rooted in a brain injury to unborn (or being born) children.

However, recent advances in the science of cell-death (new forms of cell-death, called "apoptosis") have shown that large numbers of cells can die in a manner which is so selective about which cells die, and which doesn't disrupt other cells, that it is difficult to detect by traditional means, and would not leave evidence of microglia. This means it is now quite possible that the reduced size of the temporal lobe possibly seen in some cases of psychosis could result from the death of neurons by apoptosis in response to changes in neural activity (Mitchell *et al.*, 1994, 1995). This would mean that that this difference in brain structure could easily be a consequence of the condition rather than the cause of it.

Alternatively, a reduction in volume can come about because of changes in the quality of cell, rather than cell death (e.g. neuronal size, dendrite complexity and synaptic proteins; Harrison, 1999). There is evidence that stress hormones (glucocorticoids) can bring about reduced hippocampus volume (Sapolsky, 2000), and that this reduction is also reversible (i.e. when glucocorticoids are stabilised; Sapolsky, 2000). This mirrors the way (as we mentioned earlier) temporal lobe reductions seen in psychosis seem to be reversible (Keshavan, Haas & Kahn, 1998). Biological researchers had often assumed schizophrenia was similar to Alzheimer's disease or Parkinson's disease which generally get steadily worse over time. By contrast, schizophrenia does not; for example, Ciompi analysed the life courses of 228 people with a psychosis and concluded that 27 per cent achieved complete remission, 22 per cent "minor residuals", 23 per cent intermediate outcome, 28 per cent severe outcome (Ciompi, 1980, 1981).

So the logic which forced researchers to look for events very early in life, such as mothers having had influenza during pregnancy or obstetric complications, no longer holds. Reassuringly, a recent review of work on problematic brain development during pregnancy in some cases of schizophrenia (e.g. Akbarian *et al.*, 1993, 1995) concluded that firm cyto-architectural evidence of such abnormal brain development has yet to be consistently presented (Harrison, 1999). With this work less in favour, biologists have recently elaborated ways in which brain cells might be restructured at the time of late adolescence (called the "late neurodevelopmental" hypothesis; Feinberg, 1997; Keshavan & Hogarty, 1999). These newer theories are all compatible with the idea of brain changes as the *implementation* of a psychotic state, rather than the *cause* of it.

(3)   Every new development in neurology tends to get linked tentatively to schizophrenia. Schizophrenia seems to be something of a holy grail for neurologists, holding out the promise of a practical application that they could ground their work in. Such theories tend to be 98 per cent about

neurology and just vaguely about psychosis. For example, the way in which a reduced-size temporal lobe is thought to relate to the symptoms of psychosis is almost comically vague. All manner of brain functions are carried out in the temporal lobe, particularly in the left hemisphere, from medium to high-level visual processing to speech. Enlarged ventricles have also been seen in footballers who play in central defence and head the ball too often (Asken & Schwartz, 1998) – and nobody has formally accused them of being psychotic. To our knowledge.

OTHER CONDITIONS WITH APPARENTLY PSYCHOTIC SYMPTOMS

A number of neurological conditions have been described of which a form of psychosis appears to be a part (Davison & Bagley, 1969). Neurosyphilis is thought to have a psychosis associated with it (Davison, 1983), as have certain forms of temporal lobe epilepsy (Slater & Beard, 1963) and Huntington's Disease (Garron, 1973). While the above examples are interesting and certainly show that some brain lesions cause a kind of psychosis, it would not be logically sound to say that all psychoses are caused by brain lesions. It is important to find out how similar these organic psychoses are to schizophrenia. For example, Cutting (1987) compared psychotic individuals with a known organic basis to those without and concluded that there were a number of differences in the content of the symptoms. For example, only organic psychotics displayed a theme of "imminent misadventure to others or bizarre happenings in the immediate vicinity".

For another example, the biology of Huntington's disease (HD) is known with much more certainty than the biology of psychosis. Unlike psychosis, HD has been traced back to a genetically controlled loss of specific sets of cells, in this case in the striatum. Some of the earliest signs of HD are psychological, with quite specific cognitive deficits (Garron, 1973) such as a difficulty in changing from one response set to another (people with HD often show an insistence on sameness, as they find it difficult to change tasks). Another cognitive problem in HD is in initiating new ideas. Around 90 per cent of HD sufferers are depressed (perhaps understandably in part because they face a slow but crippling degeneration until death). A very small minority (around 3%) have traditionally been said to be "psychotic" (Garron, 1973). Closer examination shows that these patients' primary problems are that they are more obsessional in a way that can seem unreasonable and bullying to others, due to their need for sameness, and reduced capacity for empathy. In fact, their symptoms show little resemblance to typical late-adolescent onset psychosis. This highlights a trend for any set of behaviours which appear unreasonable and which are not immediately understandable to be labelled "psychotic", when in fact they are not classically psychotic, and probably have more in common with head-injury sufferers. Head-injury sufferers classically show difficulty initiating their own behaviours and increases in aggression, particularly with injury to frontal lobes (known as "being a bit frontal").

NEUROTRANSMITTERS AND SCHIZOPHRENIA

Drugs that act on particular neurotransmitters such as dopamine or serotonin can be effective in reducing positive symptomatology. For example, in a classic study it was shown that the ability of a drug to reduce positive symptoms seemed to be related to the strength with which it can block dopamine receptors (Seeman *et al.*, 1976). However, this does not mean that a neurotransmitter imbalance causes psychosis. As Kandel, Schwartx & Jessel say (1989):

> It is difficult, in principle, to extrapolate from the mechanisms of action of a therapeutic agent to the causal mechanisms of a disease.

Headaches are not caused by aspirin deficiency. Rose (1984) gives an account of occasions where a drug's effectiveness has been used to hypothesise about the nature of a psychiatric condition. For example, depressives who respond to a drug have been considered to have a socially-caused depression, whereas those who do not respond have been thought to have a biologically-based depression.

Theories on the role of neurochemical transmission in schizophrenia have been refined as our biological knowledge is refined; however, the exact nature of any neurochemical imbalance in schizophrenia remains unknown. There are huge issues about the side-effects such medications bring on, many of which are almost as distressing as the symptoms themselves. Many medications appear to just mask the symptoms (people still experience unpleasant things but are just so sedated that they lose interest in them). A proportion of clients do not respond to medications at all. These issues are discussed in more detail later in the chapter; the reader is also referred to Breggin (1993).

GENETIC CONTRIBUTION

That there is a genetic contribution to schizophrenia is close to being widely accepted. However, there are extremely cogent and damning reviews of this well-established area of research, particularly with regard to the methodologies used (see Pam, 1990; Rose, Kamin & Lewontin, 1984;

Marshall, 1990). The best conclusion to draw seems to be that, while there may well be a genetic component, it may be substantially smaller than many studies have estimated. Space prevents a detailed review of the methodological faults here, but amongst other things researchers have been accused of "extrapolating" interviews with dead relatives to judge them for schizophrenia, with such "interviews" even being contradictory to up to four interviews conducted while the relative was alive. Other methodological criticisms of this work include fluctuating diagnostic categories such as "inadequate personality", and far-reaching conclusions about the nature of schizophrenia being drawn from samples where only one or two actual schizophrenia sufferers were found (Rose, Kamin & Lewontin, 1984). A smaller rather than larger genetic component would be consistent with the idea that social and environmental stimuli may go further in eliciting psychosis in some people than in others.

In summary, all the evidence for biological factors only shows at best that there are biological differences between brains of people with a psychosis and people without. The shift in the paradigms is in saying that *at least some, many or even all of these differences follow behind the psychological characteristics of psychosis.*

THE PSYCHOLOGY-CAUSES-BIOLOGY CASE

It might seem a radical idea at first, but the idea of psychology influencing biology is not remotely new. A moment's thought will bring to mind any number of occasions where biological change follows a cognitive one:

- sexual arousal, for example, following an erotic thought or image

- pupil dilation as a response to something pleasing

- placebo effects, where the expectation that a person is receiving help leads to physical improvement

- fear response, where increased heart rate, and readiness for action is shown in response to being frightened by something

- psychiatric outpatients showing an electrodermal response when a high-EE (Expressed Emotion) relative enters the room (Tarrier, Barrowclough & Porceddu, 1988)

- physical results arising from the action of a dominance hierarchy (Gilbert, 1993). For example it has been shown that people who win at tennis show an increase in testosterone, while those that lose show a decrease (Mazur & Lamb, 1980; Booth *et al.*, 1989).

In fact, it is well established that environmental conditions can influence neurotransmission in a specific manner. For example, stress has been shown to increase dopamine-mediated transmission in the prefrontal cortex and to a lesser extent in the nucleus accumbens (Thierry *et al.*, 1976; see Iversen 1995 for a review). Furthermore, it is now known that the circulating level of corticosteroids, stress hormones released by the adrenal glands, in part determines whether neurons within the temporal lobe of the adult rat undergo apoptosis (Uno *et al.*, 1994; Sloviter *et al.*, 1989; Sapolsky *et al.*, 1990).

IS THE BIOLOGY RELEVANT AT ALL?

Psychological theories can have the opposite flaw in that many psychological theorists would deny the existence of any primary lesion. For them psychosis is primarily psychological in origin. But it would be a mistake to take up the more extreme position that the biological level is not useful, or that there are no biological differences in schizophrenic brains, because (as reviewed above), there may well be at least some, and the biological level has much to contribute. There can be physical differences without these implying a primary cause. All "normal" mental processes or responses have some sort of biological implementation and the form of the mental process will be dictated by biological constraints. For example, in the blushing mechanism, when a person feels embarrassed (a cognitive judgement and emotion), there is a biological response of a blush whereby blood rushes to the cheeks. There is no *a priori* logical reason why the biological response should be the one it is. It might just as well be steam coming out of the ears and an involuntary hooting sound coming from the mouth. It would probably serve the same evolutionary purpose. Nor is there any *a priori* reason why the symptoms of psychosis should be along themes of hallucinations or an inability to concentrate, yet people in very disparate parts of the world show remarkably similar symptoms independently of each other. It seems that biological constraints are dictating the form of the symptoms to at least some extent. In psychosis, people are operating in such a different way to "normals" that it would be surprising if there was not some sort of difference in their brains.

Whatever the origin of the psychosis, be it primarily biological or primarily psychological, the best way to treat it does not have to be of the same form. Some physical illnesses (e.g. stomach ulcers) can be treated well by either medication or psychological treatments (e.g. stress reduction). So a psychological condition may be treated with drugs or psychological interventions.

HOW DO BIOLOGICAL THEORIES TRY TO EXPLAIN THE PSYCHOLOGICAL SYMPTOMS?

How would a smaller-sized temporal lobe bring about the delusion that people next door are trying to poison you? The various bits of brain damage that have been assumed over the years to cause the psychological symptoms of psychosis have relatively little to do with psychotic symptoms. The only bridge between possible structural and chemical differences and the psychological symptoms are information-processing theories. The information-processing model has been very successful over the last 30 years, and uses the metaphor of the human brain as a computer, essentially a device for manipulating information.

It has been suggested that specific "traits" of information-processing are caused by the biological differences mentioned above, and these information-processing traits are responsible for the psychological symptoms (Frith, 1992; Hemsley, 1987, has a similar theory but is more careful as to the primary cause, saying it could well be psychological; Hemsley, personal communication, 1997). Such theories carefully choose a definition of the potential information-processing deficit and describe how all the symptoms of psychosis might be explained from it. For example, there might be an unusual perception (caused by faulty brain chemistry, for Frith) which the person then strives to come to terms with in much the same way as a "normal" person might. In the information-processing model, trying to explain such an unusual event (for example, a voice produced from faulty brain connections) to themselves leads people to assume bizarre things (for example, the voice they hear is the voice of some powerful being). This normal cognitive interpretation of anomalous perceptions is proposed to lead to psychological symptoms (Maher, 1974).

These two theories are discussed in detail below from the perspective of hypothesising what might cause the "primary deficit". The accuracy of the theories themselves is not discussed and it is assumed they are useful characterisations of psychosis.

Hemsley (1987) reviewed a number of opinions as to what the nature of the cognitive impairment in schizophrenia was and, from these, hypothesised that the primary problem was

> a weakening of the influence of stored memories of regularities of previous input on current perceptions (known as "Hemsley's deficit").

The Hemsley model in theory accounts nicely for the positive symptoms of schizophrenia. For example, because people suffering from schizophrenia are less able to interpret incoming perceptual data properly – they find it difficult to integrate new data with stored memories – so there is heightened awareness of irrelevant stimuli, leading to bizarre perceptual experiences (that is, hallucinations). Delusions theoretically arise from memory having less influence in inferring causal relationships between events. Causal relationships are therefore inferred from single instances (i.e. they "jump to conclusions"; Hemsley, 1987). Hemsley's model has been interpreted by other writers, notably, Gray (1993), as being primarily biological.

However, contrary to Gray's view, Hemsley's deficit does not need to be explained by neural level dysfunction. It is possible to explain "Hemsley's deficit" from social factors, though this has not been attempted. Implicit in Gray's use of Hemsley's deficit is the idea that "healthy" people do not vary too much in the degree to which they can relate new experiences to their old ones. However, competence at this skill varies, depending on the time of day, and the emotional state. An even bigger difference is seen between different individuals! One could possibly interpret Hemsely's deficit as a weakening of the influence of "constructs" in the Kelly or Kantian sense, or "schema" in Young's terminology. Thus, individuals need to be able to impose order on the world in a way that makes sense to them and according to their own needs. These constructs are the basic results of their assimilating the world.

To help clarify this idea that people vary in the extent to which they can assimilate material cogently, consider social hierarchies (Gilbert, 1993). Ways of behaving in dominance/subordination hierarchies are thought to be driven by evolutionary mechanisms and these mechanisms are thought to be ingrained and involuntary. Social factors trigger behaviours characteristic of these hierarchies. A person at the bottom of the social hierarchy will be least likely to get resources. As part of the subordinate's role, as a hard-wired way of behaving, a lowly individual has to attend to superiors, in case they incur the displeasure of their betters, which could be physically dangerous. It is likely that there is a lot of anxiety, attentiveness and loss of control involved in the subordinate's role (Trower & Gilbert, 1989) plus a lot of adjusting to someone else's whims and desires. At a cognitive level, the person at the bottom will be less able to have the time and space to do things as they want, to make the world meet their needs, or come to terms with it (construe it properly). That individual will have to be more adept at only meeting the demands of others. In sum, he/she will be less able to integrate experiences in the way Hemsley suggests, and is more likely to get overwhelmed by everything.

To approach from another angle, sensory/emotional overload is central to Hemsley's theory. Gray sees this overload as coming about because of the basic deficit (caused by brain pathology), thereby producing an overload of perceptual data and hallucinations associated with that. It is equally possible to propose sensory and emotional overload coming about for social reasons. This overload could show itself as Hemsley's deficit, and the symptoms such as hallucinations and delusions could result from that. The difficulty in integrating everyday interactions within a bizarre, intensely personal framework may be why clients find interactions so difficult and spend so much time avoiding people.

It has therefore been argued that even if the cognitive information-processing deficit described by Hemsley is accurate, [even in most of the anatomical splendour that Gray *et al.* (1991) provide], it does not necessarily mean there is a brain-injury. A difference in cognitive processing could just as easily be brought about by social and psychological pressures.

A similar information-processing account is that of Frith (1992). His information-processing deficit can be enhanced by considering social factors just as Hemsley's can. For Frith, the primary deficit is due to a fault in "meta-representing". The meaning of meta-representing can be loosely summarised as being able to attribute ownerships to thoughts and intentions. People with schizophrenia, for example, are hypothesised by Frith to not realise that they themselves thought "I know that my car is faulty", and instead experience that idea as the thought "my car is faulty" as having been inserted into their consciousness by an external force. They are not able to label it as having originated from themselves. In this manner the theory can account for the range of schizophrenic symptoms.

There is plainly a systematic bias towards very emotionally significant ideas in the examples used by Frith, although this bias is not really drawn out by him (Frith, 1992). This bias can also be seen in hallucinations and delusions in general, and it is remarkable that a deficit in attributing ownership and responsibility to thoughts should be dealing so predominantly with material with very negative emotional tones. It is not assuming too much to say that the problems in meta-representing and filtering in Frith's paradigm could be emotionally motivated. Hingley (1992) suggests that psychological defence mechanisms can be seen as filters, or information-processing biases of sorts. Any account of hallucinations and delusions that does not account for the very emotional nature of most of them is sadly deficient. As argued at length in the next chapter, these theory-of-mind skills are developed over adolescence with repeated social experiences. These are skills in which most adults and certainly most adolescents vary a great deal, for social reasons and with social outcomes!

To summarise, it has been argued that although there are information-processing differences between "normal" people and people with schizophrenia, it does not necessarily mean that they are caused by a brain-injury as yet undiscovered. The information-processing differences may actually point to a psychological mechanism as the primary cause of the symptomatology.

EXAMPLES OF PSYCHOLOGY CAUSING EXPERIENCES AND BIOLOGY

The following examples add credence to the thesis that strange psychological states can arise without any preceding biological difference. The examples illustrate how psychological, social or environmental contingencies lead to altered perceptions in the short term.

Example A

The "fear" or "panic" response demonstrates a distinctive biological and psychological response to a psychological event. If a man were to come into the room where you are reading this book, and he was carrying an axe and had a certain look of purpose about him, you would immediately experience an enormous response biologically. This is a physical mechanism that has evolved, giving extremely useful benefits, such as the capacity for immediate fight or flight. In gaining these benefits, however, some of the abilities of the normal state have been lost. For example, it would be difficult to concentrate on this chapter with the axeman standing behind you. There would have been a trade off between things that were important and things that could be sacrificed. Almost certainly the sacrifices would be made because of biological constraints. It would not be biologically possible to have both capacity for fight/flight and capacity for intellectual thought; otherwise we would probably retain these. Therefore, in this situation there are major differences in cognition resulting from psychological factors independent of any biological cause.

Example B

The purely psychological event of bereavement can produce very distinctive psychological effects, in the absence of biological abnormality. During a period of grieving, a person may not be able to concentrate on everyday tasks, and may be overwhelmed with certain thoughts. The experience can be so intense that it is almost experienced as biological change. For example, after his wife's death, C.S. Lewis wrote:

> No-one ever told me that grief felt so much like fear . . . the same fluttering in the stomach, the same restlessness, the yawning. I kept swallowing . . . (1961)

Example C

The "trauma" or "shock" response such as occurs directly after an accident or disaster, and has recently been the focus of much research interest in post traumatic stress disorder (PTSD) also demonstrates a distinctive psychological effect. In trauma, there can be an actual physical shaking, the muscles rich in resources for action. Psychologically, there is often a feeling of things not being real, an inability to concentrate or take things in, and a brooding "shatteredness". Completely spurious and odd connections between ideas arrive that later seem totally ridiculous but at the time seem real enough. For example, a policeman at the Hillsborough disaster in Britain in 1989 (in which 96 people died at a football game due largely to appalling police incompetence) said:

> At one point it was like I was going in and out of reality. I felt as if I were seeing things and then drifting off into not noticing things even though they were happening – I just couldn't register them. I can only remember in patches. The daft thoughts that go through your head, they're not thoughts from you. I don't know how they get there. (Taylor, Ward & Newburn, 1995)

It has been proposed that people may suffer PTSD as a result of an experience of being psychotic (McGorry *et al.*, 1991). For example, individuals experiencing a forced hospitalisation on their first episode of psychosis may show symptoms associated with PTSD because of this. We suggest that the best way to understand certain symptoms of psychosis is to look at them either as PSTD-type experiences, or as experiences to do with an individual currently experiencing trauma. For example, many people with psychosis are also having many experiences which involve extreme fear, often religious absolutes like God and the Devil, and it would be surprising if this was not traumatic. Thought disorder, for example, can be seen as a natural adaptive response, similar to the loss of concentration seen in trauma. A similar way of looking at thought disorder is as a kind of natural anti-depressant. To stop themselves experiencing all sorts of damning thoughts/voices, people "numb-out", with the unfortunate consequence that they can not concentrate on or feel anything. Haddock *et al.* (1995) showed that the condition of thought-disordered clients became much more severe when they are asked to focus on emotionally meaningful material. It was mentioned above that Maher (1974) put forward the idea that delusions are formed by clients interpreting bizarre perceptions using normal reasoning. It may be that some of the only abnormal experiences that clients need to explain to themselves are these characteristics of the trauma state (sense of unreality, spurious connections etc).

In trauma there is a psychological event producing an unusual psychological state. It might be possible to conjecture about whether there was any change in brain chemistry coming with these psychological events.

For example, if it were possible to examine the brain chemistry of a person in traumatic shock, one might find that there was a dopamine imbalance there. In this case, one might want to conclude that neuroleptic medication could be used to help clear the minds of people in psychological shock and free them of the worst mental problems. If this was indeed a valid parallel to people with psychosis, one might be justified in taking the (perhaps extreme) view that this characterises anti-psychotic drugs as acting on the bruise but not the primary hurt.

CONCLUSIONS

There is a large literature on the possible biology of psychosis. It has focused on trying to find biological differences between brains from people with a psychosis and "normal" people. Such approaches have emphasised possible differences in the function of the neurotransmitter dopamine within the brain and in the size of the temporal lobe and it has been assumed that these biological differences lead to the symptoms of psychosis. In this chapter we have argued that the direction of this causal relationship has not been satisfactorily demonstrated and we raised the possibility that the biological changes may actually result from the symptoms of the disorder. Similarly, the information-processing differences between those suffering from psychosis and "normals" may arise as a consequence of the condition rather than any biological abnormality. This reversal of causality between biological difference and psychological state would parallel the reversal Copernicus championed when he argued that the earth revolved around the sun and not the sun around the earth. (This chapter was originally published under the title "Does the biology go around the symptoms? A Copernican shift in schizophrenia paradigms".)

Given the plasticity in the brain's response to psychological events, including stress, it seems likely that a descent into psychosis would involve a constant interplay between psychology and biology. We put forward the existence of a reiterative loop whereby a particular set of circumstances would elicit psychological responses which would induce specific biological events that would affect the perception and psychological reaction to the next situation, and so on. If the psychology and biology are as tightly interwoven as suggested here, it perhaps becomes less important to try and isolate which particular factor acts as the initial cause of the condition. Biological theories seem in the last few years to be moving towards a "late-adolescence" account; this would be compatible with a developmental psychological approach.

POSTSCRIPT

So much work on schizophrenia – yet is it a valid category?

A classic technique for biological research is to compare a group of people who have been diagnosed as having schizophrenia, with a group of people who have not. In fact this was so common a few decades ago that between 1959 and 1978, 15 per cent of the space in the important American journal, *Journal of Abnormal Psychology*, contained articles that compared those with schizophrenia to those without (Sarbin & Mancuso, 1980). Many biological researchers get very irritated if someone questions the validity of the concept of schizophrenia, because this is such a fundamental assumption for them. Yet the concept of schizophrenia was invented by Kraepelin in 1896 (he called it "dementia praecox"), and Bleuler in 1911 (who coined the term "schizophrenia" from the Greek words "skhizo" and "phren", literally "split mind"). They each decided they had observed a number of patients who showed similar symptoms, and that there might be a common cause in these cases. Whether they were right to make these assumptions has been comprehensively criticised (Boyle, 1990). One particular criticism is that many of the small number of people from whom Kraepelin inferred "dementia praecox" and Bleuler inferred "schizophrenia" in fact suffered from either encephalitis lethargic or Parkinson's disease, which had not been properly identified at this time. These are very different conditions from what would be diagnosed as schizophrenia today (Boyle, 1990). There is a strong argument that neither Kraepelin or Bleuler had even weak evidence on which to base their case for a valid syndrome; that is, they may have been seriously misguided in what they thought was a consistent syndrome. Further damning criticisms have been made of the concept of schizophrenia as it has currently evolved to be:

(1) If schizophrenia is a valid concept, the disorder should be characterised by a set of symptoms that tend to go together. In fact, as we saw at the end of Chapter 1, there are a large number of potentially "schizophrenic" symptoms, and whether they can be statistically grouped into clusters is very debatable. Two or three individuals may have completely different symptoms and yet the same diagnosis of schizophrenia (Bentall, Jackson & Pilgrim, 1988).

(2) Conversely, diagnostic categories should not overlap, but they do – depression and affective disorders overlap markedly with schizophrenia, for example. People originally diagnosed as schizophrenic may commonly fluctuate over time from one category to another. This does not surprise psychiatrists but puzzles clients when they are told "you used to have schizophrenia but now we think you have schizo-affective disorder".

(3)   Diagnosing schizophrenia consistently is notoriously difficult, and different psychiatrists are not unlikely to come up with different diagnoses for the same person (Bentall, Jackson & Pilgrim, 1988); this has been a long-standing issue for psychiatry (Wing, Cooper & Sartorius, 1974).

(4)   To be valid, specific diseases should be related to specific causes. Despite the fact that "nearly every variable known to affect human behaviour" has been hypothesised to account for schizophrenic break-downs (Bentall, Jackson & Pilgrim, 1988, p304), even the most widely held hypotheses remain heavily disputed.

(5)   A diagnostic label such as "schizophrenia" should allow predictions to be made about the course of the condition over time. In fact, as mentioned earlier, the outcome of "schizophrenia" is notoriously variable and unpredictable (Ciompi, 1981). How people respond to medication is also unpredictable (Crow et al., 1986). Social aspects such as social contacts, family atmosphere and duration of hospitalisation are all better predictors of future course than symptoms at first admission (Strauss & Carpenter, 1977; Vaughn and Leff, 1976; Bentall, Jackson & Pilgrim, 1988).

In summary, schizophrenia is a disease with

> no particular symptoms, no particular course, no particular outcome and which responds to no particular treatment. (Bentall, 1990, p33)

These points suggest that the current conceptualisation of schizophrenia is questionable, and that the many studies comparing people with schizo-phrenia to people without are starting from a seriously flawed set of assumptions. The term "schizophrenia" was useful in its day to give psychiatrists a common referent, but "it seems probable that 'schizo-phrenia' will suffer the same fate as 'phlogyston' and 'the luminiferous ether' which, although useful organising concepts in their time, ultimately had to be cast aside before further scientific progress could be made" (Bentall, Jackson & Pilgrim, 1988, p317). Psychological researchers have recommended that research be conducted into the specific symptoms of psychosis such as voice hearing, paranoia or thought disorder (Bentall, Jackson & Pilgrim, 1988). In this manner, researchers have a chance of actually comparing like with like. The arguments against using schizo-phrenia as a concept are at least 10 years old (Bentall, 1990), and yet many biological researchers complacently continue to sally forth using the concept! The fact that so much research persists in treating a mixed bag of people with completely different symptoms as if they had the same condition is an incredible waste of effort!

CHAPTER 3

WHY YOUNG MEN?
WHAT THE HELL IS GOING ON
IN LATE ADOLESCENCE?

The previous chapter put forward a strong argument for psychology being much more influential and important in psychosis than is often assumed at first, particularly by the biological traditions operating in most professional services. Do these discussions bring us any closer to answering the great questions about psychosis? What other clues does the scientific literature give us? If you were to look in a psychiatric textbook it would probably tell you there are three "inescapable clinical facts" about schizophrenia (Weinberger, 1987):

(1) stress is involved in onset and relapse

(2) dopamine-based medications can be therapeutically useful

(3) it is normally in late adolescence that the condition becomes apparent.

It will come as no surprise to the reader of Chapter 2 that the second aspect, the biological one, has been researched extensively. The first aspect, stress, is often invoked to mediate between general psychological pressures and biological mechanisms, in a relatively unspecified way. In truth, of the three inescapable facts, it is the adolescence angle that remains relatively overlooked. It is precisely this which will be the focus of this chapter.

First of all, we have to ask: is it actually true that schizophrenia becomes apparent in late adolescence? Perhaps the most authoritative results come from the World Health Organisation, from a study in nine countries. They found that 51 per cent of all the new schizophrenia cases they had recorded were aged between 15 and 25 (Sartorius *et al.*, 1986; Jablensky & Cole, 1997) and 82.5 per cent of participants were between 15 and 35. Most (86%) of these subjects were within 12 months of first showing psychotic symptoms. Figure 3.1 shows the distribution of age of onset for males and females (Häfner *et al.*, 1993a). However, this means a biggish minority of people who develop a psychosis do not do so in late adolescence, which is something important to bear in mind. It also tends to affect six times as

Figure 3.1 Distribution of Ages of Onset for Males and Females, Worked Out Retrospectively

A shows the age at which the first signs of psychological distress were seen
B shows the age at which first psychotic symptoms were seen

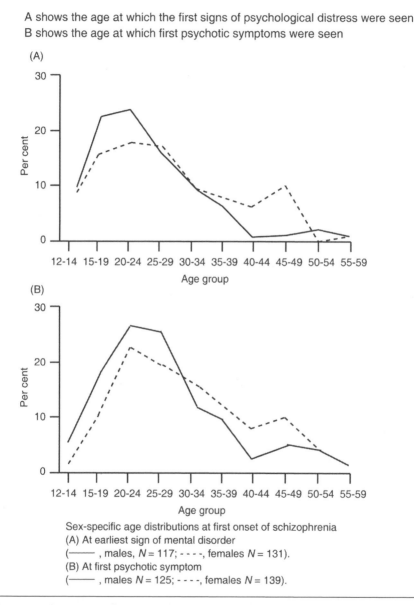

Sex-specific age distributions at first onset of schizophrenia
(A) At earliest sign of mental disorder
(———— , males, N = 117; - - - -, females N = 131).
(B) At first psychotic symptom
(———— , males N = 125; - - - -, females N = 139).

Source: Häfner *et al.* (1993). The influence of age and sex on the onset and course of schizophrenia. *British Journal of Psychiatry* **162**, 80–87. Reproduced by permission of the Royal College of Psychiatrists.

many men as women, and women tend to develop it a few years later than men.

However, for the majority of cases that do start in late adolescence, there are some interesting questions to be asked. Statistically, what are the chances of any adolescent developing schizophrenia? As mentioned in the introduction, between 0.4 and 1.9 people in 100 develop schizophrenia over their lifetime (Jablensky, 1997). How long does it take? As we mentioned in Chapter 2, retrospective accounts from people who have developed a psychosis indicate that people become unwell over a period of 1–2 years (Loebel *et al.*, 1992), with symptoms slowly escalating until a time when it is really obvious something is going wrong. The time when these problems appear to be "incubating" is traditionally called the "prodrome". What do prodromes look like? There are a number of prodromal signs that people have retrospectively reported, such as magical ideation, unusual perceptual experiences, social withdrawal and markedly unusual behaviour. These signs may seem a little woolly, and you may be wondering now whether it is possible to really notice an adolescent in the early stages of a psychosis!

An Astonishing Discovery!

Researchers in Australia wanted to answer this question, whether you could identify a small group of adolescents who were "prodromal". They surveyed normal 16-year-olds at school in the early 1990s. Because 1–2 per cent of people develop schizophrenia in their lifetime, the Melbourne group anticipated they would find 1–2 per cent of the 16-year-olds were having difficulties. What they found instead was astonishing . . .

They found that if they used fairly strict criteria for saying when a teenager was having difficulties, 10–15 per cent were prodromal. If they used rather less strict criteria, up to 50 per cent were prodromal! (McGorry *et al.*, 1995). Table 3.1 shows the sorts of signs they were picking up amongst these normal 16-year-olds. The symptoms in the left-hand column are the most common signs that are known to precede a psychotic episode.

What Can This Mean?

We saw in Chapter 1 that many people would say that psychosis is a brain disease; do these results mean that half of Australian teenagers have the beginnings of brain rot? If so, we might suspect there was something wrong with the water supply or food chain? Or is there a problem with Western societies, such that intolerable pressures are driving our young people mad? How worried should we be about hopes for the future?

The answer has to be "not too worried". As far as we know, few people in this sample of 16-year-olds were actually in contact with psychiatric services, asking for help. The teachers had not noticed any problems in unusual behaviour or learning that might indicate the students actually had brain problems. We have to conclude that they were just normal 16-year-olds, and that, in fact, normal teenagers are unusual!

In fact there is a lot of evidence to suggest that there is no such thing as a completely "normal" adult, either! Lots of researchers have surveyed apparently typical adults and found that large proportions of people without a psychiatric history endorse beliefs that could be classed as delusional (Verdoux et al., 1998; Peters, Joseph & Garety, 1999; Slade & Bentall, 1988). As many as 15 per cent of normal adults report hearing voices, although these voices do not appear to cause them problems in their day-to-day lives. Many people who have been bereaved, for example, report hearing the voice of their dead loved one (Romme et al., 1992).

However, there does seem to be a larger proportion of adolescents who show unusual beliefs. Why are adolescents so unusual? What is going on for them that disposes them to be odd? What has this got to do with psychosis? Are the same processes at work in people who do actually go on to develop a psychosis?

In this chapter we are saying that some of the signs of psychosis that seem quite unusual at first sight are in fact not so different from many experiences typical of adolescence. Over the next few pages we go through further typical adolescent phenomena, and compare normal experience with psychosis-experience. We also explain why (it is thought) adolescent experience is the way it is, and use this explanation to speculate about why psychosis-experience is the way it is. As we will hopefully

Table 3.1 Table Showing "Prodromal Signs" in 657 Teenagers (mean age 16.5 years, 95% CI 16.4–16.6)

DSM-III-R prodrome symptom	present
Magical ideation	51%
Unusual perceptual experiences	46%
Blunted, flat or inappropriate affect	21.7%
Lack of initiative	39.7%
Markedly peculiar behaviour	25.2%
Marked impairment in personal hygiene	8.1%
Social isolation and withdrawal	18%

Source: McGorry et al. (1995). The prevalence of prodromal features of schizophrenia in adolescence. *Acta Psychiatrica Scandinavica* **92**, 241–249. Reproduced by permission of Blackwell Publishing.

demonstrate, the explanatory theories of adolescence are remarkably consistent with theories of psychosis.

GET IN TOUCH WITH YOUR INNER ADOLESCENT

We'd like to remind (our non-adolescent) readers what it is like to be a teenager, for those who are not immediately in touch with that feeling. Can you remember what songs instantly remind you of teenage days? Which songs were the ones that you felt really spoke to you, really articulated what you felt better than you could yourself? Who were the most important people in your life then? How did you feel about them? How did you feel about yourself? What issues did you worry about? What did you discuss with your friends? What did you argue about, with your parents, for example? What sorts of things made you angry?

Of course, everyone is different, but it's interesting to look at what researchers have found to be general themes common to most people.

For instance, what do adolescents argue about?

ADOLESCENT PHENOMENON 1: CONFLICT AND RENEGOTIATION

There seems to be a popular stereotype that parents and teenagers argue all the time about everything. Research shows that they don't argue anything like all the time, and many families don't really argue that much at all. However, the majority of families do see a fair bit of conflict (Coleman, 1974; Rutter *et al.*, 1976; Montemayor & Hansom, 1985). This conflict is less likely to be over "big" issues such as politics or religion; typically conflict occurs over issues of rule-breaking and parental authority. For example, Smetana (1989) asked normal family members to recount their versions of family disputes and justify the stances they took. The adolescents were found to be arguing because they saw the issue as something that should now be under their control (for example "cleaning one's room" for them would have been something they should have the say over). Parents argued because they thought that the issue was something parents should have authority over. In effect, the conflicts arose because adolescents were constantly gaining ground, negotiating their way from "subordinate" to "self-ordinate" beings. This is difficult for parents, who are unsure about relinquishing the protection they give their child. It has been said that: "the parental task is to accept as best they can the adolescent's call for greater freedom" (Coleman & Hendry, 1990, p84). Parents are also having to come to terms with another major role for themselves, that of middle-aged people with grown up children.

So conflict comes about because of all the renegotiation of roles. Why do adolescents need all this renegotiating? They need to renegotiate roles because they eventually need to be independent; they need to be able to progress from the family. They need to be able to enter the adult workplace, to go to university or college, to perhaps move to different areas. What would be the use of a married 40 year old still doing everything their parents told them to? (That would be a situation their parents probably wouldn't want either; of the many feelings parents feel when their children leave home, one is often a relief, as their energies are freed up for them to look after themselves again.) Gaining independence ("individuation") from parents is thought to be one of the fundamental tasks of adolescence.

Having negotiated independence from parents, where does this leave the young person?

For most people, the evidence shows that teenagers attach themselves instead to their peers. They progress through same-sex gangs, to mixed-sex gangs, to the formation of "romantic pairs". Obviously there's a lot of variation between individuals and between genders, but it can be generalised that peer relationships (heterosexual or homosexual) become far more important and usually in the larger part replace parental attachments (Berndt, 1979). Forming attachments to their peer group is seen as the other great task of adolescence.

Having introduced the two fundamental tasks of adolescence, we now go on to consider more experiences typical of adolescence, and to compare them to experiences of people who have experienced psychosis.

Conflict in Psychosis

For example, we discussed earlier how families renegotiate roles so as, gradually, to give adolescents more independence. How much of this renegotiation/apparent conflict goes on in families of people with a psychosis? Data on this sort of topic are difficult to collect. It appears there is a lot of variation, from families with no discord at all, to those with much (Birchwood & Tarrier, 1992; Leff & Vaughn, 1985; Wearden et al., 2000; Wynne & Singer, 1963). In one of our studies, we found that a majority of adolescent-onset psychosis sufferers were highly anxious about arguments; clients were significantly more likely than a comparison group of students to endorse questionnaire items reflecting this difficulty, such as "People who argue with Mum are awful", "I never say things my Mum may not want to hear" (Harrop, 2000). On the whole, they shied away from disagreements. (As we mentioned, there was a very small number of psychosis sufferers who really shouted at their families a lot.) Our data suggest that psychosis-sufferers worry a lot about conflict (this is different to saying that this is the parent's fault, which we are certainly not saying).

By way of contrast with the striking anxieties most psychosis-sufferers felt about conflict, it appears most clients would like to be more independent and empowered regarding their families (Barham, 1993). For example, theories from the 1960s are very popular with clients (even though they are around forty years out of date), partly because they seemed to blame the parents for the client's illness, and in doing so empowered the clients (e.g. Laing, 1965). It also seems that many clients are really looking to have an issue on which they are allowed to oppose their parents, as if they were trying to start on the process of rebellion and individuation outlined above. Indeed, much of the psychosis literature resembles a battle between parents and their offspring as to who is "right" or who is "to blame" for the illness.

ADOLESCENT PHENOMENON 2: DE-IDEALISATION

We said above that conflict reflects a need to move towards normal independence; what changes psychologically to enable normal adolescents to start this process?

It would be difficult for people to be able to stand their ground and win their battles unless their perspective on their parent's behaviour had changed. When they were younger, adolescents may have thought very highly of their parents, and just assumed they were great people; younger children are thought to "idealise" parents. As the process of gaining independence gets underway, adolescents come to re-evaluate this idealistic view of their parents. A writer called Peter Blos (1962, p91) phrases this nicely:

> Whereas previously the parent was overvalued, considered with awe, and not realistically assessed, he now becomes undervalued and is seen to have the shabby proportions of a fallen idol . . . The adolescent becomes arrogant and rebellious, defies rules because they are no longer universal absolutes, but have to be tested for being inventions of a deranged despotic parent.

Does it happen? Steinberg & Silverberg (1986) devised the Emotional Autonomy questionnaire, based around the writings of Blos (1962). One of the subscales is de-idealisation, and this was shown to increase steadily with age, for the 865 teenagers who completed it. The young adolescent begins to be aware of the fallibility of their parents (p185):

> What used to be the centre of his world and an authority on everything now becomes something human and motivated by hitherto unsuspected human motivations.

Younger children idealise their parents because they just don't have much experience of noticing their parents doing less impressive things, and because to young children, parents do seem to know everything and understand everything. Children can be amazed how parents seem to even read their minds and perhaps appear to have "eyes in the back of their head". By the time the child reaches adolescence, the knowledge gap is not so wide, and parents appear much more human. The more experience adolescents have of their parents, the more likely they are to become aware of any weaknesses and flaws; before, they might have just assumed flaws were not there. Can you remember the first time you realised your parents were just human, perhaps the first time you realised you didn't agree with their views or they didn't seem to know something?

> When I was a boy of fourteen, my father was so ignorant I could hardly stand to have him around. But when I reached twenty-one, I was astonished at how much the old man had learned in seven years.   (Attributed to Mark Twain)

Idealisation and Psychosis

We have data that show psychosis-sufferers are more idealistic than university students: in a recent study (Harrop, 2000), we found that, compared to university students, clients with psychosis who were under 40 years of age were significantly more likely to endorse items reflecting idealisation such as "My Dad is always fair" and "I have never known my Dad to lie" ($p<0.05$). Compared to comparisons matched for gender, age and educational level, they scored significantly lower ($p<0.05$) on the de-idealisation subscale of Steinberg and Silverberg's (1986) Emotional Autonomy scale (Harrop, 2000). On their overall scores on this scale, the psychosis group resemble 13-year-olds more than older adolescents (Harrop, 2000).

ADOLESCENT PHENOMENON 3: DEPRESSION AND LOSS – "HEAVEN KNOWS I'M MISERABLE NOW" (MORRISSEY, 1984)

When people think about their adolescence, they often see it in particularly rosy terms, but there are a lot of very strong negative feelings around at adolescence as well. Many readers may remember times of acute misery at adolescence. There are a number of potential reasons for this. When adolescents de-idealise their parents, this is not an entirely positive experience, because in return for the greater personal freedom that adolescents gain, they lose a lot in terms of security and attachment. This can lead to a sense of loss, depression and uncertainty, amongst other things. Losing one's image of one's own parents as ideal can be a great loss indeed. Often clients are reluctant to relinquish this comforting image. Some researchers have suggested it is as traumatic as bereavement, as it is a bereavement of a kind.

There is a lot of evidence that a number of negative experiences such as depression and loss go hand in hand with the development of autonomy. For instance, the Emotional Autonomy scale mentioned earlier has correlated very well with some apparently negative phenomena such as the amount to which adolescents said their parents did not accept them, and their lack of "felt security"; it has even been argued that this scale measures more negative factors to do with detachment than autonomy (Ryan & Lynch, 1989).

Depression and Psychosis

There is a significant prevalence of depression and anhedonia in psychosis. Often, when the more florid symptoms of psychosis are in remission, there is a depression still present – in fact, it is shown in a third of such people (Birchwood et al., 1993). Depression is so common following psychosis that there is a separate category in the ICD-10 diagnostic criteria for "post-schizophrenic depression" (WHO, 1992). It has traditionally been thought that this emotion is a response to the losses involved with breakdown, such as loss of career aspirations, and loss of respect and standing amongst one's family and friends. It is suggested here that it may also be due either to thwarted needs for autonomy and the associated need to rebel against parents. Alternatively, depressed feelings may be due to the losses involved in a partial rebellion.

ADOLESCENT PHENOMENON 4: EGOCENTRISM, GRANDIOSITY AND SELF-CONSCIOUSNESS

When you considered the defining features of adolescence, you might have thought about how sure adolescents feel about issues, or ways in which adolescents can be quite grandiose?

This has been termed "adolescent egocentrism", and is another important area of adolescence research that has enormous relevance for psychosis. For example, it has been suggested that adolescents behave as if they carry an audience around in their imagination (Elkind, 1979). The idea of the "imaginary audience" would explain many aspects of adolescent behaviour. For example, teenagers often have a certain grandiosity (Elkind, 1967, p1031):

> Possibly because the adolescent believes he or she is so important to so many people (the imaginary audience), they come to see themselves, and their feelings as very special, even unique.

The stereotype of the self-absorbed teenager is well known, but is it realistic? Empirical testing has shown that in "normals", egocentricity is high in early

(13 years old) and mid (15 years old) adolescence, and then declines from mid to late adolescence (17 years old) (with a further peak in a college-age sample). Self-consciousness increases from mid to late adolescence (Enright, Shukla & Lapsley, 1980; Lapsley *et al.*, 1986).

Why are adolescents egocentric? Elkind (1967) suggested adolescents find it difficult to distinguish between *what others are attending to* and *what they themselves are attending to*. Adolescents assume if they themselves are obsessed by a thought or a problem, then other people must be obsessed by the same thing. Elkind suggested that this is because they have yet to develop that cognitive capacity. The paradigm Elkind used was based on Piaget's work on adolescence (Inhelder & Piaget, 1958). To help readers understand Inhelder and Piaget's theories for adolescence, we'll have to take a brief diversion into Piaget's theories on younger children:

Piaget saw cognitive skills as being learnt in fairly discrete stages, as the child progresses to being a fully equipped adult. He observed that children appear to stop wanting objects once that object is out of sight, and theorised that very young children's knowledge of the way the external world works is so limited that that they do not know that an object out of their sight continues to exist. A child a few months or years older will continue to search for objects even when the objects are hidden. This suggests that they are able to form representations of the object which can stand independently in their minds, hence they "know" that objects exist independently – this is called the stage of "preoperations". The stage after preoperations ("concrete operations") is where children have developed the ability to have two or more symbols for the same thing. An example of this stage at work is when children show that they realise the amount of a substance stays the same even if its appearance is altered (called the "conservation tasks"). For example, older children are able to predict that pouring water from one shaped glass to another does not change the amount of water. Their understanding of how external things, such as how water "works", has got deeper.

The same learning process goes on in the domain of learning about other people's minds. At the final stage of Formal Operations individuals are able to represent abstract ideas to themselves, rather than concrete object-based thought. They start to develop reflective abilities (the ability to "think about thinking"). For example, when younger children have information that a character in a story does not have, they have difficulty realising that the story character will not make decisions based on that information (Mitchell *et al.*, 1996). Inhelder and Piaget suggested that young adolescents have difficulty conceptualising other people's thoughts and opinions, and that this skill is developed over adolescence.

From this point of view, young adolescents behave as if they have an imaginary audience because they do not know enough about other people's minds to realise that other people have different perspectives, different interests and limited interest in them (Elkind, 1967). They may perhaps understand *in principle* the concept that other people may have a covert inner life and opinions, but *in practice* they have difficulty

> differentiating between the objects toward which the thoughts of others are directed, and those which are the focus of their own concern. (Elkind, 1967, p1029)

In other words, unless they make an effort to work out what other people are thinking of, they automatically assume that other people think the same way they do about everything. Hence they are egocentric because they see their perspectives and needs as practically the only existing ones. Similarly when an adolescent

> attempts to cognise the thoughts of others, he fails to suppress his privileged information, his own perspective intrudes, with the result that he reproduces his own perspective rather than anticipating the perspective of the other. (Lapsley & Murphy, 1985, p206)

Egocentrism diminishes in late adolescence; this is presumed to be because adolescents learn from repeated social interaction and experience (Lapsley & Murphy, 1985).

De-idealising is about learning to take a more sophisticated view of all other people, not just parents. As adolescents progress to "debunk" their parents, they are left in a situation where the rest of the adult world then also needs to be debunked. This is a difficult task, all the more so because they are losing the protection of the parents (as parental credibility is being eroded). They are left exposed in front of a set of authorities in the adult world who are still somewhat idealised and quite frightening, without anyone to appeal to if it all goes wrong. As we pointed out earlier, peers gradually take on a whole new importance, and are not as kind and supportive as parents are. Individuals are left much more open to criticism. For example, adolescence is a time when a person's self-esteem can be frighteningly dependent on the attitude of opposite-sex peers (Arkowitz *et al.*, 1978). Parents worry about naive teenagers falling romantically for a person who may not treat them well. When they are older and have more experience of romantic relationships, they may be less likely to accept poor treatment.

Egocentricity and Psychosis

The relevance of such egocentricity for psychosis is enormous. Many of the diagnostic criteria for schizophrenia are like egocentricity taken to an extreme, for example the ICD-10 includes persistent delusions . . . such as religious or political identity or superhuman powers and abilities (e.g. being able to control the weather . . .). (WHO, 1992)

Many people with a psychosis show extreme grandiosity, often to the extent that they believe they are important figures, such as Jesus. Many sufferers spend so much time on their own that it is, in a way, true for them to say they are the most important people in the world – they are virtually the only people in their world environment! Also, delusions of reference (where sufferers feel passers-by or televisions are referring to them) are quite egocentric experiences. In reference experiences, innocuous things that other people do are interpreted as other people only being interested in the person with the psychosis. Voices can be seen as more severe versions of reference experiences – other people are assumed to be so preoccupied with the psychosis sufferer that they neglect their own lives (and bodies) to devote all their time to communicating intimately with the sufferer.

A classic observation of someone with a psychosis is that they have lost touch with what the people around them are really thinking, and become caught up in what they project onto other people as thinking. Laing (1965) described the way that people with a psychosis relate to other people as "fantasms" – that is they had a rather strange and unusual image of the other person in their heads and hence were not really relating to the other person at all. Of course, people are so complicated that anyone's understanding of what makes other people tick is always going to be an approximation to the complexity other people actually experience:

> *Object relations theory*, broadly defined, rests on the assumption that in our relationships we react according to the internal representations we hold of people important to us, in the past as well as the person actually before us now . . . Thus our responses to those before us now may have only the vaguest of associations with present tense reality. (Kroger, 1996, pp50–51)

Psychosis research has already tried to include these sorts of concepts. These empathic skills have been called "theory of mind" skills (i.e. whether the person has a theory about what is in other people's minds; Frith, 1992). Unfortunately, as discussed in Chapter 2, *theory of mind skills* have been seen as having a biological origin, rather than, as the adolescence literature strongly suggests, a social origin.

In summary then, we have said that the ability to mentalise-for-others is something that develops during adolescence. Without this ability, and during its development, adolescents will be egocentric and self-conscious. It has been proposed that people with a psychosis remain egocentric (and get much worse) because they never develop a more sophisticated understanding of how other people work, such as is vital for gaining independence and "feeling like an adult"; without it, the adult world is a difficult place to operate. More than any other adolescent phenomena, egocentricity virtually *defines* schizophrenia.

ADOLESCENT PHENOMENON 5: THE "PERSONAL FABLE" OF SIGNIFICANCE, UNIQUENESS AND INDESTRUCTIBILITY

Adolescents report experiencing many profound occurrences that seem to occur just for them, such as seeing particularly striking scenes in nature. For example:

> Mother nature becomes a personal respondent to the adolescent; the beauty of nature is discovered and exalted emotional states are experienced. (Blos, 1962, p93)

This sense of uniqueness and indestructibility has been called "the personal fable" (Elkind, 1967). Adolescents have a belief in their own indestructibility (e.g. "pregnancy will never happen to me/I will never die").

> They believe that their thoughts or feelings are understood by no-one, least of all by their parents. (Elkind, 1967, p1031)

Presumably these feelings of loneliness and uniqueness come at times when they are forced to realise that everyone else does not see the world as they do, as their egocentricity had led them to believe.

Did/do you experience *personal fable* ideas such as feeling invulnerable or particularly heroic? There is much empirical evidence to suggest that most people do. Enright, Lapsley and Shukla (1979) showed that a measure of "personal fable" followed the same pattern as egocentricity – decreasing from mid to late adolescence. The personal fable was explained by Elkind as deriving from the "imaginary audience".

> The emotional torments undergone by Salinger's Holden Caulfield [the lead character in *The Catcher in the Rye* by J. D. Salinger] exemplifies the adolescent's belief of his own uniqueness of experience. (Elkind, 1967, p1031)

Many adolescents keep diaries; these are used to confide thoughts and events that cannot be shared with real people:

> posterity looks over his shoulder as he writes. (Blos, 1962, p95)

The personal fable suggests that, just as adolescents need to learn about others, they also need to develop an understanding and acceptance of how they themselves work. For example, they may also need to learn things such as how their body copes with alcohol, what sleep routines are best for them, what times of day they feel most able to concentrate. Another example is that they might find role-conflicts make it confusing for them to know what they want (for example, an adolescent boy might want to be independent and devil-may-care towards his parents to impress his friends, while also wanting to be seen as a dutiful and respectful son to please his parents; Thomas, 1968).

Personal Fables and Psychosis

As the personal fable is roughly akin to egocentricity, it should hardly need pointing out that experiences of uniqueness and loneliness, feelings of indestructibility, and a sensation of things being especially significant, perhaps spiritually, are fundamental experiences in psychosis; in fact they are intrinsic to the diagnostic criteria (ICD-10; WHO, 1992). A passage about *adolescence* by Barker (1951) cited by Blos shows this admirably:

> Those exquisitely melancholy afternoons of my adolescence when I used to walk with the abstraction of a sleepwalker through the damp avenues of Richmond Park, thinking that life would never happen to me, wondering why the banked fires of my anticipations, burning in my belly worse than raw alcohol, seemed not to show to strangers as I wandered in the gardens. And often it appeared to me, the frustration, in the disguise of an hallucination: looking between the trees that dripped with hanging mist I sometimes saw classical statues take on an instant of life, turning their naked beauty towards me; or I heard a voice speak out of a bush: 'everything will be answered if you will only not look around'. And I have stood waiting, not daring to look around, expecting a hand on my shoulder that would tender an apotheosis or an assignation. But there was only the gust of wind and the page of a newspaper blowing breezily up and past me like a dirty interjection. Or a bicyclist flashed by, offering possibility until he reached me and decamping with it when he had passed. For I was suffering from a simple but devastating propensity: I was hoping to live. (Barker, cited by Blos, 1962, p92)

The author's eloquence testifies to his sanity, and yet within the context of normal adolescence, here there are reference experiences, anhedonia, voices, apocalyptic cognition and others.

ADOLESCENT PHENOMENON 6: MENTORING AND SEEKING "NEW GODS"

After the loss of the idealised image of their parents, adolescents are in a position where they are used to having parent-type figures, and are now left without them. It is common for them to seek new authority figures that take on a profound significance and are held in idealised esteem. Famous writers or statesmen, religious or moral leaders, footballers, pop-stars or perhaps figures in the young person's immediate environment can become powerfully important mentors (Hendry, 1983). Readers might like to have a think about who was particularly important in their lives when they were adolescents!

Mentor characters can be idealised to the extent that it can be a bit like a crush. The need is for a perfect person to replace the perfect authority lost.

> If a ten-ton truck
> Kills the both of us,
> To die by your side,
> Well the pleasure, the privilege is mine. (Morrissey, 1986)

In psychosis, a powerful and omnipotent character is nearly always assumed by the individual to be behind the voices or thought manipulations (Chadwick & Birchwood, 1994, 1995). Usually it is God or the Devil or somebody famous who is telepathically communicating with the client; by implication the client is a very important person for someone so important to be in close contact with them. Could such experiences be serving a mentoring need?

ADOLESCENT PHENOMENON 7: PSYCHOSIS-LIKE EXPERIENCES

At the start of this chapter we mentioned the Australian study in which up to half the 16-year-olds seemed to be mildly psychotic; we ourselves have replicated the Australian study twice, in both 17-year-olds and 22-year-olds, and found again that there are high levels of psychotic-like thinking in young adult samples. Our study also included some broad measure of attachment and psychological independence which seemed to link psychological development with psychosis scores (people with higher scores on the prodromal signs measures were those who had the highest parental autonomy scores and those who had either very high or very low peer autonomy scores for their age; see Table 3.2). This is consistent with the notion that the more psychologically developed teenagers were experiencing the turbulence associated with such development, particularly if they were unusually distant from (or dependent on) their peers.

In a further study, we compared psychosis sufferers (aged under 40 and without a diagnosis of drug-induced psychosis) to a normal comparison group matched for age, gender and educational level. Psychosis sufferers scored significantly lower than those in the comparison group on parental autonomy, but not peer autonomy, although a significantly greater spread

Table 3.2   Men and Women with High Psychosis Scores have Higher-scoring Autonomy Profiles (mean age=21.9 years, sd=3.7)

	Schizotypy		Early Signs	
	Rest of sample (schizotypy <25, n=54)	Highest ½ s.d. (schizotypy >25, n=6)	Rest of sample (Early Signs ⩽50; n=47)	Highest ½ s.d. (Early Signs >50; n=12)
Parental Autonomy				
mean (s.d.)	53.4 (7.1)	58.2 (10.3)	52.6 (6.2)	59.9 (10.0)
2 tailed	p=0.17, (t=1.37)		p=0.002, (t=3.2)	
Peer Autonomy				
mean (s.d.)	37.3 (2.6)	39.7 (1.4)	37.3 (2.6)	38.8 (2.6)
2 tailed	p=0.04 (t=2.16)		p=0.09 (t=1.7)	

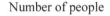

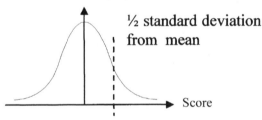

Figure 3.2   Figure Showing How Participants with Highest Scores on Psychosis Measures were Selected, for Table 3.2

was seen for peer autonomy of psychosis sufferers. The psychosis group was much closer to 13-year-olds than 17-year-olds on these measures of psychological development (Harrop, 2000).

SUMMARY

At the start of the chapter, it was noted that many adolescents have unusual experiences and asked why. The question was: what is going on for them that disposes them to be a "bit odd"? It was wondered whether the same processes were at work in people who do actually go on to develop a psychosis.

We hope that the arguments have convinced you that adolescence is a particularly unusual time and that it is "normal to be unusual" at this time. Hopefully it has also shown that some of the apparently incomprehensible experiences of psychosis have a lot in common with typical features of adolescence.

Here's a recap of some of the key ideas:

● At the start of adolescence, people are often egocentric and experience "personal fable" cognitions, which were both shown to be closely related to them having a limited, idealised understanding of other people.

● Building a more elaborate understanding of others is part of normal adolescence. It helps people gain independence, but doing so can be a depressing and stressful experience. Conflict between parent and offspring during adolescence is a normal part of gaining independence.

● The same issues of adolescence are relevant for people who develop a psychosis; similarities were drawn out between the normal troubled teenager, and the individual of a few years older who is actively psychotic.

WHAT CONCLUSIONS CAN YOU DRAW FROM THIS?

Our conclusions are that psychosis is not that big a departure from normal adolescence. Many of the features of psychosis seem to be extensions of typical adolescent phenomena. People seem to be stuck in the middle of the uncomfortable turbulent experiences of adolescence such as loneliness, grandiosity, depression and delusion-like fantasy, yet unlike most adolescents they do not emerge from them. This would mean that the self-same teenage "troubles" now deteriorate into the emergence of psychotic symptoms (Harrop & Trower, 2001).

Hypothesis 1) Some people with a psychosis are not very independent, and have an idealised, less elaborate view of their parents and others. Their viewpoint means that it could be difficult for them to operate autonomously in the adult world. For example, still having idealised views of one's parents as especially powerful, knowledgeable "gods", (as a younger child perhaps does) would make doing the things that adults do – cooking, driving and so on – very intimidating. Many in this group would not have shown any particularly remarkable problems during early adolescence; many possibly achieved very highly at school.

Gaining independence from parents is one half of the tasks of adolescence. The other task is creating closer peer relationships that can replace the closeness lost with parents. In normal adolescence, part of the resolution of the uncomfortable period of adolescence comes with bonding to peers and leaving the family. This leads us to our second hypothesis . . .

Hypothesis 2) Some individuals with a psychosis have gone part way towards an adult, autonomous view of their parents, but cannot relate to their peers and end up stranded in a social and psychological "no man's land". For these people, their relationship with their parents has been renegotiated, and they are experiencing common adolescence phenomena (for example, conflict with their parents and de-idealisation). Unfortunately, the situation does not get resolved, because their peer relationships are not well developed enough, perhaps because they have not de-idealised their peers yet (this will be explored later in the book). In these circumstances the condition of being a troubled teenager may gradually and insidiously deteriorate to become a partial or full psychosis.

In one of our studies, admittedly with just a small number of participants (reported at length in Section Three), we found that 86 per cent of the people we were working with who had a psychosis fitted the first hypothesis, whereas the remaining 14 per cent fitted the second (Harrop, 2000). Clients in the former group (not being independent) reported being anxious about ever expressing anger towards their parents, and had strong rules about how they should behave towards their apparently-idealised parents. Clients in the smaller second group (partially rebellious) had no qualms at all about expressing anger towards their parents and behaved in an almost tyrannical fashion.

Our argument goes further than just saying that as the condition arises in late adolescence, adolescence issues will be important to consider in treatment. Our argument is that the symptoms of psychosis can arise directly from the phenomena of blocked adolescence.

Our argument will now hang from how well we can explain the symptoms of psychosis from these postulated blocks to development and this is covered in brief in the next chapter, and at length in the next two sections.

CHAPTER 4

WHY MIGHT SOME PEOPLE BE BLOCKED?

In the previous chapter, it was speculated that late-adolescent onset psychosis might be understood as an exaggerated form of typical adolescent experiences. For most people, adolescence is a transition period. It was suggested that people who develop a psychosis get trapped in this period of their lives. We described two situations in which this might happen:

- Some people with a psychosis have not gained independence from their parents, and continue to understand parents and others in an idealised manner, with only a broad-brush understanding.

- Another small group of people with a psychosis have partially individuated from their parents, but have not managed to bond to peers, and hence have not got the resolution of their problems that bonding to peers can bring.

In this section we attempt to explain the blocks that may occur in the development process that leave some at-risk teenagers stuck in this psychotic-like state, and why the blocks may come about. We also start to investigate how these blocks might lead to psychotic symptomatology, something we continue in much greater depth in Section Two.

WHY MIGHT IT BE DIFFICULT TO INDIVIDUATE FROM ONE'S PARENTS?

So why might it be so difficult for some at-risk adolescents to gain independence? The perspective changes of adolescence may be unpleasant and difficult for an individual to accept, as Rosenberg pin-points:

> Once the individual seriously attempts to fathom what others think of him, the conclusions that emerge are by no means palatable . . . In the early years the child has accepted the idea that others think well of him and has given the matter little thought. In early adolescence, when he is able to get outside his own viewpoint and see matters, including himself, from the perspective of others, he

recognises the complexity of others' attitudes towards him; he becomes aware of both their qualms and their sources of appreciation. (Rosenberg, 1979, p238–9. Reproduced by permission of Krieger Publishing Company.)

There might also be other reasons why such transitions may be more difficult for some people.

SELF-CONSCIOUSNESS

Adolescence is a time when people feel particularly self-conscious (Rosenberg, 1979). Experimental studies have shown that it is impossible to be "other aware" when a person is feeling "self-aware" (Duval & Wicklund, 1972). Being locked into an awareness of one's self-as-presented-for-others prevents other-awareness judgements. Also, the same researchers argued that it is inevitable that someone who is feeling self-aware for a length of time will start to feel very self-critical:

> . . . we would argue that the objective state will be uncomfortable when endured for considerable time intervals. As the individual examines himself on one dimension after another, he will inevitably discover ways in which he is inadequate, and at such a point he will prefer to revert to the subjective state. (Duval & Wicklund, 1972, p4)

Hence, for a shy teenager who is particularly self-aware, an "agent perspective" (where they could step back and actively judge the behaviours of the other people in their life) may be nearly impossible. This would mean that they will have difficulty gaining an understanding of others which they would need to help overcome their natural youthful egocentricity (see Adolescent Phenomenon 4 in Chapter 3, page 41). Their energies are more likely to be taken up dwelling on their deficiencies. It can be seen that de-idealisation and independence are going to be difficult for someone locked into this self-aware state.

Some people with a psychosis hear critical voices that comment on their actions nearly all the time. A person under such continual threat is going to find it very difficult to get out of the object state, because their voices are always with them. In Chapter 10 we investigate the experience of extreme self-consciousness as "feeling like an object in the other person's gaze", an experience described as *"objectité"* by Sartre (1943/1957).

IDEAL PARENTS

It may seem unfair to rebel against "good" parents. It has been argued that it is almost better for adolescents pursuing independence if their parents are harsh, because it will then not be so difficult for adolescents to find issues on which to oppose them, nor will they need much reassurance about how right they are (Blos, 1962). (Here, for instance, peer groups can serve as a particularly potent source of outside validation; Berndt, 1979). However, with parents whom the adolescent has a close relationship with, it may feel insulting to try to take control and be assertive. After all, parents generally think they have their offspring's best interests at heart. Normally parents have to put up with a lot of apparently unreasonable behaviours and conflicting messages:

> No individual achieves independence without a number of backwards glances. (Coleman & Hendry, 1990, p84)

One moment adolescents can be unusually adult and taking the high moral ground on some issue against the parent. The next they can be acting like a small child again, and using ways of behaviour thought by the parent to be long since gone, perhaps seeking reassurances like a much younger child would (Kroger, 1996). The rapidly-fluctuating nature of adolescent moods can be exasperating for parents. We have observed a similar pattern of rebelliousness cycling with guilt and more childish, reassurance-seeking behaviours operating in people with a psychosis (see Section Three).

Many clients idealise their parents, and are particularly anxious to protect them. Thus it is hard for these clients to individuate against them and do their own thing. To de-idealise them may seem like an aggressive act against a God, or against someone they have a genuinely warm and close relationship with.

For example, Alan had been floridly ill for a period a year ago. He had been so in awe of his mother that he passively did whatever he thought she wanted of him. Every few months he would have built up such resentments and frustrations that he would have an angry verbal outburst. His mother took this as signs of a setback in his illness after a period of having been "doing well". Al usually felt chronic guilt and shame after his outburst, and would return to being totally compliant for a few months.

> Opposition is true friendship. (William Blake)

Some parenting traditions have held that conflict in families is a bad thing. Research has shown that although conflict can be unpleasant and difficult for all parties involved, it is actually a good thing because it reflects healthy self-assertion and rights to self-actualise on both sides (e.g. Lamborn *et al.*, 1991). A political system in which dissent is voiced and tolerated is generally held to be healthier than one in which no-one is ever allowed to disagree. Conflict is good here because adolescents have rights to assert their needs as adults against their parents. They also need to practise their arguing skills if they are to bond with peers successfully. To reiterate, an interesting implication of this theory is that one does not have to take sides in the debate of parents vs. child mentioned at the start of Chapter 3. It reconciles the two sides because it says it is natural for both parties to have grievances with the other. (Also, it implies that in many cases, the parenting is actually very good, so the child does not want to leave home!)

INTIMIDATING PARENTS

Another situation where the adolescent may not feel able to individuate is in situations where the parent is frightening. Some parents take disagreement and difference as a threat to themselves, and try to disallow it. For instance, it has been suggested that people sexually abused as children are particularly at risk from schizophrenia spectrum disorders (Hunter, 1991). This could be because a child living with a dominating and abusive parent perhaps copes by being extremely subordinate and wary of adults. A person who is stuck in an involuntary subordinate role (Gilbert, 1993) may find this role impossible to break out of, even though it might later be possible to escape painful circumstances. The life transition and role renegotiations of adolescence for such a frightened person would be too difficult to attempt. Stuck in such a subordinate role, maintained by fear of adults, and unable to enter the adult world as one of the adults, and yet seeing all their friends successfully becoming adults, it can seem that there would be nowhere for the adolescent to go. They remain trapped in a child-like role when, in their eyes, everyone else is authoritative and powerful.

INDIVIDUATED FROM PARENTS BUT FACING PROBLEMS WITH PEERS?

Peer relationships may be so difficult and threatening that parental relationships are preferred, in the sense that clients are too anxious for them to be able to move away from the home base. In the same way that it is easier for individuals to interact with their parents when they have de-idealised them, there is a similar need to de-idealise and understand peers. Peers are often less tolerant, more competitive and perhaps more likely to be punitive.

Evolutionary theorists have suggested that losing one's peer group invokes all the built-in fears of being alone and vulnerable ("left to the wolves"; Gilbert, 1993). It also means that they are then trapped in the safety of the family, but feeling unbearable anguish and despair over their failure to individuate and all this failure implies in terms of not being able to bond to peers.

Although some (mainly female) clients actually get married and have children (Sartorius et al., 1986), most (mainly male) have enormous problems with romantic relationships. Around 90 per cent of male clients asked in a recent study had never been on more than a couple of dates (Harrop, 2000). Our interviews showed that dating was such an impossible goal (though desperately desired) that it was never attempted (see Chapter 14). Some clients were terrified of dating; as one client put it:

> If you want to know the truth, I've never really had a girlfriend. I'd like one in principle but not in practice. Mostly when I talk to girls I feel sure they hate me, they think I'm a load of old rubbish, and how could I possibly think I am normal?

Dating is one of the most important and common ways of gaining security, support and recognition from one's peer group. It is also the path to marriage and parenthood – the next "life-stage". The consequence is that major life stages are cut off and opportunities for self-construction are lost.

To sum up: we have described why some people with a psychosis might get stuck – they could be unable to appropriately refine their understanding of other people. This would mean they find it difficult to gain independence and to leave the family and attach to peers.

A POSSIBLE BIOLOGICAL NEED FOR INDEPENDENCE?

Why is it that the first group of psychosis sufferers (the group of non-autonomous individuals who remain bonded to their parents) do not just live happily in this state? Why do they show any distress at all? Part of the answer might be that there has evolved a powerful sexual and maturational propensity to individuate from one's parents, the thwarting of which creates enormous emotional turbulence.

The motive for autonomy is not just an intellectual pursuit, it is also a biological goal. All group animals show a desire to be at the top of the hierarchy, and to find a mate. However, Gilbert (1993) has described an opposing mechanism, where an individual assumes a low-ranked position when threatened or defeated by a dominant other. Gilbert calls the latter the "involuntary subordination" response, and it includes the tendency to be submissive, appeasing and to have low self-esteem. This low-ranking can have serious effect: in ethology, there is considerable evidence that sexual maturation can depend on attaining status in group hierarchical relations. In many old-world monkeys, males do not sexually mature while they are in the company of dominant males. In stump-tailed macaques, males do not show an adolescent growth spurt until the dominant male is removed; soon after this the next-highest ranking male begins sexual development (Steinberg, 1987, 1988). Effects have been shown amongst female tamarins and marmosets; young females living in proximity to their mothers show suppressed periods, and yet if they are removed from this proximity they develop regular periods within four weeks (Evans & Hodges, 1984).

Here we have another example of the ideas from Chapter 2 – profound biological changes induced by social and psychological experiences. In humans, it has been shown that the timing of puberty can be influenced to a large extent by psychological factors. It was found that a higher percentage of ballet dancers than non-ballet dancers were "late" maturers (55% vs 29%; although this effect may be due to anorexia as much as maturation). In a longitudinal study, Steinberg (1987) assessed how physical maturation and relationship measures developed together over a year. He found the usual results of more arguments, less cohesion and increasing autonomy with increasing physical development. He also found the reciprocal relationship in girls – autonomy and distance between parent and child resulted in increased physical development. Hence there is evidence that, as in ethology, a person's psychological environment can strongly affect puberty (see also Brookes-Gunn & Warren, 1985).

One of the seminal findings in psychosis research concerns people who have recovered from a psychotic episode in hospital and return to live in the parental home – they are twice as likely to relapse as those who leave hospital to live independently (Brown & Birley, 1968). It has been shown that people suffering from schizophrenia perceive themselves as being in a low-ranked position and show all the features of Gilbert's involuntary subordination response (Birchwood et al., 2000b). A degree of associated sexual inhibition is also likely to occur as part of this response. It would not have to be as extreme or dramatic as actual maturational or pubertal inhibition or even ovulation suppression to be relevant; though this might be happening. One of the many ingredients integral to this maturational process is the role of sex-hormones; some sort of effect might be expected in the sex-hormone levels of people with schizophrenia; interestingly, there are now a number of reports on the connection between sex-hormones and psychosis.

Variations in sex-hormones have been shown to correspond to variations in psychotic symptoms (Häfner et al., 1993b). Other researchers have used rats to attempt to show a relationship between symptoms and sex-hormones. Riecher-Rössler, Häfner, Staumbaum et al. (1994) found injecting rats with "schizophrenia" (i.e. a psychoactive drug) had less effect after they had been injected with oestrogen. They concluded that oestrogen raised the threshold for vulnerability for "schizophrenia". One could speculate further on the biology involved (e.g. whether or not sex-hormones could be used as anti-psychotic medications). The current hypothesis is served well by the conclusion that there is some sort of irregularity in the sex-hormones of people with a psychosis. A proponent of the ethological theory could speculate that it is a biological drive to reach adulthood coming into conflict with a biological suppression effect that is due to the proximity of dominant parents, and because, psychologically, clients "do not feel like adults". They may still idealise their parents, and peers, and yet they may be experiencing the same self-construction and individuation urges against their parents that normals have. This may cause some discomfort because they may not feel that these urges are acceptable against idealised others.

SOME PRELIMINARY PRACTICAL IMPLICATIONS

Practical and therapeutic implications of the developmental theory discussed in these last two chapters are considered at length in Section Four (particularly Chapter 15). However, here are some preliminary conclusions for now . . .

The adolescence Literature may be Useful for Normalising

Our experience has been that some clients are very much in awe of their parents, and this creates problems for them because they find it difficult to be around them. Other clients have urges to rebel against their parents but feel very bad about doing this. Such clients may benefit greatly from knowing more about normal adolescent development, especially given their isolation and lack of a normalising peer group. For example, it would be important for them to hear it is not unnatural to rebel against one's parents, or to think ill of them. It is also permissible to have differences of opinion with them on major issues. Wild mood swings in this context are not evidence of going mad, but may be taken as typical occurrences during adolescence. Like normal adolescents, it may be comforting for clients to know that although these experiences seem unique to themselves (and many will be!), the feelings themselves may be typical for people undergoing adolescence. (Obviously, there are clients for whom anger is a problem, but therapy – such as Rational Emotive Behaviour Therapy – can be used to help them develop "healthy" adaptive anger; Ellis, 1994; Dryden, 1990.)

Parents could be encouraged to see the client in the light of being like a rebellious teenager. This would certainly be less worrying than a label of schizophrenia. This might help them feel less bad about any conflict that arises, and help them feel less alone too, as conflict is something most parents experience, and would not reflect on their parenting skills. Particularly shy clients might benefit from being encouraged by their parents to let go a bit, and being reassured the world would not end if they fell out with their parents briefly over something. Many clients in our sample feared dire consequences, such as being thrown out of the house or being sacrificed to the devil, if they stand up to their parents even once or even in a mild way (Harrop, 2000; see Chapter 13).

> Adolescents could not grow into adults unless they were able to test out the boundaries of authority, nor could they discover what they believed unless given the opportunity to push hard against the beliefs of others. (Coleman & Hendry, 1990, p89)

Peer Relationships and Romantic Relationships as Important Focuses

Another common adolescent phenomenon is a need for acceptance amongst peers as well as parents; how ironic it is that a diagnosis of schizophrenia realises clients' worst fears of being different in a most malignant sense. Much research to date has focused on parental and family relationships in psychosis, and the goal of this work seems to be a slightly unnatural situation of parents and offspring living together in harmony. A greater emphasis on achieving peer relationships and leaving the family might be helpful. Most clients have very few friends, and those friends they have are often fellow users of psychiatric services. The area of romantic relationships is also of paramount importance to clients; many clients see a romantic partner as the most important thing (along with rewarding employment) that they would want for themselves in the long term (although many clients find it too threatening in the short term). Professional services are cautious about the area of romantic relationships (perhaps understandably so), and this is an area where much research is needed. It is suggested that clients may gain much from knowing more about the opposite sex, about whom some know very little. It often seems that the opposite sex is a source of fear for them; it cannot be healthy for them to be intimidated by such a large proportion of the population. Many clients would benefit from being tolerably encouraged by their parents to look for romantic partners, as many seem to think this is something their parents would not allow.

People with a Psychosis may Benefit from Working on their Understandings of Others

It was argued earlier in the section on egocentricity that a fundamental skill that people with a late adolescent psychosis have not developed (that usually develops during adolescence) is an understanding of the psychology of other people, or "theory of other minds" (ideas on how to go about this are described at length in Chapter 15). Understanding others is intrinsic to the person becoming an independent agent – to be able to objectively judge the world and others around us – enabling the person who might be very much in awe of their parents to individuate and rebel, something they probably want to do but don't know how to go about. For people who have individuated from their parents but are still scared of their peers, a more thorough understanding of their peers will be a useful tool to enable them to gain the acceptance (and perhaps employment) they want. A better understanding of one's peers means one is more likely to be able to manipulate them to get what one wants in terms of meeting autonomy and attachment needs. It has been shown that when people are less self-aware, they are more likely to be able to respond appropriately to social cues (Gollwitzer & Wicklund, 1985). It is also a good general rule that when one feels criticised and badly judged by others, looking at the causes, motivations and authority behind the judge's actions will be very valuable in understanding it.

Clients who hear voices are often locked into a state of extreme self-consciousness described earlier ("objectité"). Many are self-focused to the extent where anything that enters their consciousness seems to portend critical references to themselves (e.g. planes going overhead, messages from the television). They may appear hyper-aware of others as the ones looking/judging and themselves as the one looked at and judged (for example, as they watch for threats from others as they walk down the street), but they often do not have a good understanding of others as separate psychological beings with vulnerabilities, motivations and beliefs of their own, which have nothing to do with the client. Clients typically need to be encouraged to watch other people and to come up with explanations of their behaviour that are internal to these other people (see Chapter 15). They could perhaps concentrate specifically on understanding their parents, as a start to the process of de-idealisation, if necessary.

A good example of what has been proposed in this section comes from an autobiographical tale from Bertrand Russell:

> In adolescence, I hated life and was continually on the verge of suicide . . . Now, on the contrary, I enjoy life; I might almost say that with every year that passes I enjoy it more . . . Largely it is due to a diminishing preoccupation with myself. Like others who had a puritanical education, I had the habit of meditating on my sins, my follies and shortcoming. I seemed to myself – no doubt justly – a miserable specimen. Gradually I learned to be indifferent to myself and my deficiencies; I came to centre my attention increasingly on external objects: the state of the world, various branches of knowledge, individuals for whom I felt affection. External interests, it is true, bring each its own possibility of pain: the world may be plunged into war, knowledge in some direction may be hard to achieve, friends may die. But pains of these kinds do not destroy the essential quality of life, as do those that spring from disgust with the self. (Russell, 1930, p14)

This chapter has attempted to describe some potential ways in which the normal psychological developments of adolescence might be blocked in people with a psychosis. The next section describes in much detail how such blocks might lead to the formation of psychotic symptoms.

SECTION SUMMARY

Let us take stock. In this section we have discussed:

- the disparate ways the various parties involved regard schizophrenia
- the idea that biology is the only important thing to look at – we rejected this idea, and it was concluded that the psychology has been neglected, particularly the adolescence angle
- similarities between normal adolescence experiences and typical psychotic ones
- the suggestion that adolescent development can be blocked in various ways, for example, through difficulties in understanding others
- that when these blocks are severe enough, they can lead to all sorts of mental-health problems, of which the most severe is psychosis (psychotic symptoms).

How can that happen? Our explanation is that the blocks in adolescent development can cause a profound breakdown in the development of the self. We address this in the next section.

SECTION TWO

PSYCHOSIS AND THE SELF

So why does schizophrenia arise during adolescence? In Section One we painted the background to this question – that adolescence is a period of crucial and, literally, *self*-development, which can easily be derailed. When this happens, the person is vulnerable to a number of mental-health problems, the worst of which is psychosis. But what actually happens to bring on psychotic experiences? In this section, we paint in the foreground in our picture-analogy by addressing this question directly. How could psychological blocks in adolescence actually give rise to symptoms of psychosis? We believe these blocks can severely disrupt the process of constructing a self – arguably the most important single task of human existence – and that symptoms of psychosis can be one of the consequences. In the next five chapters we discuss the process of self-construction and how these blocks can disrupt the process. Adolescence is *the* time in life when the individual grapples with the enormous psychological changes involved in the transition from being a dependent child into a full blown mature "person in the world".

This section deals with the complex ideas concerned with the self that have been occupying philosophers for many centuries. What is "the self"? Does it exist? Does it matter? What do we mean by "self-esteem", "self-image" and "self concept"? Do we just *have* a self, or if not, how do people go about *getting* "a self"? These are key questions facing adolescents – and the adolescent within all of us. What happens at the extremes of this process where people are having difficulty "getting a self"?

The first chapter, Chapter 5, introduces the idea that *study of the "self"* is important in psychosis.

Chapter 6 contains some *experiential exercises* that the reader might like to try, to get an insight into the centuries-old debate on the meaning of "self". These thought experiments should be able to help shed some light on psychotic experiences.

Chapter 7 explores some of the ways in which *self-construction* works. For example, people tend to want to create selves that, for example, serve attachment needs or fit in with drives for independence.

Chapter 8 describes *the intimate detail of our quests to establish authentic selves in the world* – how we negotiate the fact that everyone else also wants to create a self as well, the trade-offs and compromises that we all make.

Chapter 9 describes *what can happen if a person's self-construction needs are not met* because there is no-one to co-operate with this process. The extreme isolation and sense of nothingness that this threatens can certainly bring about some experiences which seem typically psychotic.

Chapter 10 focuses on the opposite tendency – *when a person's self is not defined by them as agent, but instead feels forced on them by someone else.* When agency and ownership of a person's own role feels imposed, some experiences can result that seem typically psychotic in a different, engulfing way.

CHAPTER 5

THE CRISIS OF THE ADOLESCENT SELF

> For youth in particular, self-presentation is likely to assume the function of testing and attempting to validate one or more self-hypotheses . . . In a groping and tentative way, different selves may be rehearsed – the glamour girl, the caustic wit . . . Hence the common sense question 'What is he trying to prove?' has profound psychological significance, for that is precisely what the adolescent is trying to do. A girl wants a date in order to have evidence that she is attractive . . . When an adolescent – or anyone else – tries to achieve a certain goal, he does so not simply for the advantage it affords, but because it enables him to *prove* something about himself to himself. What concerns them is the uncertainty about what they are like, and what motivates them is the desire to know, to achieve certainty. Yet ultimate certainty forever eludes us so that the responses of others are required not only for confirmation but for the lifelong reconfirmation of our working self-hypotheses. (Rosenberg, 1979, p48. Reproduced by permission of Krieger Publishing Company.)

According to Rosenberg, adolescence is a time at which many adolescents focus on the question "who am I?" It is a time when they can find things out and play with possibilities for the future. As Rosenberg relates, this is a difficult task for most people. We suggested in the previous section that people who go on to develop a psychosis have particular difficulty with this process. So what sort of a sense of self do people who develop a psychosis have?

Few would doubt that people with a psychosis have a problematic, often quite devastated sense of who they are. We know from personal accounts that they can feel they are someone who is intensely threatened by the outside world, by what they believe to be massive conspiracies, by gangsters, secret police and other powerful agencies intent on destroying them. They may believe themselves possessed by evil spirits, in danger of divine retribution because of their own wickedness or feel they are being scapegoated by other evildoers. They often feel so vulnerable that they misinterpret and greatly magnify any criticism from within their own family as extreme hostility, and experience the behaviour of worried parents as a personal invasion. Even worse – because they cannot escape from it – many experience constant attack from hostile voices that condemn them and tell them to do dangerous things, mainly to themselves.

In response to this perceived relentless attack, some may try to defend themselves by attributing all the blame onto malevolent others; this lets them see themselves as innocent victims of this persecution. Others will blame themselves and see themselves as bad or evil, fully deserving their punishment. And some may go backwards and forwards, one time blaming themselves, other times blaming others.

That is one extreme – the extreme of feeling the self to be invaded, intruded, oppressed, even engulfed by a world of hostile people, agencies, spirits and voices. The other extreme is as intolerable – of the empty self, of feeling abandoned and marginalised by an indifferent and rejecting world, cast out into some kind of wilderness for unwanted, unworthy life forms. Sometimes the very experience of having a diagnosis of schizophrenia, and being (sometimes forcibly) hospitalised, leads them to identify themselves as almost less than human, unacceptable in the world of ordinary people – as "mad", as "freaks", as unwanted "outcasts" from society. Depression is a common consequence, and even suicide (Birchwood *et al.*, 2000).

These consequences of schizophrenia seem bad enough, but the "schizophrenic episode" itself – the acute psychotic crisis – can possibly cause even worse consequences. Some schools of thought believe that a psychotic episode can have such a catastrophic effect that sufferers show not just low self-esteem – which assumes an intact self to be threatened – but fundamental problems with the very essence of self. As we shall later explore, the very boundaries of the self seem to break down, together with loss of agency. Alternatively, at the other extreme, an illusory self is created with great omnipotent powers. Some of the psychotic symptoms can be understood as manifestations of this breakdown or disturbance in the self – thoughts no longer seem one's own and sound like voices or appear to be placed in one's head, or thoughts are broadcast for all to hear.

It is precisely this apparent fundamental breakdown in "normal" perceptual, cognitive, affective processes – the partial or complete disintegration of the "fragile self" (Mollon, 1993) – that often seems to characterise the "psychotic episode".

What then causes the disturbance in or even disintegration of the self in psychotic episodes? Given our preparatory arguments above, we think it is time to put forward a psychological explanation.

Our explanation argues:

- That all humans have a fundamental need to be a "self", to have a social identity, recognised and valued by others

- That this "self" is not an entity (isn't something we are born with which resides somewhere in the mind), but has to be continuously constructed

- Therefore this "self" is fragile and can be damaged or even destroyed.

- We would like to take the reader through these steps in some detail in the next chapters, citing evidence that we believe supports the theory.

CHAPTER 6

THE MYSTERY OF THE SELF: WHY HAVE IT? WHAT IS IT?

Do we need a self? Is there such a thing as the self? If there is, what is it? These are strange and difficult questions which some never think about, but others become preoccupied with. We believe they are good questions to ask, and in this chapter we explore them and try to find some answers, often surprising answers.

If we didn't have a self, surely we wouldn't even exist! Even objects, chairs and tables have an identity, not only as a member of a class (e.g. chair, table) but also with is own unique identity – this chair in this place with these scratch marks given to me by my grandmother, etc. So it is certainly true we also have and need an identity, in the simple sense, as we wouldn't otherwise exist. But the question is not only "do we need an identity?", but "do we have, and do we need to have, a self?" Tables and chairs have an identity, but they don't, as far as we know, have or *need* a self! We also have an identity in the same sense – our physical bodies – but we humans, probably uniquely among the species, believe we have, and need to have, a self. We care about our "self" probably more than almost anything else. This is what all people need and work so hard to achieve. We strive to make something of ourselves. Most of us want to stand out from the crowd, to be someone in life, make an impact. We will have much more to say about this in the section below on the motivations and limitations of self-construction. Let it suffice for now to say that the motivation to "self-actualise" is the most fundamental motive, since it involves no less than the motive *to be*. To quote one of Shakespeare's most famous lines, at the beginning of Hamlet's soliloquy:

To be or not to be – that is the question.

WHAT IS THE SELF? DOES IT REALLY EXIST?

What then *is* the self? And does it really exist? Even given the distinction between simple identity and self, the questions still seem strange ones to ask. We are talking about what I *am* – surely nothing can be quite as certain, fundamental, and familiar? If this were true, we would have no difficulty answering the questions, and on the face of it, it does seem obvious – any of us can answer the question what am I? I am a man, Caucasian, psychologist, a husband, a father, and more psychologically, I hope I am reasonably caring, sociable, ambitious and so on. But these are qualities or attributes I *have*. It still leaves the question, what am *I*, the self that *has* all these attributes? Is the self some kind of thing or a spirit? It has to be one or the other, and yet it doesn't feel satisfactory to say it is one *or* the other. And if it is a thing or a spirit, where is it located – in the head, in the mind, in the brain, in the heart? One person might say the self is everywhere, it is all of him, and in a sense that is true. But another person might say it is nowhere, in that he *doesn't* want to say it simply *is* in any one part of the body, for example, pointing to his eyes and saying "it's just behind here!" And that is true too, because if it was, say, just behind the eyes, and a clever surgeon could open up your head and look behind your eyes, what would he see – a little version of you? Probably not!

So it seems the self is everywhere and nowhere, and we can't easily decide whether it is a thing or a spirit. Actually the more we ask these questions, the more puzzling it becomes.

How do we find out the answer to our question, what is the self? The 17th Century French philosopher René Descartes believed he had the answer. His answer was so persuasive and compelling that it remains highly influential to this day, particularly in the field of mental health. To paraphrase Descartes, he might say that in a science like physics, if we want to know something, we usually have to go to an expert, a physicist, because we don't have the expertise ourselves. But surely we don't need to ask an expert "what is the self?"? We only have to examine our own conscious experience. Descartes reasoned that one way of being certain of our answer is to be absolutely radical and to try to doubt absolutely everything, including whether we even have a self at all. This was his "method of doubt". Imagine that an evil genius has managed to deceive us into believing there is a world and that we exist, whereas maybe there isn't anything, it is all an illusion. Is there anything left that we cannot doubt? The only thing that we cannot possibly doubt is that we doubt! And if we doubt we must think and if we think it is self evident that we exist. This is what is meant by Descartes's famous "proof": *cogito ergo sum*, or "I think, therefore I am".

But Descartes's idea of the self being "I am" (or "I think") is that the self is pure consciousness, what he called "pure thinking substance", and that nothing else is a necessary part of the self, since all else could be doubted. And this is how he came to what we call dualism, the distinction between mind and matter, that the self is basically made purely of non-material "mind stuff" (consciousness, thought, mental events) and everything else, including our own bodies, is made of material stuff which we can see and touch and measure.

It is important to know if Descartes is right or not for many reasons, but in particular because the answer has major implications for the explanation, diagnosis and treatment of schizophrenia. Dualism has been very influential in mental health because it has led to a focus on *mental* illness, an illness of the mind (and therefore by implication the self) as distinct from the body. Thus people with a diagnosis of schizophrenia are often viewed (and view themselves) as *being* schizophrenic (i.e. in their self-identity) (Estroff, 1989).

How do we find out if Descartes is right? If he is right then every one of us should be able to verify we have a pure non-material self by looking within our conscious experience. The argument is that what we experience is self-evidently true, e.g. if we have a headache we cannot doubt it. So here is an experiment to try:

> Close your eyes, empty your mind completely, and get in touch with your Cartesian self – the "I think therefore I am" – just pure thinking substance. Spend a few minutes concentrating on bringing your self into consciousness.

Most people in our experience find this task very difficult, if not impossible. Instead of finding the Cartesian self, they keep coming across anything but – images, worries, thoughts about this and that, sounds, smells, sensations. Or they just nearly catch it but it slides away and seems to vanish. This self seems extraordinary elusive.

This was exactly what another philosopher, David Hume found. In the 18th Century, this Scotsman wrote that all he could identify in experience were perceptions of things like heat or cold, light or shade, love or hatred, pain or pleasure. In fact Hume put forward the opposite argument to Descartes. He also examined his conscious experience – a method he called his "empirical" method of doubt, and concluded that there is no such "thing" as the self. His challenge was that if there was a self we would be able to identify it in experience, but there is no such self – only sense perceptions. Therefore we are no more than a bundle of perceptions, and the concept of self should be "cast to the flames" along with all other metaphysical nonsense.

We seem to have gone from one extreme to the other. Descartes found the self and showed it was purely mental; Hume got rid of the self altogether! Who is right?

The debate has been raging for nearly 300 years. Indeed, out of this intellectual battle between the Cartesian "rationalists" versus the Humean "empiricists" grew the modern debate in philosophy and psychology about the nature of the self. The debate has traditionally been fought between the radical behaviourists on the one hand who eschew the metaphysics of internal entities, and the "mentalists" who account for behaviour in terms of personality, "mental" disorder and the self.

However, recent philosophical analyses show both positions to be misled (McCulloch, 1994). There is no need to take up one or the other position if one rejects the doctrine of Cartesian dualism – the doctrine that there are two kinds of "stuff" – mental stuff and physical stuff.

One way of seeing this is by considering one of the criticisms of Descartes's "proof" that the

> 'I' was a substance whose essence or nature is to think and whose being requires no place and depends on no material thing. (1642/1951, p26, cited in Levin, 1992)

However, consciousness (the "self-evident" basis of Descartes's proof) has no content of its own but "intends" objects (Brentano, 1995/1874), i.e. consciousness is always consciousness *of* something. This is what we discovered when we tried the experiment earlier, when we looked for the Cartesian self in our consciousness but, like Hume, only came up with perceptions of things.

Our experience therefore tells us that consciousness is not an independent substance as Descartes claimed, but rather strangely seems to be both connected to, and yet separate from, the objects of which it is conscious. Elaborations of this idea have been developed by a number of philosophers (e.g. Mischel, 1975; McCulloch, 1994) and are the essence of the notion of the seemingly paradoxical connection between separation of concept and object, thought and action, and in the present case, consciousness and its objects (Trower, 1984).

It is time for another mental experiment which accommodates this new discovery.

> We couldn't find the self by emptying our minds; maybe we should try filling our minds with something and then look. So this time keep your eyes open, and focus on an object in the room. While doing so, try to find your "self".

What did you experience? You will have experienced the straightforward awareness of the object – here is this lamp. That is simple perception. But you might also have experienced being aware of your awareness of the object. This second awareness is often called meta-awareness, a kind of looking at yourself looking at something! This is a kind of self-awareness – here I am looking at this lamp. We can even go a level further – here I am looking at myself looking at this lamp! We come close here to the distinction between what William James, one of the founding fathers of psychology, called the "*I*" and the "*me*". The "*I*" is the part that does the looking, the "*me*" is the part that "*I*" am looking at. The "*I*" is the subject, the "*me*" is the object. This is an important discovery about the self.

The self appears to have these two parts: the *"I"* and the *"me"*. Let us look more closely at what we might have discovered about these two parts in the above experiment. First, the *"I"* has a strange quality, namely it doesn't seem to have any identity of its own. This is because it is pure consciousness. The only way of identifying the *"I"*, as pure consciousness, is as a reflection of something or things which it isn't. The *"I"*, or consciousness, has no content or substance of its own and can only exist as a reflection of something outside. The nearest analogy is a reflection in a mirror. The reflection of the chair in the mirror doesn't mean the reflection (or the mirror) has a chair in it. The reflection, like consciousness, is itself empty, and is no more than a reflection of . . .

Modern philosophy says that consciousness is always consciousness *of* something, and there can never be a consciousness which exists independently of the world it reflects upon. Similarly the *"I"* can never be a "self" in the sense of a real being in the world, but only an awareness of that world.

But what about the *"me"*? Didn't we also discover the *"me"* in our experiment? Isn't that the real self that we are looking for? Yes and no. When I look at myself in my mind's eye, or literally in the mirror, I have a sense of *me* – this body sitting here, this face that is my face. But it is a very private me, and seems to lack the substantiality that I attribute to the real self in the world that I know I really am. This private me is a rather pale and lifeless thing by comparison!

We seem to be half way there in our search for our self, in that we have identified the subjective *"I"*, and we have found a *"me"* which has no substance, no sense of realness. But I still haven't found the real solid, tangible, hungry self, the self as we normally know it – a real person in the real world.

We therefore suggest a third and final experiment. This one is taken from the twentieth century French existentialist philosopher, Jean-Paul Sartre.

> This time, imagine that you are peering through a keyhole, totally absorbed in a scene on the other side. Hold this idea in your mind for a couple of minutes. Now imagine that, all of a sudden you hear footsteps in the hall. Someone is looking at you! What do you experience? (Sartre, 1943/1957: p222)

First, you will have a straightforward awareness of the scene you are peering at. You may or may not have also experienced meta-awareness as before, looking in your mind's eye at yourself as *"I"*, looking through the keyhole as *"me"*. But what happens when you hear the footsteps? Sartre says:

> By the mere appearance of the Other, I am put in the position of passing judgment on myself as an object . . . I recognize that I *am* as the Other sees me. (Sartre, 1943/1957)

In other words, I have at last found my self, albeit not a very pleasant experience in this case! As a contemporary British philosopher Greg McCulloch puts it:

> In feeling shame, now, I acquire a new kind of self-awareness, of myself-as-object, which is routed through the Other's consciousness of me. (1994)

Of course becoming aware of myself as object need not be through shame – it can equally be through pride – but the principle is the same.

So it seems that to have a sense of self I need an audience or Other, who looks at me, and in that look makes me, literally, *self-conscious*. This experience can be exhilarating or humiliating, depending on what I am doing at the time and how the other evaluates my behaviour. How does this happen? Sartre says that it is only through the other's look (or equivalent perception) that I can gain what philosophers call *ontological status* – that is status as a "real" object. This status is one that we all hunger for – recognition, validation, even adoration, and without which we feel empty. Sartre (1943/1957) says that it is only through the Other that I can experience my self as an object in the world, or in his rather technical language, the Other

> is the concrete, transcending condition (p274)

of the objectivity of the self.

This is a profoundly important point, for it means that the presence of the Other is a necessary condition for the existence of a self. Hence this theory of the self is radically interpersonal. The constructivists similarly argue (Stevens, 1996) that the self can only exist in a social context, in a community of others.

We have finally clarified what it takes to be a "self". Let us take stock of the arguments so far. Uniquely among the animal species, we humans seek to become truly real "selves" in the real world but since we are not born with a self we have to construct it. How do we do that? It seems that the basic essentials are that "I" as conscious agent must continually present my "self" or "me" to you or some other person and you must give me some recognition or acknowledgment. What does this mean in detail?

THE THREE ESSENTIALS FOR SELFHOOD

We think (see also Trower & Chadwick, 1995) that within any one individual there are three essentials for selfhood, namely:

• an objective self which is constructed

- a subjective agent which formulates and presents the self-to-be, and

- the Other who is "the audience".

The Objective Self

The objective self is the "product", as it were – the self that is constructed. This, the most familiar aspect of self in everyday life, refers not to some mysterious inner entity, but to the observed, behavioural, public self, or what William James (1891) called the empirical "me". The objective self as defined here is also close to Sartre's concept of Being-For-Others (*Être Pour Autrui*).

The Subjective Agent

In order to construct an objective self, I, as conscious agent, must first present my "self" i.e. perform self-presentational acts, which sociologist Erving Goffman (1959) likened to performing a role in drama. As subjective agent I choose the roles, the rules and the subsequent actions – the self-presentation behaviours – that constitute the objective self, and I monitor (i.e. observe and judge) those behaviours, and also monitor the feedback from the other. I guide my own behaviour according to social and moral rules of conduct which as agent I believe the other (and the social community) will recognise and value (Leary, 1995). But I also guide my behaviour according to the idea I have of an ideal for myself (Markus & Nurias, 1986). These evaluative functions are particularly complex, and entail not only the direct evaluation of my own actions, but the meta-level evaluation of the other's evaluation of my own actions (Mead, 1934). In addition I can evaluate the *other's* action (these meta-appraisals were mostly clearly drawn out by Laing, 1969). These appraisals have important ontological (self-objectifying) implications, as explained in the next paragraph. The subjective agent as defined here is close to Sartre's concept of Being-for-Itself (*Être Pour Soi*).

The Other

In order to become an objective self, the presented self must be recognised as a legitimate social and moral self by the other (Harré, 1979). The other therefore has two interlinked powers . . .

- The first power is to be able to reify the presented self into an objective self, for in the very act of observation, the appraiser *objectifies* that action, that self-presentation behaviour, and thus objectifies the other's self, turning him into a Being-For-Others (*Être Pour Autrui*).

- The second is the power to define or redefine the presented self, and thereby influence how the self is presented. The second power enables the other to implicitly or explicitly state the social and moral rules according to which self-presentations must conform in order to be recognised as a legitimate social self. The other of course is also an agent, and I (subjective agent) am also an *other for him*.

For our present purposes, we are defining the other's role and function as observer, and emphasising the power of providing the "public" objectivity of an audience which transforms the presentations of self into the objective self. This transformation is a vital part of the theory, and asserts that there can be no objective self without recognition by the other.

Implications for the Self-image

What implications does our theory have for the self-image?

This is an important point since it shapes the kind of therapy we propose in Section Four. The dictionary definition of self-image is "one's own idea or picture of oneself, especially in relation to others". However, we argue that an image of self (as a social object) must be an image of self as observed by another. These images of self are therefore all necessarily images from an observer perspective. It means a person's self-image is an image in which he represents to himself how the other is seeing him (image-of-self-through-the-eyes-of-the-other).

We therefore support a long tradition of thinking that the concept or image of self is necessarily a reflected self or "looking glass" self (Cooley, 1902/1922), i.e. an image of self as we imagine others see us (Mead, 1934). This is because the self can only be a social object through the eyes of the other (Sartre, 1943/1957).

A second important point is that the term "self-image" is often taken to be a description of some kind of internal entity – a label for "what I am". In the previous chapters it will hopefully be clear that there is no such "thing" as the self, and therefore the "self-image" refers to no more than what I and the other believe my self-presentations show at any point in time. We will explore the importance of these issues when we discuss therapy in Chapter 16.

So in summary, we have argued:

(1)   yes, we do need a "self", but

(2)   no, it does not exist as a ready-made internal entity but we have to construct it by

(3)   presenting ourselves in endless sequences of social rule-following behaviour to an Other or Others who need to give us affirmation or recognition.

But suppose the Other doesn't give us that recognition, or tries to change us? This is the topic of the next chapter.

CHAPTER 7

THE POTENTIAL AND THE LIMIT

Why don't people just go ahead and construct their ideal selves all the time? Few of us seem to do this, and many seem to fail miserably in that task! One reason for this is that we are always up against the problem of having to persuade someone to affirm the ideal self we so desire to have recognised – and they often don't comply!

In this chapter therefore we are going to talk about two opposing motives involved in the process of self-construction. The first is the motivation that I, as agent, have a basic human need to construct an objective self, in accordance with my desired self concept, and which entails gaining the other's affirmation. We call this *the existential motive* – existential because it is about our very sense of being. The second is the motive to construct a self that conforms to the other's desired self-concept for me and which supports or promotes his or her own desired self-construction. This we describe as *the moral motive* – moral because it concerns what we believe to be our duty to the other. This distinction has similarities in common with the distinction drawn by the American psychologist, E. Tory Higgins (1987), between the *ideal self* (one's hopes, aspirations and wishes) and the *ought self* (one's sense of duty, obligations or responsibilities), and is a distinction that, as Higgins points out, has been made by a number authors.

THE EXISTENTIAL MOTIVE

By "the existential motive" we are referring to the claim that the making of a self is the most fundamental human passion and drive. This idea is perhaps most explicitly expressed by the humanist-existential thinkers, with such concepts as the drive toward self-actualisation (Rogers, 1967; Maslow, 1954), and the concept of being-for-itself (*Être Pour Soi*) (Sartre, 1943/1957), and by the "self" school of psychoanalysts with the concept of narcissistic need (Kohut, 1972).

Rogers (1967) describes the motive to become a self as

man's tendency to actualise himself, to become his potentialities. (p351)

By this he means

> the directional trend which is evident in all organic and human life – the urge
> to expand, extend, develop, mature – the tendency to express and activate all
> the capacities of the organism, or the self . . . it exists in every individual, and
> awaits only the proper conditions to be released and expressed. It is this
> tendency which is the prime motivation for creativity as the organism forms
> new relationships to the environment in its endeavour most fully to be itself.
> (p351)

Rogers identifies a number of components of becoming that self which one
truly is:

The first is self-direction or autonomy, by which a person gradually chooses
the goals toward which *he or she* wants to move. He becomes responsible for
himself. He decides what activities and ways of behaving have meaning for
him, and what do not.

The second is what he calls "toward being process". This concerns being
more openly in a process, a fluidity, a changing, flowing current. He quotes
Kierkegaard's description of the individual who really exists – of someone
constantly in the process of *becoming*.

The third is "toward being complexity", that is to *be*, quite openly and
transparently, all of ones complex and changing and sometimes contradictory feelings, with nothing hidden.

Fourth is "toward openness to experience". This involves being in a close
relationship to one's own experiences rather than being closed off to them –
a child-like acceptance.

The fifth is "toward acceptance of others". Closely related to this openness
to inner and outer experience in general is an openness to and an
acceptance of other individuals.

Sixth is "toward trust of self". This involves developing

> more trust of the processes going on within themselves, and have dared to feel
> their own feelings, live by values which they discover within, and express
> themselves in their own unique ways. (Rogers, 1967)

Psychoanalysts within the school of "self-psychology" express the drive
to become a self in rather more dramatic terms. Kohut (1977) argues that,
at infancy and throughout life, all people have a primitive narcissistic
drive or ambition within them to be grandiose and exhibitionistic, to
have a tendency to regard themselves as omnipotent and to become
enraged or thrown into despair when thwarted. These "archaic" drives
are healthy and necessary, but must be modified through appropriate

experiences with mirroring and idealised self-objects – significant others who are functionally part of the self – to a mature realism with a stable and secure self. Kohut (1977) sees it as essential to the child developing a self that he has a dependable "mirroring" parent (mother). The child performs and thereby seeks confirmation of its valued self by the mirroring self-object. The self will only develop if he receives loving, valuing reflections from the other. As Miller (1979, cited in Mollon, 1993) puts it:

> The child has a primary need to be seen, noticed and taken seriously as being that which it is at any given time, and as the hub of its own activity.

For the existentialists the drive to become a self is *the* fundamental human project. If we take Sartre's (1943/1957) account, any individual's passion is to become a real, tangible being-in-the-world. His account emerges from the phenomenological nature of consciousness. As we described this account above, consciousness has no identifying characteristics, no content, no "being" or essence of its own, but can only reflect upon objects outside of itself (the notion of Intentionality discussed earlier). This emptiness or *"nothingness"* of consciousness is what I experience, according to Sartre, as anguish, and underlines the need to *become*, i.e. to fill the gap and become a real object. From this comes the drive to construct a self, to become a real me in the world. In technical terms, the being-for-itself (*Être Pour Soi*) seeks to become a being-for-others (*Être Pour Autrui*). How does he try to achieve this? There are various ways, but one way is to play a particular role or act a part. *For example:*

> . . . he is playing at *being* a waiter . . . . The waiter plays with his situation in life in order to *realise it.* . .

But since I (and the waiter) can only *play* at being x, I can never actually *become* x. So the project to *become* is a never-ending project, with all the implications this entails, of a continuous process, of freedom to change, of insecurity and so on. In addition, I cannot realise or become a self alone, but only through the other, a feature we shall elaborate on later, and which echoes the principle discussed by Kohut of the necessity of the mirroring self-object.

The existential motive to construct a self is, we claim, a healthy, indeed necessary motive and purpose. It can become a problem however when the motive turns into an imperative, a compulsion to self-actualise at all costs and without restraint, and often with one particular other or others. We focus on this problem – the problem of the existential imperative – in Chapter 16.

THE MORAL MOTIVE

Almost in opposition and in a never-ending tension with the existential motive is the moral motive. The moral motive means that any individual will, to varying degrees, experience a pressure to construct a self which the other wishes them to construct. Among others, Harré (1979) has argued that people construct themselves and each other according to "moral" rules that specify and guide the behaviour required to be a "warranted and legitimate social being". This works at the macro level – the level of the social group or generalised other, where it reflects general social rules or norms of conduct – or at the level of the specific other, where it may reflect the personal wishes of the individual other. The reward for conforming to the rules of the other (both the generalised and the specific other) is that the other is more likely to give the recognition that is needed to become an objective self. The other may evoke the moral motive in order to try to make sure that the individual will present himself in the way he ought. The punishment for refusing to conform to the rules is that the other is more likely to refuse to give recognition, or will attempt to redefine the actor by means of a shaming label – two types of threat which are described later. The problem with the moral motive, then, is that it can be in direct conflict with the existential motive. To interpret Sartre (1943/1957) this is because I wish to found my own being – to be the author of my own self-construction – but the other (who I need to achieve this) may wish to be the author of my self-construction, and uses the moral motive to try to achieve this control.

INTERACTIONS OF THE EXISTENTIAL AND MORAL MOTIVES

In co-operative relationships, we negotiate our existential and moral wants and duties without undue conflict – though we rarely do it as explicitly as we are describing here. If I want you to affirm my presented self, you may agree to do so if I also agree to modify my behaviour to conform in significant ways to your requirements, which may include giving you affirmation of your presented self. In this way we affirm each other but maintain mutual respect. It's a process of give and take, maintaining an equilibrium between the existential and moral motives, and it is how long-term, "healthy" relationships can be maintained. How does this process work? We turn to this question in the next chapter.

CHAPTER 8

HOW IS THE SELF CONSTRUCTED?

Given the dynamics of the existential and moral motives, how does this self-construction process work in social interaction, in our day-to-day conversations? The sociologist Erving Goffman's idea (Goffman, 1959), like Sartre's, draws on the metaphor of drama – a person attempts to construct his self by means of self-presentation performances before an audience.

The process begins with so-called "self-presentation behaviour for others". Self-presentation is defined by Schlenker (1980) as the attempt to control images of self before real or imagined audiences, and thereby to influence how audiences perceive and treat the actor. This means I attempt to get you to affirm my self as presented. This usually involves a compromise between the existential and moral wants and oughts, namely the self I really wanted to present and the self you want and I ought to present.

For example: I want to relish my victory over you in a game of chess but compromise by saying you played a fine game and I was lucky!

The second stage is the perceived, anticipated or imagined evaluation by others of the self so presented. This is where I judge whether you accept or are indifferent to my presented self, or even worse, you reject and attempt to redefine my presented self, on the grounds that I have breached a moral rule.

For example: I gloated too much and you redefine me not as a worthy champion but an arrogant pig!

The third stage is the evaluation of self by the actor him or herself, consequent upon the other's evaluation. This is where I accept, am indifferent to or reject the other's affirmation or redefinition of my presented self.

For example: I try to discredit your evaluation of me by labelling you a poor loser!

In co-operative relationships the process may be simple, almost like a game with all winners and no losers. First, I present my "self" to you as the "other". Second, you observe and thereby "objectify" my presented self as an objective self; third I appraise and feel, for the moment, at least secure and at most elated with my objective self-through-the-eyes-of-the-other. Here I have succeeded in my self-construction goal at this moment in time. Then, in ordinary conversation (as opposed to, say, an interview situation) it will be your turn, and we will go on to take turns in a kind of game of mutual and reciprocal self-affirmation, not only today, but tomorrow and the next day and the days, weeks, months and even years that follow. In this way the insecure temporality of the process comes to feel like secure permanence, though the sense of permanence is illusory in that either party can bring the relationship to an end at any moment.

In competitive relationships the process is a more traditional game with definite winners and losers, as we saw in the example from chess earlier. The system may become strained at times, particularly in competitive situations, but will usually function robustly enough such that most participants, most of the time, feel sufficient self-affirmation from their social group. Even in the example above about chess, we can make it work by making light of the exchanges and reframing apparent disaffirmations as merely teasing. However, the process *can* go badly wrong. In the following section we explore ways that this process can break down for at least one, and sometimes all, the participants in disturbed relationships.

CHAPTER 9

THE INSECURE SELF (*LE NÉANT*)

THREATS TO THE SELF

The construction of the objective self in the way described above occurs in an ideal world. In the real world the process often falters or breaks down, resulting in a variety of what Goffman called "spoiled identities". Social psychologists, philosophers and others have identified a whole range of sophisticated ways that people prepare for, recover from or repair identities, such as giving "justificatory accounts" like apologies or reframing what "actually" happened (Harré, 1986; Snyder, Higgins & Stucky, 1983). However, further along this continuum we come into the realm of dysfunctional "selves" (e.g. as in personality disorders) or worse, into the failure to construct a self or the collapse of self, as may be the case in some types of psychosis.

There are three major forms that self-construction failure may take:

(1) The first we call the *Insufficient Self* where the self as agent apparently lacks the skill repertoire, the social knowledge and sufficient theory of other mind skills to construct behavioural self-presentations which are effective in expressing the authentic self (the existential motive) but in a way that takes account of the needs of the other (the moral motive) and the rules of the situation.

(2) The second we call the *Insecure Self* in which the agent has escalated his existential motive into an absolute imperative (a demand), and though able to produce behavioural self-presentations finds that the other rejects the presented self or withholds recognition and thus the individual cannot achieve the status of objective self which he demands.

(3) The third we call the *Alienated or Engulfed Self*, where the agent constructs self-presentations but receives affirmation only on condition that the presented self conforms to the requirements of the other rather than the agent (i.e. objective self is imposed and controlled by the other by means of the moral imperative).

We shall not enlarge further here on the Insufficient Self but focus on the second and third forms of vulnerability, briefly outlined in Trower and

Chadwick, 1995 and in Dagnan, Trower & Gilbert, 2002. We include a measure of these vulnerabilities in the Appendix, called the Self and Other Scale, page 203.

THE INSECURE SELF AND SCHIZOPHRENIA

An individual may fail to construct an objective self due to the lack of the attentive, "objectifying" or "mirroring" Other. We showed earlier we need the other in order to *be* – to be an objective self in the real world. This is normally not a serious problem in the give-and-take of everyday encounters – we win some, we lose some. But if the individual (as an Insecure Self) finds his existential need has become an *imperative* which must be met, but that the other is indifferent – does not value, nurture or even attend to the self as presented, or worse still is completely absent – then we have a problem. The person has (or anticipates that he will have) an experience of failing to *be,* in the profound sense of Sartre's *le néant,* or *nothingness* – or more exactly "no-thingness", of not being a thing, or object in the world . . .

> a man evaporates without an eye witness. (Sartre, 1962: p168)

The late psychiatrist R.D. Laing (a guru of the anti-psychiatry movement during his lifetime) called this *Ontological Insecurity* – the insecurity of no-thingness. Most existentialist writers refer to this as "existential anxiety", but see it as the source of the motive to construct ourselves and those who are important to us. As existential psychotherapist Emmy van Deurzen (1998) points out, existential anxiety in itself is a normal, healthy and indeed essential aspect of human nature. But it *can* become the source of severe problems. Laing, drawing on Sartre's concept of no-thingness, believed ontological insecurity reached such severity in many people diagnosed with schizophrenia because they have few or no such trusted others to affirm them. Hence they stare their no-thingness in the face, and see no way of coping with it.

The essence of the insecurity threat then is that the other leaves me *unconstructed* (consistently neglected) or *deconstructed* (inconsistently neglected, mirroring sometimes, and then withholding), but either way, not being an objective self. This level of insecurity becomes a problem when it is intense and persistent.

A dramatic example of this failure of mirroring (failure to affirm and value the self of the other) is given by Kohut (1977). In responding to her young child, the mother

> . . . responds – accepting, rejecting, disregarding – to a self that, in giving and offering seeks confirmation by the mirroring self-object. The child therefore

experiences the joyful, prideful parental attitude or the parent's lack of interest . . . as the acceptance or rejection of his tentatively established, yet still vulnerable creative-productive-active self. If the mother rejects this self just as it begins to assert itself as a centre of creative-productive initiative (especially of course if her rejection or lack of interest is only one link in a long chain of re-buffs and disappointments emanating from her pathogenically unempathic personality) . . . then the child's self will be depleted and he will abandon the attempt to obtain the joys of self-assertion and will . . . (p76)

In the psychoanalytic literature this phenomenon is known as "narcissistic vulnerability", referring to the fragility and uncertainty in the sense of self. This leads to strong reactions to the "narcissistic injuries" of feeling slighted, ignored or treated without respect or empathy. The most prominent reaction is of narcissistic rage (Kohut, 1972) – with secondary reactions of depressive withdrawal or of a retreat to an arrogant, grandiose and somewhat paranoid state of mind. According to psychoanalyst Phil Mollon (1993), these overt reactions seem to be protective responses to a more fundamental injury or break-up of the sense of self.

Mollon (1993) gives examples of clients who felt unreal, who had a sense of disappearing, who had a dread of evaporating, of having no sense of self etc when significant others ignored them or looked through them. He gives a specific clinical example of a client who, if she felt unfocused upon by another person, would feel overwhelmed with an uncertainty over who she really was, or even have doubts about her own existence. Her response was often to fly into a rage (the narcissistic rage which comes from a need to make other's obey one's will).

The origins of this problem are thought to be found in the early life of the child, when the parents, particularly the mother, made the child feel very insecure, and fearful of abandonment. The eminent attachment theorist John Bowlby (1969) usefully distinguished various stages in the response to breakdown in bonding – the first two being protest and despair. During the protest stage the person may vigorously pursue the other, try to compel, coerce etc the other to be securely *there*. They may use care-eliciting or care-giving manoeuvres to establish the bond; they may use guilt, attraction, power to bring the recalcitrant other into line, i.e. they may take the role of masochist or "poor me" to "pull" from and thereby lock the other into the reciprocal role of sadist or persecutor. Using our present concepts, we would describe these manoeuvres as emanating from the moral imperative. However, once they have entered the despair stage, the scene is set for future psychopathology and what Masterson (1989) calls "abandonment depression". This arises when the mother's continuous unavailability produces the climate in which the child's real self will not be able to emerge. From this point the person may go on to develop personality disorder or a psychotic breakdown.

What is the Evidence for this Insecurity Threat in Early Development?

In a review of the extensive parent–child interaction research literature, Blatt and Homann (1992) characterise one pattern of parental style as one of being psychologically unavailable, uncaring and neglectful, and if affection was given, this was inconsistent. They related this to what they call "anaclitic depression", in which the individual intensely and chronically fears being abandoned and left unprotected and uncared for. Goodman and Brumley (1990) found lack of maternal responsiveness and affectional involvement were characteristics of mothers diagnosed with schizophrenia.

What is the Evidence for the Unavailability Pattern in the Families of People with Psychosis?

Both Vaughn (1976) and Smith, Birchwood, Cochrane & George (1993) have written about a small subgroup of "burnt-out" relatives in inner city areas where their low level of "expressed emotion" (usually a good thing) reflects apathy and indifference rather than calm concern, and may be engendering this apathy, negative symptoms and increasing levels of social impairment.

CHAPTER 10

ALIENATED/ENGULFED SELF (*OBJECTITÉ*)

We have seen that the Insecure Self may not be able to construct an objective self due to significant others being persistently absent – indifferent, disinterested, preoccupied and generally unavailable. But an individual may fail to construct an objective self due to a diametrically opposite reason, namely the other being excessively present and intrusive – not so much mirroring the objective self but of taking possession of it, by means, we would argue, of the mechanism of the moral *imperative*. This is the situation of the Engulfed or Alienated Self.

To be *my* objective self, "*I*" as agent, must construct the self-presentation *for* the Other, and the Other must empathically recognise and value this self as *my* self, freely constructed. But if the objective self is controlled and indeed constituted by the Other, then it is not my self but an alien self imposed upon me.

Sartre develops this notion of alien self in his analysis of being-for-others (1943/1957). First he reminds us that we can only become a real object in the world by being recognised as such by the other. But secondly he states

> . . .we must recognise that we experience our being-for-others in the form of a possession. I am possessed by the Other; the Other's look fashions my body in its nakedness, causes it to be born, sculptures it, produces it as it is, sees it as I shall never see it. The Other holds a secret – the secret of what I am. He makes me be and thereby he possesses me, and this possession is nothing other than the consciousness of possessing me. I, in the recognition of my object-state, have proof that he has this consciousness. By virtue of consciousness the Other is for me simultaneously the one who has stolen my being from me and the one who causes "there to be" a being which is my being. Thus I have a comprehension of this ontological structure: I am responsible for my being-for-others, but I am not the foundation of it. (1943/1957, p364)

Remember the experiment of peering through a keyhole, totally absorbed in a scene on the other side when you suddenly hear footsteps in the hall and you realize someone is looking at you? In other words, you as person A are being looked at, evaluated and labelled by person B, and thereby become an objective self – *defined*, *labelled* and constituted by B. You *feel* like an object, labelled, experienced through shame and self-consciousness.

Sartre uses the term "objectité" or *objectness* to identify this quality or state of being an object.

This experience is part of normal psychological life, and we normally cope with it in ordinary relationships in ordinary everyday life. But when relationships are not so normal, as in so-called "high expressed emotion" (EE) families, the experience of being engulfed can be overwhelming.

For example, one of our clients, Jane, diagnosed as paranoid schizophrenic, said one of her main fears was being taken over:

> everything being taken from me, your personality. You can't be yourself. You're not in control of your own person.

She dreaded the idea of someone

> telling you what to do. Like you *have* to do what someone else says all the time. I'd just run away. I won't let anyone get near me. If someone cared for me I'd feel they want to take my life over, be swallowed up, and overwhelmed. That would be *possessive caring – being the other's property.*

In reviewing the expressed emotion and social-support research in schizophrenia, Davidson and Strauss (1992) comment that a

> "highly critical and over-involved family milieu can be seen as interfering with the development of an active sense of self by fostering negative appraisals and undermining a person's efforts at establishing his/her own sense of agency" (p142).

To recap, if you are in the *objectité* state, you, as object, can lose your sense of agency to the other as subject, i.e. you can lose the ability to stand back and be an observer and hence judge of yourself and creator of your actions. According to Sartre, when you are object for the other, you experience the other as being able to control your being as object, much as a puppeteer controls the puppet. In the extreme forms just described, we have examples of clients who feel so deeply penetrated by the other that the other can control their thoughts, movements and sense of self.

It is not difficult to imagine that a person, when in such a phenomenological state, will fail to attribute thoughts and actions to self as agent and will instead attribute thoughts and actions (which are in fact their own) to the other (whether real or hallucinated). The notion of being an object possessed and constituted by the other may help to explain a number of psychotic symptoms which have external control as their theme. These would include voices referring to the individual in the third person, voices criticising, delusions of influence – both control and somatic passivity – and some of the thought disorders, including thought insertion, thought broadcast and thought withdrawal. It might explain how some feel that spirits can get inside the body and control the person's movements. Chadwick and Birchwood (1994) found that malevolent voices were extremely powerful (omnipotent) and all-knowing (omniscient), and in the case of command hallucinations, individuals felt compelled to carry out the voice's commands (Birchwood *et al.*, 2000b).

An extreme form of the state of *objectité* would give an explanation for the mysterious disorders of willed action that researcher and clinical psychologist Chris Frith and his colleagues have identified (1992), and attribute to a dysfunctional brain mechanism, as we discussed in Chapter 2. A loss of willed action is the loss of agency in other words. This perspective also helps explain the perceived omnipotence and omniscience of the voice and the compulsion to obey. The only "defence" for such a vulnerability is avoidance or withdrawal – the common feature of the negative symptom profile.

Indeed, this approach may explain what Frith calls the "disorders of willed action" including *abulia* (no will), *alogia* (no words), *athymia* (no feelings) – inability to generate appropriate behaviour of their own will, behaviour elicited by irrelevant external stimuli. Frith suggests how specific features of schizophrenia (such as listed above) might arise from specific abnormalities in "metarepresentation". This is the cognitive mechanism we discussed earlier under "what is the self?". This meta-level of awareness, or consciousness of consciousness of . . . is what enables us to be aware of our goals, our intentions, and the intentions of other people.

We have also already discussed the nature of consciousness as intentional. The lifelong experience of being intrusively controlled, and of having an alien and not an authentic (self-constructed) self, and the concomitant loss of a centre of initiative, is indeed likely to cause profound dysfunction in the normal operation of consciousness and the way social information is processed. We suggest that this may be the psychological origin of Frith's failure of willed action. It may similarly help to explain the externalisation (i.e. caused by powerful and hostile agents) of a person's own intentions, thoughts and actions which, it has been suggested, may account for some of the anomalous experiences that arise in psychosis (e.g. by Garety & Freeman, 1999).

How do clients respond or cope with the experience of alienation? There are at least three ways – constructing a false self, avoidance or withdrawal, and by turning the tables and alienating the other.

The first way of coping with the experience of being the other's object is by constructing a false self, behind which the true self may hide. Winnicott (1960) introduced the term "false self" into psychoanalysis. He saw this as a part of the personality based on *compliance* to an environment which did not respond to the infant's own inner initiative. For example:

> ... the mother who is not good enough ... repeatedly fails to meet the infant's gesture; instead she substitutes her own gesture which is to be given sense by the compliance of the infant. This compliance on the part of the infant is the earliest stage of the False Self and belongs to the mother's inability to sense her infant's needs. (p145)

Another way of dealing with being the other's object is to escape or avoid the other, as in the case of Jane (see page 84). A study by Egeland, Pianta and O'Brian (1993) showed this to be true of children with over-intrusive mothers – they developed a characteristic "defence" of avoiding interaction.

Such a response pattern also appears to be fairly typical of those relapsing psychosis sufferers whose relatives are intrusive, critical, or hostile (known as "high EE" behaviours).

Some examples:

- A mother waves her hands and snaps her fingers in front of her daughter's face in an attempt to elicit some kind of response; disregards requests for privacy, walks into the patient's bedroom unannounced, monitors her routine activities such as bathing and dressing, offers unsolicited advice. The common response was protective withdrawal.

- A young man spent more and more time by himself, retreating to his room or going for solitary walks. During arguments he ceased to speak at all – he would cower in a corner of the room and put his hands over his ears as if to shut out the noise. (Interestingly, a comparison group of people who were depressed tended to seek out comfort and support) (Leff & Vaughn, 1985, p114).

- In a detailed micro-analysis of verbal and nonverbal behavioural sequences, Altorfer *et al.* (1992) found patients displayed evasive reactions to negative affective style of the relative. Specifically, they found a decrease in patients' nonverbal behaviour following negative affect statements, and an increase following positive statements. They interpret this as the patient's way of withdrawing from the communicative situation, eventually resulting in "freezing" behaviour. Enabling separation and modifying such communications is a key part of family intervention and helps reduce relapse.

In the examples above, those with psychosis do not seem to feel allowed to argue their corner, or even assert their rights not to engage. However, there are additional problems with those who have internalised/incorporated a critical parent, particularly when this takes the form of a malevolent voice, from which the client cannot escape. This isn't a problem of simply not being able to argue, it is a question of not being able to conceptualise or hold onto a self-supporting point of view. It is as if they become so overwhelmed by the other's view that it literally becomes their *own* view, *their* self.

The third way of dealing with alienation is by turning the tables and absorbing the other; Sartre again:

> . . . if in one sense my being-as-object is an unbearable contingency and the pure 'possession' of myself by another, still in another sense this being stands as the indication of what I should be obliged to recover and found in order to be the foundation of myself. But this is conceivable only if I assimilate the Other . . . Thus my project of recovering myself is fundamentally a project of absorbing the Other. (1943/1957, p365)

Person A may try to "absorb" person B by not only observing B's self-presentations but labelling them bad, worthless or even wonderful etc, hence constituting B's objective self and thus having control of it. In this way, A is free of control and controls the other in turn (though in the process he has lost his own objective self, but that's another story).

It is most likely that this third way of responding to alienation would be the strategy of someone with perceived high self-esteem or moral superiority or specialness, such as the narcissist, or the manic or the angry paranoid. The other two strategies will be most likely used by those who are low in self-esteem and powerless.

Of course a more functional way is by getting a deeper understanding of the other without belittling and rubbishing – either oneself or the other. This strategy will be discussed in Section Four.

The effects of increased self-consciousness are likely to vary depending on the perceived self-esteem of the individual. We know something about those with low self-esteem. Hope, Gansler and Heimberg (1989), looking at self-awareness and social phobia in particular, reviewed a number of studies showing the effect of this state: being painfully aware of one's physiological arousal, for example, sweating, disrupted performance at a task, amplifying whatever emotional state one was in, heightened sensitivity to negative feedback such as rejection, and tending to attribute negative outcomes to the self – a reversal of the usual self-serving bias. Furthermore, the self-focused anxious person becomes more aware of discrepancies between ideal and actual performances (alias selves) and an increased likelihood of disengaging from the desired course of action.

However, the effects of increased self-consciousness on people with perceived high self-esteem is likely to be different. As Richard Bentall and his colleagues have shown, deluded subjects showed an *increase* in the self-serving bias effect (blame others and not themselves for negative outcomes), which supports what we speculated earlier about turning the tables on the other. This is in line too with the finding of Morf and Rhodewalt (1993) that narcissistic personalities reacted to threat to self by rating the *other* more negatively than less narcissistic individuals.

INTEGRATION AND CONCLUSION

We have described insecurity-threat and alienation-threat in terms of dispositional vulnerabilities, such that for any given individual, threats of one type will predominate over the other, leading perhaps to "sociotropic" (dependent) versus "autonomous" (independent) interpersonal styles, as defined by Beck (1983).

However, there are likely to be intra-personal cycles – where a person oscillates between insecurity and alienation, as may occur in certain types of borderline personality disorders – and interpersonal cycles: insecure person A tries to ensnare person B as his Other by means of the moral imperative, thereby creating alienated self-experiences in B, who withdraws, avoids etc, leading to further insecurity in A, and exacerbation of this particular vicious cycle. This interpersonal cycle would not only maintain, for example, high EE (expressed emotion) interactions, but probably lead to an exacerbation of them, to the point where a "breakdown" may occur, leading to yet another hospital admission for the family member who is in the subordinate position in the interaction.

Furthermore, there are probably simultaneous occurrences of insecurity and alienation. For example B imposes an alien objective self on A, but ignores or in other ways devalues any attempt by A to present an authentic (i.e. their own) self to B or anyone else. A is thereby caught in a complete trap – entrapped in an alien self and blocked from constructing an authentic self. One of the few options left is to withdraw into a vacuum of non-being, which may help explain negative symptoms, or wildly procrastinate between approach and avoidance. In fact, this latter is the type of picture that Masterson (1989) paints in his portrait of the borderline (inter-personally intense and unstable) personality – that mothers show both over-involvement (uses the child for her own dependency needs) and inconsistent (stops the child "individuating" i.e. authentic self-presentation). Indeed Bezirganian, Cohen and Brook (1993) showed this to be true in a large-scale study – that both child-rearing practices had to be present together to be "pathogenic".

We have argued that many problems, particularly in psychoses, will at least involve a problem in the construction of self, and have described two of the major threats to this – the unavailability of the mirroring other, or the intrusive possession by the other. Cognitive psychotherapy has rather neglected this topic. This approach would suggest a new research agenda, examining the specific ways that people with schizophrenia are failing to construct their selves, and to develop therapy in the direction of enabling them to repair the process and begin again – or for the first time – to construct a self.

One area that is ripe for development is concerned with self-consciousness or self-focused attention – a major part of the phenomenology of being an "engulfed" object for the other, and which also magnifies the experience of emptiness of the insecure self, discussed above. Duval and Wicklund first developed the notion of self-consciousness into a theory known as Objective Self Awareness Theory in 1972. More recently Ingram (1990) showed that heightened self-focus was associated with a wide range of psychopathological states, including alcohol abuse, depression, and various forms of anxiety, and Wells (2000), and Segal *et al.* (2002) have, in their different ways, developed exciting new attentional control therapies that enable clients to disengage from the self-focused interlock. We believe these methods are relevant for the insecurity and engulfment traps discussed here, and our own approach is discussed in Section Four, namely working to switch attention from a self-focus to be other-focused.

SECTION SUMMARY

To summarise: this section has focused on the centuries-old debate on the nature of the self.

- We have said that there is a fundamental need for a self but the self is not a given and has to be constructed.

- We are dependent on the Other for affirmation and the construction of a tangible self, and therefore the self is always vulnerable.

- We described two threats to self: the threat of insecurity and the threat of engulfment/alienation, and described how insecurity (*le néant*) and engulfment (*objectité*) can lead to psychopathology. In Chapter 16 we look at therapeutic strategies to counter these problems. But first, in the next section, we present evidence for these threats in action in real life.

SECTION THREE

PERSONAL ACCOUNTS

Do these self-construction problems happen in practice? In the previous section we put forward a theory about how people construct their selves. We said we believed this process is severely disrupted in the lives of people who have had a psychosis, and is indeed an integral part of psychotic disturbance. But that is a theory (albeit with quite a pedigree, historically from the literature). How could we set about testing these ideas empirically? What actually happens in the actual lives of the people we work with who have had a psychosis?

In the four chapters in this section we report the detailed accounts of conflicts that actually happened in the lives of 21 of our clients. The clients agreed to participate in a study in which we sought to find out what kinds of interpersonal experiences they had, and whether these experiences could be accounted for in terms of our theory.

In the first chapter (Chapter 11) we describe the methodology with which data was collected. This chapter will mainly interest academics who want to know how the study was conducted.

In Chapter 12 we provide the main results from the detailed interviews through which people gave their accounts of the main significant conflicts they had experienced.

In Chapter 13 we report the actual accounts of the conflicts, and bring out the main themes that we believe link the results to the psychotic symptoms people experience; this chapter will interest both lay-people and professionals as it should feel like a novel treatment of familiar material.

Chapter 14 will also be of general interest as, in it, we look at conflicts that relate to peer interactions and romantic relationships.

CHAPTER 11

HOW WE ASKED PEOPLE TO GIVE THEIR PERSONAL ACCOUNTS

(This chapter may primarily interest researchers who want to know exactly how the study was carried out; the interested general reader may want to dip in and out of this chapter, or perhaps skip to Chapter 12 and refer back if and when necessary.)

We wanted to find out if young people who had had a psychosis really had the experiences our theory predicted. Did they experience threats to self-construction in their key relationships? Did some feel a sense of emptiness and nothingness, others a sense of alienation, and yet others perhaps both? Were they thwarted from being truly themselves in these or any relationships? This was quite a difficult methodological task if we were to be scientifically sound. We approached the problem by trying to answer some key questions.

(1) *Where are the fundamental dynamics to be found?* That was easy to answer in light of the previous chapters: in the minutiae of key interpersonal interactions, particularly those interactions with those most important people, parents or peers, which seemed to that person to be "epoch-making" – especially important. Family relationships have (unsurprisingly) been shown to be very important in psychosis by many investigators. One of the most scientific approaches to this has been the field of research focusing on a characteristic found in families called "expressed emotion" which we referred to a lot in the previous section. A large number of studies have consistently found a significant relationship between psychotic *relapse* and *certain types of attitudes* held by family members towards the index client (Bebbington & Kuipers, 1994; Hashemi & Cochrane, 1999). In the late 1960s, researchers extensively interviewed many relatives of people with a psychosis, and distilled down what were initially 10-hour interviews to a number of key traits and attitudes. They then looked to see which attitudes were statistically related to relapse in the psychotic family member over the next few years (Brown & Birley, 1968). Those that were linked were called "high expressed emotion" (EE) attitudes, and included behaviours rated as critical, hostile or emotionally over-involved towards the index client.

Nowadays, EE is assessed during a much shorter structured interview called the *Camberwell Family Interview* (Vaughn & Leff, 1976), and high EE has been linked with poorer outcome over and over again (Wearden *et al.*, 2000); it is one of the most robust findings in psychiatry.

Our theory of self-construction might be able to explain the crucial effect these high EE communications have, i.e. they might be intimately related to one or other (or both) of the two types of threat to self-construction. In addition, at least some of the symptoms of relapse may be construed as forms of defence against such threats (such as paranoia) or manifestations of an actual breakdown in autonomy of the self (e.g. delusions of passivity and control). Of course, specific EE communications may not bring about relapse, but they may have an accumulating effect, by, for example, blocking self-development, causing the individual to become trapped in a dependent role without self integrity, with consequent negative symptoms or at least a pattern of chronic social withdrawal. Given this line of reasoning, the aim of the following study was to identify, analyse and compare accounts of significant interactions, particularly those which could be labelled as high EE, and to analyse these interactions in terms of our model of interpersonal threats to self.

(2) *How do we get a full honest report of what the person involved thought and felt?* In quantitative research studies, it is usually the case that people with a psychosis simply tick boxes in a questionnaire or at the most get interviewed just once by a complete stranger; the guarded comments they make in this situation are often taken as a true report of how they feel. Like anyone, it is likely that psychosis-sufferers need time to get to know their interviewer before confiding some of their more intimate ideas. Hence this study is unusual because the interviewers spent a lot of time getting to know the person involved. Obviously this raises the question of "leading the witness", and interviewers had to be careful not to do this; the trade-off between being able to observe and effects caused by the observer's involvement was thought to be worth it. The extensive rapport-building at the start of the interviews was undertaken in order to get more valid reports from the participants, which would hopefully more accurately reflect their thoughts and feelings.

Another way in which this study differs is that it doesn't use a common technique in psychology, namely taking isolated snippets of thoughts or feelings away from the context they were experienced. Such reduction of the data takes away some of the "understandable-ness" from the person's own particular understanding of the situation. In a sense, it takes away from their narration of their own story. In order to carry out these analyses, a structured interview was developed to encourage participants to describe their conflicts as unfolding stories of specific interactions between themselves and a significant other (parent or peer), with a focus on how the client saw his "self" being constructed, reconstructed or deconstructed, and the psychological sequelae of this process in terms of beliefs, actions and emotions. This methodology was based more on the paradigm of discursive psychology (Edwards & Potter, 1992; Harré & Gillett, 1994) rather than traditional experimental psychology, with the former's focus on the social construction of everyday situations, and the emphasis on an individual's particular construction of conflicts. However, at this point a problem was encountered . . .

(3) *How can the insight of people with a psychosis be enhanced?* It was suspected that many people with a psychosis do not have great insight into their own thought processes, and were also as likely as any of us are to censor what they report to appear socially acceptable. This was particularly likely if the subject matter was sensitive (and arguments with the most important people in their lives were likely to be sensitive). To counteract this we used a slightly unusual technique of Rational Emotive Behaviour Therapy (REBT; Dryden, 1995) to justify structured probing, to get a more accurate report. One important feature of REBT theory (and other cognitive therapy theories) is that if a person reports an emotion, there must be images or cognitions driving that emotion. For instance, if a person reports feeling angry, this has to come from two different cognitions: of how things *currently are*, and how things *should be* (Ellis, 1994). If the subject reported feeling angry, but then reported only cognitions that fitted with feeling sad, that justifies gentle persistence from the interviewer as, logically, there have to be angry cognitions. Typical probing was along the lines of:

> Given that you said you were feeling angry, what thoughts or images were in your mind at that time?

This sort of probe typically produced more appropriately angry cognitions, such as

> I felt put down, treated like a shit; he shouldn't have treated me like that.

THE STRUCTURED INTERVIEW

We needed people's genuine, personal accounts but some of our participants tended either to speak for a very long time, or alternatively say very little, so for this reason, and the fact that we needed a standardised set of data so we could compare people, we developed a clearly structured interview. The interview (available from the authors on request) starts from the point where participants started to feel an emotional reaction to a specific interpersonal event ("tell me about a time when you felt very uncomfortable (perhaps angry or anxious or down) with someone you were interacting with''), and continues up to the moment when they judged the incident had ended. We called this the ''emotional episode''. The aim was to help the participant to identify at least two and up to five chained sequences or stages within an emotional episode, each of which may have contained perceived threats to self of either the insecurity or alienation types. (See Chapters 9 and 10 for a more detailed discussion of these terms, or the next few pages for a briefer working summary. The interview itself may be easier to understand with a completed account, such as in Chapter 13.) The first sequence begins with a description of an interpersonal event, e.g. a critical comment by the other. The participant gives their appraisal of this event in terms of a threat to self, and a description and rating of how they themselves felt and what action they took or wanted to take, e.g. anger and a critical counter-retort.

At the outset, this first sequence was designed to be followed by the identification of a second, in which the participant was to be asked to describe the other's reaction to his response behaviour. In fact, during piloting it appeared that a great many participants did not respond in the conflict as they wanted to; instead they appeared to only imagine what would happen if they did. For this reason, the natural progression of the sequence includes the imagined response, for those people who did not actually act as they wanted.

After this second sequence, the interview logs the Other's response to their response (for example, an escalation of criticism). This response is the subject's prediction of how the other would respond in the imaginary sequence. This next sequence would also include the participant's appraisal of this second reaction (again in terms of a threat to self) and their emotional and behavioural reaction to this (e.g. a counter-escalation of anger and angry behaviour). There may be a third, fourth or even fifth sequence, each linked to the preceding one to make a complex chain. The final sequence explores the participant's cumulative self-construction outcome, and the emotional and behavioural consequence of that outcome.

HYPOTHESES

The main prediction of this study was that a typical sample of people diagnosed as having schizophrenia (especially those who are living with or are closely attached to a family with high expressed emotion communications) would report emotional episodes which would clearly demonstrate blocks to self-construction. The study aimed also to identify types of blocks, to unravel the psychological pattern of these blocks, to explore the relationship between self-construction problems and psychotic symptoms, and explore connections between these phenomena – self-construction blocks and symptoms – and family relationships. It was hypothesised that these blocks contribute to the formation of symptoms, and also to the maintenance of symptoms (hence we have also included participants older than adolescence, so as to look at maintenance issues). To focus on the key "high expressed emotion" interactions, the Camberwell Family Interview was used (Vaughn and Leff, 1976); this interview was also useful for the sake of getting a balanced picture, because it gave the viewpoint of the other family members involved in the conflicts.

METHOD

Participants

Participants were consecutive referrals to the study from psychiatrists and other mental health workers in three NHS Trusts in the Midlands of the UK. (Ethical approval was obtained from all three Trusts.) In all there were 35 referrals, of which 9 were excluded because they fell outside our inclusion criteria, and 5 did not want to participate. The *inclusion* criteria were:

(a)   an ICD-10 diagnosis of paranoid schizophrenia or delusional disorder

(b)   age range 17 to 40

(c)   living with or in "regular and meaningful contact" with the parental family.

People were *excluded* if:

(a)   they had primary organic impairment

(b)   they were currently misusing drugs or alcohol.

The *number* of participants was 21, including 17 men and 4 women, aged between 17 and 45 (mean age = 30 years, SD = 1.9). Six had a history of drug misuse (but not currently). All clients had had at least two and at most five acute admissions, and a psychiatric history ranging from six months to seven years. All were receiving neuroleptic medication.

Procedure

All participants were approached in accordance with ethically approved guidelines. All patients volunteered for the study, and were approached to meet with a psychologist for a number of sessions "to discuss relationship and family issues". The confidentiality of what they might disclose was emphasised, as was the fact that nothing would be entered in their case notes, and that the interviews would not have any effect on their medication or future treatment from the services. All participants were seen on an outpatient basis. The interviews were conducted by the authors. Permission to publish was obtained (names and some details have been altered to preserve confidentiality).

MEASURES

The ABC Structured Interview

The ABC interview protocol is described in detail below. (A summary of how it should be administered is available on request from the authors.) The interview is based largely upon, and conducted according to, the ABC cognitive assessment procedure of REBT (Dryden, 1995). Since all the data was provided by the participants, and no ratings or judgements were made by the interviewers, inter-rater reliability checks were not relevant. Sample interviews from both interviewers were rated by two external experts in REBT as to how the interviews were conducted. The experts were Dr. Antoni Diller, a trained REBT therapist and Dr. Andrew Jahoda, a senior lecturer in clinical psychology, who were unaware of the hypotheses of the study. Tapes were rated for:

(1) *fidelity* (how faithfully the interviewers implemented the guidelines for the ABC sequences

(2) *skill* (how skilfully they implemented the guidelines)

(3) *bias* (how much bias they demonstrated).

Rater's reports showed that both interviewers were rated to have performed well and equivalently with each other on these criteria.

Camberwell Family Interview

The Camberwell Family Interview (CFI) (Leff & Vaughn, 1985) is a semi-structured interview completed with the relatives of clients. The complete transcript of the interview is rated using strict criteria for scores on five categories of communication:

(1) critical comments

(2) hostility

(3) positive comments

(4) warmth

(5) emotional over-involvement.

Seven or more critical comments, any presence of hostility observed as generalisation of criticism or a rejecting attitude, or a score of 3 or more on emotional over-involvement is rated as "high" expressed emotion; otherwise the expressed emotion rating is "low". In deciding the rating scores, behaviours referred to in the interview and non-verbal communications during the interview are also taken into account. Rating scores are then most commonly used to divide relatives into two categories, high and low expressed emotion (EE), the dichotomous nature of the categorising reflecting the fact that the most frequent use of the scales is to predict relapse in the future in a yes/no manner. Clients whose relatives are classed as "high EE" are generally twice as likely to relapse (Bebbington & Kuipers, 1994) as others. The CFI has good psychometric properties, and Chris Harrop was trained in administering and rating it by its originator, Christine Vaughn, to an acceptable criterion standard on blind-rated tapes.

THE ABC STRUCTURED INTERVIEW AND INTERVIEW PROCEDURE

As described earlier, the interview is designed to capture, in an operationally-defined way, the two main threats to self-construction, and the participants' cognitive, emotional and behavioural responses to them, as well as the Other's reaction to the participant's own reaction and the repeating chains of such sequences during a complete conflict episode. The interview accommodates threats that occur in a complex sequence, and responses to threats that were inhibited as well as those that were executed. To recap, the two main threats are:

(1) Insecurity (I), where the Other fails (for example, through indifference) to recognise and objectify the presented self

(2) Alienation (α), in which the Other either coerces the client to construct a false self that is usually perceived by the client to be of demeaned status (coercion subtype) or defines the client as bad or flawed (redefinition subtype). There may even be a complex dynamic interaction of the two, where indifference is followed by control or vice versa, depending upon the situation, and the response of the individual to the initial threat. A fictitious illustration of each of these types follows (below).

First Situation: Insecurity Threat

John (excited and expectant): "Hey Mum, look what I've made!"

Mum (watching TV): "Not now, John, Just be quiet a minute, will you?"

John (angrily and under his breath): "Piss off then."

In this situation, John makes his "self-presentation" and looks for affirmation from Mum. Mum however is indifferent, leaving him "unconstructed" with the consequence of angry feeling, angry behavioural intentions and critical thoughts about Mum.

Second Situation: Alienation Threat

> Dad: "God, you are a lazy young man. Get out of bed and find yourself a job!"

> John lies there, says nothing.

In this situation Dad "constructs" John's self by defining him with the phrase "lazy young man". By saying nothing, John allows this definition to be true, and is alienated negatively from his "true" self-construction goals ($\alpha-$).

Alternatively, Dad might actually praise John in some way, and define him in what he (Dad) thinks is a positive way, but John doesn't. If it isn't a role that John would have chosen for himself according to his own self-construction needs, and if it is odious to him, then this is defined as an experience of positive alienation ($\alpha+$). For example:

> Dad: "Your room looks so much better now you've tidied it – you really are an obedient young man."

> John fumes.

Third Situation: Alienation-Insecurity Complex Threat

> Husband: "Look at this dust. Some wife!"

> Wife: "Sorry dear, I've been cooking you this nice meal instead – would you like some?"

> Husband: "No thanks, I'm off down the pub."

In this situation both threats are in the same interaction. Husband "constructs" a bad self for his wife by the term "some wife". By apologising, she allows this definition of herself. She then makes a self-presentation, to which he is indifferent, leaving her unconstructed.

Clients were taught the concept of self-construction and threats to self-construction; most clients grasped the ideas fairly quickly. In the conflicts reported, the categorisation as to whether the conflict is an α or I (or whatever) was made by the client themselves. In some cases, the interviewer described the types of threats very carefully and the client said which (if any) applied to their situation (there were a number of situations where no category applied; see results).

How the Types of Threat Were Used to Build Up Sequences

The main aim of the interview is to elicit from the client an account of an entire emotional episode, usually a family conflict, defined as any interactive incident between themselves and one or more members of the family (usually a parent) or peer group, in which the client feels significantly distressed. A wide range of conflicts were reported, and an attempt was made to get something in each of the following categories – an important issue with parents, a day-to-day repetitive issue with parents, an issue with their friends. Some clients did not talk about family issues; however, after a lengthy engagement process it usually became clear that there were issues, but the client was reluctant to disclose them for whatever reasons. For example, some clients initially claimed to never feel uncomfortable in their relationships with their parents, and yet spent the best part of their day avoiding their parents at all costs. Obviously, clients were not coerced and were free *not* to talk; clients were also continually reassured that they were free to discontinue the interviews at any point, an option some chose. It was important during engagement that it was essentially client-led, and that they felt able to talk freely and be supported; the interviewers were careful not to put words in the client's mouth. For example, it was vitally important that the client felt able to contradict and disagree with the interviewer should the need arise (and most clients did this).

The framework for the interview is the ABC (A for Activating event, B for Beliefs about the event, C for emotional and behavioural Consequence of the beliefs, given the event) method from REBT, but modified in a number of ways.

- Firstly, the client is asked for the initial emotional reaction they experienced at the beginning of the selected incident. Key aspects of the emotional response are then explored (noted under C for Consequence). Clients identify the general emotion or mood they experienced (see Figure 11.1 for a map of the interview results sheet; the *emotion* is identified as item 1 on this Figure).

- Secondly, the client identifies the *emotional impulse* – the behaviour that they felt they impulsively wanted to carry out at the time, such as aggression in anger, or avoidance or escape in anxiety (item 2).

- The triggering event that set the emotional reaction off is asked for, and key aspects of this noted, particularly verbal or non-verbal communications by the significant other towards the client (noted under A for *activating event*; item 3).

The next part of the interview is concerned with the client's beliefs (B) about the activating event (A) which cause the emotional and behavioural

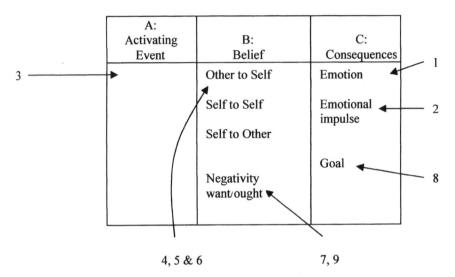

Figure 11.1   Map of Conflicts Interview Results Sheet

responses at C. Beliefs are divided into those that constitute the appraisal (or evaluation) of the event (which we term the primary belief), and those that constitute the coping response to the event (which we term the secondary belief) – a distinction borrowed from Lazarus (1992). The three main appraisal or primary beliefs are the three person evaluations:

• *Other-to-self* (what the other thinks of me; item 4)

• *Self-to-self* (what I think of me; item 5)

• *Self-to-Other* (what I think of the Other; item 6)

(Chadwick, Trower & Dagnan, 1999).

The questioning begins with the first of these – the client's appraisal of the other person's explicit or implicit evaluation of him – and continues to the second and third. A number of other measures are taken such as conviction level in the beliefs, and *"negativity"* (in a sense the badness potency of the evaluation; item 7). The coping response or secondary beliefs are those beliefs that define the actions that the client wants to take, given the appraisal of the event and their emotional reaction to it. The first of these beliefs concerns the emotional *goal* (item 8). For example, the emotional goal for anger, given a negative appraisal, may be to stop, coerce or discredit the other. Finally, the action beliefs are rated for the intensity with which they *want* or must achieve this goal (item 9).

Although each sequence has the ABC structure, all sequences subsequent to the first are "chained" to the one before, in that the behavioural C of the previous sequence becomes new A of the next. This can happen in two ways:

(1)   First the client may report carrying out a behavioural C (e.g. getting aggressive such as throwing cups, shouting), which become the first part of the A for the next sequence. The client reports the other person's reaction to their aggression, and their own reaction becomes the second part of the new A. The interviewer explores the emotional and behavioural Consequences to this new A, and finally the appraisal and coping response beliefs.

(2)   Second, the client may report that they inhibited their behavioural impulse at C (e.g. they had an impulse to be aggressive, but inhibited this behaviour). In this case the client is asked to imagine carrying out the inhibited aggressive behaviour as the new A in an imaginary ABC sequence. The client reports how he imagines the other would have reacted (second part of the A), how he would have felt and behaved at C, and what appraisal and coping response beliefs he would have had at B.

The final sequence in the chain is the one in which the client judges that the episode comes to an end. In truth, sequences have no ends and no beginnings – actual conflicts have histories of preceding sequences that set the scene, and following sequences that set the conditions for the next conflict, but we believe our method enables us to focus on the more significant segments of interaction.

CHAPTER 12

RESULTS I:
ANGER AND CATASTROPHES

Twenty-one people who had had at least one psychotic episode agreed to give us detailed accounts of what were for them the most significant conflicts they had experienced. These accounts were extraordinarily rich and often surprising in the information they gave us. In this chapter we report those findings for the group as a whole and for subgroups where the results consistently differ.

All names and other such identifying details have been changed to preserve anonymity of the participants. In all, 50 conflicts were recorded. Each conflict started with an engagement between the client and someone close to them, such as a family member or a peer and ended with disengagement. Each conflict also had an internal structure, consisting of a linked series of between two and five sequences, each of which in turn consisted of a sequence of activating events, beliefs, and emotional and behaviour consequences – the ABC structure as described in Chapter 11. Each conflict contained within it a "difficulty" in self-construction, and the descriptions show the unfolding process of this difficulty. The results and interpretations are presented sequence by sequence, beginning with the first and continuing through the last, in a way that tracks the unfolding process in a mini-narrrative. Parental conflicts and peer conflicts appeared to be substantially different and so these are considered separately.

FIRST SEQUENCE

The first sequence encompassed the interpersonal events that marked the opening of the conflict (the Activating events or As), the appraisals of those events (the Beliefs or Bs) and the emotional and behavioural consequences (the Cs) that followed from the Bs, given the As. The first sequence therefore captured the first, immediate impact of and response to the other's behaviour.

Activating Events (the "facts" as perceived by the client)

As predicted, many, if not most of the activating events were from what might be termed "high EE" communications from others.

Consequences (emotional and behavioural)

This section reports the emotions and behaviours that clients reported in response to the actions by the significant other that started the conflict. The main finding here from parental conflicts was that a majority (79%) involved the client getting angry in response to the activating event, usually intensely so (average of 7.5 out of 10). Of this group, just over half (52%) also wanted to shout something angrily. However this was inhibited in all but two cases (88%).

Only 42 per cent of peer conflicts show clients reporting anger (5 out of 12); of these, none actually expressed their anger behaviourally, although two did resolve not to have anything to do with their friends again.

The finding that there was a lot of anger in parental conflicts is consistent with the notion of the existential imperative, which would predict some degree of annoyance/anger and assertive/aggressive intent as the immediate normal response to the thwarting of self-construction. In an unpublished study using a similar methodology, 91 per cent of students responded with irritation or annoyance to criticism (Huber, 1997) from parents. People with a psychosis responded with roughly the same level of anger as the students (both had an average anger intensity of 8). Students also inhibited their aggressive impulses, but to a lesser degree – 61 per cent of students inhibited their impulses, compared with 83 per cent of clients. Students also expressed a more moderate and appropriate level of assertion.

Beliefs (primary and secondary)

Thus far results show that a majority of clients responded angrily or with aggressive but inhibited impulse to perceived criticisms or hostile or indifferent communications. However, to gain an understanding of the psychological mechanism – in particular whether this really was a response to a thwarting of the existential imperative – it is necessary to examine the types of beliefs.

Almost the entire sample (92%) perceived the Other (other-self) as communicating a negative evaluation of one form or another. A majority were classic put-downs, defining the client as bad or flawed in some way

($\alpha-$) but about a third were interpreted as coercions to fulfil, and thereby be defined by, a menial role which, to the relative and outside observers (for example, staff) often could be seen as evaluatively neutral or even positive (α or $\alpha+$), and thus the patient's interpretation would be regarded as surprising or simply paranoid. The Other's evaluation of themselves was not endorsed (self-self evaluation) by the majority of clients (55%), though this majority group did think that the negative evaluation was "potentially" true. However, 61 per cent also expressed critical put-downs ($\alpha-$) of the other (self-other). The interpretation is that these data reveal an anger-driven defence of the self, (shown by the clients' refusals to endorse these evaluations) against a perceived threat to the desired self or imposition of the undesired self (Markus & Nurius, 1986). In other words they attempted to protect their desired self and reject the undesired self.

We think the Beliefs connecting A to C show a picture in which clients (i) perceive the other as rejecting or indifferent to their desired self and/or imposing an undesired self (negative other-self), (ii) return the rejection, indifference and/or negative labelling of the other and thereby attempt to discredit them as evaluators (negative self-other) and thereby (iii) protect their evaluation of their desired self (self-self).

First Sequence Interpretation

The first sequence showed the participants perceived threat to, and attempt to defend the constructed self (i.e. paralleling Bentall's concept of attributional biases as evidence of psychological defence; Bentall, Kinderman & Kaney, 1994). The angry response, rejection of criticism, and externalising of negative evaluation (external attribution) are consistent with the notion of the existential imperative – the insistent psychological motive to have the desired self-affirmed (constructed) and the undesired self-*dis*affirmed (deconstructed). The first sequence typically described motivations which fit with the idea of the existential imperative.

SECOND SEQUENCE

The second sequence started where the first left off, that is, the consequence (C) of the first sequence was the triggering part of the activating event (A) for the second. It might be expected that the second sequence would have embraced a second line of defence of the desired self if the first had not been successful. As we mentioned earlier, there were two quite different types of second sequence – those reporting actual events, beliefs and consequences, and those reporting imagined events, beliefs and consequences.

Activating Events

The two types of second sequence (actual and imagined) were immediately apparent in two types of activating events:

- those *actual* responses of the Other when the client actually responded impulsively

- those *imagined* responses of the Other anticipated if they (the client) had not inhibited their impulse.

Plainly, there was a large discrepancy in the majority of cases (89%) between what they would have liked to have done, and what they actually did.

Consequences

The "existential imperative" having been thwarted in the first sequence, most clients had strong impulses to do something about this, but in the second sequence the majority did not in fact respond. What stopped them acting were strong feelings of anxiety at C, in both parent and peer conflicts (especially in peer conflicts). Most of the anxious Consequences emerged from how they imagined the Other would have responded had they (the client) really expressed their anger. It is interesting that the only two "happy" emotional outcomes were from the only two real instances of acting upon the initial self-affirming urges.

Beliefs

The form of these anxieties becomes clearer when the Beliefs behind the emotional Consequences are considered. Seventy per cent of clients held Beliefs that could be considered as catastrophic. It seemed that the people who inhibited their angry impulses did so because they were scared of having their self constructed in an extremely negative/catastrophic way if they expressed their anger. Some of these negative evaluations might not appear to be that bad to an outside observer, but certainly seemed catastrophic to the client in his/her situation.

For example: Sandra felt that to be seen as a tart (in her second conflict, with her peers; Chapter 14) was the worst thing that could happen to her. It is also interesting that five out of six clients who showed guilt as their second sequence C showed a Self-Other belief that viewed the other positively; their guilt appears to reflect a belief of having wronged someone virtuous.

Second Sequence Interpretation

Taken as a whole, the second sequence shows that many clients have enormous fears of impending catastrophes which they feel may occur if they were to act on their existential imperative urges. Even without catastrophe, all but a few of the clients experience anxiety provoking beliefs around themes of having their self constructed in a very pejorative way, and loss of social support. These beliefs therefore are consistent with the idea of the "moral imperative". It seems as if the moral imperative stymies the existential imperative, with the effect that the existential imperative is driven elsewhere. So what is the result of this "double-bind"?

THIRD SEQUENCE

In what was predominantly the final sequence, clients told how they actually acted and how it left them feeling. In this study, 67 per cent of participant's conflicts went to a third sequence (the other remaining at two sequences); on the whole these (with three sequences) were the people who had an imaginary second sequence.

Activating Events

The activating events of the third sequence were how the client actually responded at the time of the conflict. In most cases, what clients actually did was nothing. Eighty two per cent showed submissive or appeasing withdrawal responses, where the client apparently did what was required of them by the other, or remained motionless.

Consequences

The majority of the clients whose conflicts went to a third sequence felt depressed (62%). Without the benefit of knowing what emotions and beliefs had gone before in the previous sequences, these emotional responses appear as typical negative symptoms – anhedonia, depression, withdrawal, apathy. This was the prevailing picture for most of the time (i.e. the first two sequences were generally over quickly, the third sequence extends in time to hours, possibly days, and was typically the "presenting" picture). In these situations, the final feelings make more sense when the beliefs which are driving them are known.

Beliefs

Again, to understand the link between A and C it is necessary to look at B, and B here for 65 per cent of clients was typically the belief of being useless and impotent. In other words they interpreted their own submission as helplessness and were forced to finally accede to the negative self-construction. The remaining 35 per cent were left with the more extreme belief that they were bad people as a result of the submission and withdrawal.

Third Sequence Interpretation

In the majority of cases the clients did not construct their desired selves because of the fear of being reconstructed in extremely negative terms and ended up submitting to the lesser of two evils – submitting to the alien definition of self which they so angrily wanted to resist. Having being thwarted in their self-construction needs, and unable to do anything about this, they were left feeling depressed and, in their eyes, their selves were valueless. In effect, not being able to throw off the imposed self created for them, they were left "wearing" it.

WHOLE CONFLICT INTERPRETATION: SUMMARY OF MAIN THEMES

The activating events cover a variety of situations, but with the REBT paradigm, it is possible to make useful comparisons between conflicts in terms of the underlying beliefs and emotions. Conflicts can usefully be described in terms of self-constructions, failures and defences. As the initial conflict was to do with either ignoring the client's self-presentation, or steam-rollering it into an alien and unpalatable form, then the end product of the first sequence was the resultant angry and self-assertive urge, the "existential imperative".

However, very few clients actually acted on this impulse, and therefore could not construct a desired or even more bearable self thereby. For the vast majority of clients there was an overwhelming fear of the consequences of self-affirming action; the consequences were all along the lines of being reconstructed as a terrible person and thereby losing one's social support, often to a catastrophic extent. The catastrophes were far more extreme than anything found in a student comparison study (Huber, 1997).

In the final sequence, therefore, the client was prevented from taking overt defensive action, and hence the majority were, on the whole, blocked from self-construction, trapped in an alien construction and consequently depressed. They also showed – as the pathway to this fate – submissive and avoidant behaviours, of a sort which have been thought to be characteristic of one major form of post-psychotic depression (Birchwood *et al.*, 2000a). A conventional psychiatric view of this data would be that the clients are showing that particular manifestation of the underlying illness that commonly emerges after recovery from an acute episode and which is marked by negative symptoms and depression. However, putting two of the findings together – that conflicts are initiated by abrasive communications and end with depression/dysphoria – an alternative and more psychological picture appears, namely that patients get depressed because of the style of communications and the calamitous self-constructions, and not because of any underlying illness.

Function of the Conflict as a Whole

As a whole, the conflicts generally represented a type of entrapment in which clients cannot self-construct, because they feel coerced either into abandoning the struggle for self-construction or accepting an alien self-imposed upon them or both. Most of these conflicts were either frequently occurring or infrequent "defining moment" occurrences which set the precedent and pattern for future interactions. As such, a sense arose of how such conflicts perpetuated on a larger time scale could certainly contribute to the emergence of "negative symptoms" – apathy, withdrawal, and anhedonia were all amongst the majority of end-products.

What some people may find more surprising is that the thwarting of the self-constructions themselves, and the alien selves sometimes taken on by clients (under perceived duress), and the search for a mirroring other, also contribute to symptoms, but this time to the creation of the "positive symptoms". The next section looks for themes within the individual cases and reports in a more qualitative manner, using specific single cases to speculate about the formation of positive symptoms. Initially consideration goes into the issue of repression of anger and self-construction needs. Other clients did not seem to have problems expressing anger (in fact they almost have a problem with being too angry); in these cases, the moral imperative seems to be the one awry. Finally, some clients never get angry at all; these clients are then considered.

CHAPTER 13

FURTHER RESULTS: LINKING CONFLICT INTERACTIONS TO SYMPTOMS

The results reported in Chapter 12 compared the underlying fundamental beliefs held by clients across a number of situations using the data from the ABC Interview. In this section, clients are grouped by themes, each illustrated with typical case studies, including biographical information and symptom profiles. In looking for themes in the way clients functioned in terms of the self-construction process, two broad groups appeared. In the first, majority grouping, despite wide variation between individuals, there was a broad theme of inhibition of self-construction. In the second grouping there was an opposite theme of uninhibited self-construction.

INHIBITED SELF: ANGER HELD IN

As we saw in the previous section, the largest group of clients (12 out of 21) felt they could never get angry because they were too scared of the consequences. Since anger appears to be driven by thwarting of the existential imperative, it is proposed that this group are characterised by inhibition of self-construction, because of fear of consequences. Some of these clients would rarely express anger, and when they did it tended to be in an extreme form. The illustrative case studies that follow are described using a particular structure: how the client presented at first interview, then the content of their conflict with their parents. Some information about the parents from the Camberwell Family Interview completes the dyadic picture, and finally the client's symptoms are described. This is followed by an interpretive summary of all the inhibited-self cases (Table 13.1).

DAVID

Presentation

David presented as an affable, white 24-year-old dressed as a skinhead. He had been unwell for six years and was diagnosed as suffering from paranoid schizophrenia (ICD-10; section F20.0). He left school aged 16 and attended a local technical college for two years; he later worked in an office for a year. He was first admitted to hospital aged 21, has had four re-admissions since then and has been unemployed since his first episode. He was the youngest child of four and lives with his Mum and Dad.

Family Background

From the Camberwell Family Interview, David's mother was rated as High EE. She was very critical of him ("he really is bone-idle", "he is the most selfish person"), scoring 16 for Critical Comments and 1 for Hostility (generalisation of criticism from one-off instances to long-standing character traits). Both of these scores qualify for a rating of high EE. She scored 2 for Emotional Over-Involvement (this would be low EE, as the cut-off point for high EE is 3 on this scale; however, she was already rated as high EE on the basis of her critical comments and hostility scores); although she prompted him to do things a lot, and felt sure he couldn't exist without her, she fully accepted his right to his own life and to do independent things such as leave home (eventually). She rated as 3 for warmth, and 3 for positive comments, which are not used in the rating of EE (but are included to give a fairer picture of her).

Conflict

David's first conflict seems on the face of it a quite mundane, ordinary, everyday event of little apparent psychological interest. However, a detailed look at this episode shows otherwise.

In Figure 13.1, David was asked by his Mum to make a cup of tea (Activating event or point A), and that the request was made in such a way that he took angry exception to this (Consequence or point C). David was angry because although his mum liked him in this role as dutiful son, he felt he was being treated like a slave (Belief or point B, coded $\alpha+$), a self-construction which he far from endorsed (remember how David dressed as a skinhead!). Therefore his action impulse was to refuse to do such a thing and "tell her to piss off" (point C). However, when he imagined the consequences of this in a second sequence, he experienced anxiety (point C), because he predicted that if he told her to "piss off", she would define him as a totally bad person (point B, coded $\alpha-$). If this imaginary outcome actually happened, he would have largely endorsed this definition (actual = 4/10; potential = 9/10), and he would have experienced a very intense level of shame (9). Hence in reality, in order to avoid this traumatic reincarnation, in the third and final sequence he said nothing and did as he was told (point A). Consequently, David felt

Figure 13.1   David's Conflict

Activating Event	Beliefs	Consequences
Mum said: "Go and make me a cup of tea."	*Primary* Other-Self: "*There she goes again, using me – treating me like a slave, worth nothing. How dare she, the bitch!*" Categorise: α− Confidence: 9 Self-Self actual endorsement: 4 Self-Self potential endorsement: 9 Negativity: 9 Self-Other: "*She's selfish.*" *Secondary* Preferred goal: "*No way I am going to be her slave.*" Action choice: "*Refuse – tell her to 'piss off'*"	*Emotion* General: Angry Specific: Insulted/ hurt Intensity: 9 *Action Impulse* "*Refuse, tell her to 'piss off', tell her to 'bloody make it herself'*"
"*Imagining I said "No, fetch it yourself", and didn't get the tea.*" Describe other's reaction: "*She'd say 'God aren't you a nasty sod!'*"	*Primary* Other-Self: "*She would hate me. She would be hostile and critical. She thinks I'm bad. She's right; I would 'feel' (experience myself) as a bad person.*" Categorise: α− Confidence: 9 Self-Self actual endorsement: 7 Self-Self potential endorsement: 9 Negativity: 9: Self-Other: *Secondary* Goal: "*Not to do anything that would make her think I'm really bad.*"	*Emotion* General: Anxiety Specific: Shame apprehension Intensity: 9 *Action Impulse* "*Do as I am told – make the tea*"
"*I say 'Sure, that's fine.' I go fetch a cup of tea like she wants.*" Describe other's reaction: "*Pleased with me.*"	*Primary* Other-Self: "*She's pleased with me but it sticks in my throat. She's treating me like a slave, like I'm worth nothing. And by doing what she wants I'm being like one*" Categorise: α+ Confidence: Self-Self actual: 10 Self-Self potential: 10 Negativity: 10 Self-Other: *Secondary* *Failed* want goal: "*Not being her slave*"	*Emotion* General: Depression Specific: Intensity: 10 *Action Tendency* "*Give in and just do what I'm told*"

depressed (point C) because he was trapped in a construction of himself which was demeaning and which by now he fully endorsed (10/10): "She's pleased but it sticks in my throat" (point B, coded α+).

Symptoms

David's symptoms on acute admission included command hallucinations, episodic severe depression, suicidal urges, and ideas of reference. His voices were mainly expressing anger at his Mum, and others, sometimes commanding him to kill his Mother and others, but also to kill himself, because "everyone is against me". There were periods of aggression, during one of which he was retained at a secure unit. At that time he kept a collection of knives, and there was also an incident when he trashed the late-night garage where his parents had got him a job. At other times he felt ashamed for this behaviour and became very low. At these times David was severely depressed, and was hospitalised after a number of suicide attempts. David's history then showed an oscillation between anger and aggression on the one hand, and low self-esteem and depression on the other. The interpretation is that the command hallucinations functioned as a kind of "solution" in allowing him to express the existential imperative (to be the person he wanted to be, i.e. manly) that was being thwarted by the moral imperative in his interactions with his mother, and which he was too anxious to express directly. In other words, the voice enabled him to be strong and independent without the normal consequences. The conflict analysis described above and summarised in Figure 13.1 helps to uncover the entrapment that David experienced and the role that the command hallucinations may play in "resolving" the conflict.

ALAN (AL)

Presentation

Alan was 19, and had been diagnosed as having paranoid schizophrenia with his first hospitalisation occurring only a few months ago. He became overtly unwell as he left school and started working in a butcher's shop. He had also experimented with drugs such as LSD and Ecstasy, but reported he was "losing it" before that. At interview, Alan presented as being very meek, shy and "small", despite being a heavily built person; if anything his behaviour was reminiscent of a small child. He lived with his Mum and younger brother.

Family Background

Prior to his first acute episode, Al spent most of his time with his mates, experimenting with drugs and hardly ever at home. At this time his Mum felt she had "lost" him. After the acute episode this situation markedly changed and Al became very dependent on his mother. During the CFI, she expressly said that

> I feel I have my 12-year-old back, who I lost years ago. I've got my son back, and he's lovely. He's nothing like the child he was before, he was so self-centred and . . .obviously I don't want him as he is, but now he's so loving, so concerned. He was never concerned about anyone before. And this is what I always believed was inside him. Although it's really painful to see – I could cry sometimes, just weep and weep – I'm like a mother hen with him now, like he's 12 years old again.

Whereas the self that Al wanted for himself was trendy, fairly manly, unconventional and independent, the self his Mum wanted for him was of a good boy who respected and looked up to his mother. She rated for high EE on critical comments (scored 13: critical of nearly everything he initiated), hostility (rated 1: generalisation of criticism: e.g. "He does nothing, now, absolutely nothing. I can't even get him to wash up after tea") and emotional over-involvement (rated 5: dramatising, self-sacrificing behaviour "there's no point me getting a job", "I say to him – "yours isn't the only life ruined by this you know, Al", wants to do everything for Al and knows everything he wants). She also scored a number of positive comments (4) and warmth (3). Of this conflict situation, she said "it was a real battle to make him do anything. It was a real shouting match".

Conflict

In his first conflict (Figure 13.2), Al reported an incident in which his Mum attempted to get him to get up, to get him to the hospital gym. He felt that he hadn't slept very well that night and did not want to get up (he liked to sleep a lot, and when he did get up he would mostly sleep in front of the TV). He said he resisted his Mum's attempts to get him up, until she got angry with him. In terms of the ABC sequence, in sequence 1 he said she urged him to get up, that he ought to get up (point A; perhaps appealing to his sense of the moral imperative). He felt that although she wanted him to be a "good boy", he would experience it as being a silly kid (point B, code $\alpha+$). He himself certainly rejected this demeaning definition of himself (self-self: 1/10), and felt really angry (point C: rated 8/10). Yet the second sequence showed that he felt very anxious about his angry impulses (point C), because he imagined (at point A) that if he acted on his anger his mum would get even more angry and label him as a "little shit" (point B; code $\alpha-$). He would largely accept this definition of himself (rating 8/10), and would have felt great shame (rating 10/10). This anticipated consequence was what caused such anxiety, and because of this Al got up and did as she wanted. Finally, in sequence 3 he felt very depressed (point C; rating 9/10), because he had yielded to and become the "good little schoolboy" that he so despised. In total, Al showed a very typical pattern of anger repression brought about by the anxiety he felt from how he imagined his assertive actions would go down.

It transpired that rebellious episodes such as this one happened every few months, and that usually he later become so ashamed of his earlier "outburst" (as defined by his Mum), that he set about "winning back her good opinion". He did this by doing things he thought his mother wanted him to – continuing from sequence 3 of Figure 13.2. Alan was especially compliant and meek until he had another angry episode, which his Mum saw as a setback after a period in which he had been "doing so well"; as she said to him to override his anger "Al, I'm doing everything in my power to stop you becoming a vegetable". But why was Alan so vulnerable to being defined as "bad"? The extent to which Al feels ashamed of himself if he incurs her wrath and how he spends months trying to win back her good opinion is unusual – if his behaviour is seen as typical of adolescents (Smetana, 1989), then it is only natural for people his age to be contrary and changeable and to exasperate their parents. (Parents also have every right to be annoyed by such behaviour!). Such problems certainly should not be the cause of as much life-enveloping shame as it was. Alan thought at these times that he was so worthless that everyone else was conspiring to sacrifice him to the devil, as we shall see.

Symptoms

Moral theme

The power that Alan's anxiety sequence had over him is apparent in his symptoms. At times he was convinced that he was very bad, that everyone hated him and was intensely ashamed of himself. Al was obsessed with the devil, and at times feared everyone else was in league with the devil and were plotting to have him ceremonially sacrificed. He told of how, while sitting in a pub he had seen the Devil's face reflected in his pint glass, about to sacrifice him, and that he, in sheer terror, fled the pub, and ran screaming down the street. He also saw people as having one red eye, which meant they were half in league with the Devil. At night he could hear people chanting (preparing an altar for him), and said "I could see hoofprints and smell the goat". Earlier we considered David who heard angry voices against his mother, which we interpreted as being due to the existential imperative for self-assertion. In contrast to David, Al's hallucinations seemed to come from his sense of the moral imperative. Hence many of his delusions and voices came from the idea that he was awful and deserved

Figure 13.2   Alan's Conflict

Activating Event	Beliefs	Consequences
Alan: *"I hadn't slept all night. Mum woke me and said 'Get up, you have to go to the gym'. I tell her I've had no sleep and don't want to get up"* Mother: *"Come on get up now! I don't care if you have had no sleep"*	*Primary* Other-Self: *"Undermining my views: Therefore treating me like a worthless child. What I say is bullshit."* Categorise: $\alpha+$ Confidence: 7 Self-Self actual endorsement: 1 Self-Self potential endorsement: 8 Negativity: 8 Self-Other: *"She is being unfair. Bad person"* Categorise: $\alpha-$ Conviction: 7 Negativity: *Secondary* Preferred goal: *"Refuse to comply to unreasonable demand. By refusing in effect refusing to be a silly little kid."* Action choice: *Stay in bed*	*Emotion* General: Angry Specific: Intensity: 8 *Action Impulse* *"Stay in bed and say 'For God's sake I've had no sleep!', shout etc?"*
"Imagining staying in bed and saying 'I haven't slept' " Describe other's reaction: *"She would say: 'Do as you're told you little shit. Don't be babyish' "*	*Primary* Other-Self: *"As a bad child. I'd feel terrible."* Categorise: $\alpha-$ Confidence: 9 Self-Self actual endorsement: 8 Self-Self potential endorsement: 8 Negativity: 8 Self-Other: *Secondary* Preferred goal: Action choice: *Obey her and get up*	*Emotion* General: Anxious Specific: Anticipatory shame Intensity: 8, 10 *Action Impulse* *"Get up reluctantly but quickly"*
"I get up quickly." Describe other's reaction: *"She's surprised but pleased: 'Good boy'"*	*Primary* Other-Self: *"Treating me like a little school boy doing what he's told, again – aargh!"* Categorise: $\alpha+$ Confidence: 9 Self-Self actual endorsement: 9 Self-Self potential endorsement: 9 Negativity: 10 Self-Other: *She's wicked* Categorise: $\alpha-$ Conviction: 9 Negativity: *Secondary* *Failed* preferred goal: *"Didn't ignore her and stay in bed. Gave in to her and became a little kid"*	*Emotion* General: *Pissed off* Specific: Intensity: 9 *Action Impulse* Describe: *"Carry on getting up; glum, slow, reluctant"*

punishment. For Al, the moral imperative was to both avoid being labelled as bad, and thereby preserve the social support of his Mum, because he was very dependent on her; he had to a large extent lost contact with his friends and was scared of them (see later). One function of the delusions was to squash any actions that might jeopardise her continued mirroring and validation.

Existential Theme

Incongruent with Alan's anxiety and shame behaviour was a story his mother told of a terrifying physical assault where Al actually threatened her with knives and picked her up by the throat (she weighed about 18 stone at this time). On this occasion, Al was speaking in a way that suggests he felt he had been taken over by the Devil. At interview, the most he would say about this was that it was something he feared; he was reluctant to talk about times when he got angry, but this incident suggests that he did have much anger. There is too little evidence to do more than speculate, but it is plausible that at this time he felt he had been taken over by the Devil, and that this could be some kind of transformation of, and measure of the strength of, the existential imperative. Al's existential imperative to self-assert therefore refuses to be quashed and manifests itself in hostility towards his mother and psychotic episodes along the themes of the devil. One might wonder why this might happen, but as Horney (1950) said:

> There is simply nothing that may not be invested with pride . . . One person is proud of being rude to people, another is ashamed of anything that might be construed as rudeness. (p93)

It would seem unavoidable that a purpose of these themes would be to give him a level of power against his Mum. Alan's Mum gave him a lot of consideration (in fact bent over backwards to accommodate him) when he was in this psychotic episode. In his role as the Devil, he was very abusive, insulting and demanding; at one point he insisted she stay with him at all times. His Mum had to really wheedle him to be allowed out of the house.

The conflict shows that in the final sequence, Alan was left feeling thwarted and impotent. This was reflected in his long-term behaviour, because he withdrew as much as he could from interaction with his Mum, although he didn't want her to know that he was withdrawing from the interactions because that too would be a source of shame (he preferred to be up at night, when there were no people about). If one was unaware of the power struggles involved, this social withdrawal, anhedonia, depression and perhaps "bizarre behaviour" could only be explained by a disease model.

But the alternative proposed here is that it is the entrapment created by the conflict of the imperatives, revealed in the analysis of the sequences, and the subsequent thwarting of Al's efforts to construct a viable self that bring these behaviours about.

DISCUSSION

These two cases are representative of a number of clients in that all these clients felt thwarted in their self-construction urges and yet repressed their anger. In Table 13.1, 12 clients who fitted this pattern are shown, with an abbreviated account of their conflicts. An attempt is also made in each case to show a functional link to symptoms. This group all follow the same theme in that they repressed their angry impulses to assert themselves because of their sense of the moral imperative. As mentioned in the previous section, in many cases the moral imperative took the form of fearing catastrophic consequences, an especially common worry for clients (for example Imran and Alan feared being thrown out of the house or sacrificed to the devil). The anxieties they experienced led them to feel trapped and unable to pursue their self-construction needs. As a result they acted submissively, allowing themselves to be constructed by the other, and they felt depressed. The anger repressed in these instances is driven underground, but it doesn't just disappear; instead it seems to reappear in symptoms.

For example, David (and possibly Alan) heard voices expressing hostility towards their parents. Such voices might be described as malevolent (Chadwick & Birchwood, 1995), but a closer examination reveals that much of their malevolence was directed at their mothers or other people they felt controlled and defined by. In this context, even malevolent voices might be seen as supportive, if they are serving a need. Alan heard voices that were hostile and critical of himself, which seem to partially reflect the moral imperative (i.e. his guilt and anxiety for asserting himself) and a need for some sort of mirroring of his self (as if the anger from Sequence 1 gets directed at himself, to stop him being ignored and unconstructed).

Most people will be able to empathise with the unstoppable nature of unexpressed anger, as most people will have had the experience of coming away from an argument and finding themselves ruminating about all the good argument lines that they wish they had thought of at the time, perhaps even saying them out loud or acting them out (Bentall et al., 1994). In fact this "rehearsal" is a popular coping strategy in normal people, for dealing with stress (Roger & Najarian, 1989). Rehearsal and efficacy of emotional coping have been shown to be positively correlated (Roger & Schapals,

Table 13.1 Table Giving Interpretative Summary of All the Conflicts which Fitted the Category of Inhibited Self

Name/Parental EE	Sequence 1	Sequence 2	Sequence 3	Speculative link to symptoms
Martin *Father:* high EE Criticism: 7 Hostility: 0 EOI: 1 Warmth: 5 Positive comments: 7	Dad: *"Not now son."* *"He thinks I'm a 'waste of space. He mustn't. He's a bastard!"* (αI) Anger 9 *"I'll do something bad – that will make him sorry"*. Goes with prostitute. (Existential imperative to reject αI by rebelling)	*"He might think I'm a pervert"* (α–) *"Am I? I mustn't I let him find out"* Anxiety shame 9 Anticipatory shame 9 *"Say nothing; Interrogates friends, check radio"* (to cover his tracks) (Moral imperative to conceal α–)	*"I've covered my tracks, but now he thinks I'm a 'waste of space again. He mustn't"* (αI) Angry 9 *"I'll do something that will make him sorry!"* (Swings between existential and moral imperatives)	Believes there is a conspiracy to put him away. Police and the media are following him. Believes they will put him on trial as a pervert and it will be in all the newspapers, to his father's great shame. This exemplifies the moral imperative – punishment for his badness
David (Figure 13.1) *Mother:* high EE Criticism: 16 Hostility: 1 EOI: 2 Warmth: 3 Positive comments: 3	Mum: *"Go and make me a cup of tea"* (α+) *"She's treating me like a slave again. How dare she, the bitch!"* Anger 9 *"Tell her to piss off and do it herself!"* (Existential imperative to reject α+ by asserting manly self)	*"If I do that she'll say I'm a nasty sod. I would be"* (Would become α– as defined) Anxiety 9 Anticipatory shame 9 *"Sure, that's fine"* (Moral imperative to avoid being α– by behaving submissively)	*"By doing what she wants I'm behaving like a slave. That makes me feel I am one"* (Yields to α+) Humiliation 8 Anger 9 Sullen withdrawal, goes to bedroom. Angry ruminations (trapped in α+ role by moral imperative)	Voices tell him to harm or kill his mother but he doesn't tell her this for fear of hurting her feelings. By attributing such thoughts to voice(s), David is released from guilt caused by moral imperative, allowing expression of existential imperative i.e. desired macho and powerful self
Alan (Figure 13.2) *Mother:* high EE Criticism: 13 Hostility: 1 EOI: 4 Positive comments: 3 Warmth: 3	*"Mum tells me to get up."* (α+) *"Treating me like silly kid"* Angry 8 *"Want to shout, 'for God's sake I've had no sleep!'"* (Existential imperative to reject α+ by shouting indignantly)	*"She'd say 'do as you're told, you little shit.' I'd feel terrible"*. (Would become α–) Anxiety 8 Anticipatory shame 10 *"I got up reluctantly"* (Moral imperative to avoid being α– by behaving submissively)	*"I'm a good little school boy again – aargh"* (yields to α+) *"Pissed off"* 9 Glum, obedient	Delusions of Mother and others seeking to sacrifice him to the Devil as a punishment (exemplifies the moral imperative – punishment for his badness). Occasional delusions of being the Devil, which are possibly driven by the existential imperative

Louise, Did not want Camberwell Family Interview done on husband	*"Husband said 'you're not having the tablets'"* (She wanted to take an overdose). *"Treating me like I'm silly, pathetic. A nutter"* (α+) Angry 9 Aggressive outburst – punches, kicks and shouts (Existential imperative to reject α+)	*"He thinks I'm horrible"* (Becomes α−) Shame 9 Guilt 8 Hugs husband and says sorry. Husband: *"It's OK"* (Moral imperative to seek release from α−)	*"I've given in. Still treated like a child; helpless and powerless. I feel trapped"* (Yields to α+) Depressed 10 Humiliated 9 Angry 9	Angry voices tell her to kill husband. (Experiencing this as a commanding voice perhaps lessens guilt from moral imperative, and embodies expression of existential imperative to angrily reject marginalised self)
Luke *Mother: Low EE* Criticism: 2 EOI: 1 Warmth 4	*Policeman and Dad grab me by the arms.* *"They're treating me like I'm a criminal"* (Define him as α−) Angry 9 *"Wanted to lash out with a hammer, tell them to f . . . off"* (Existential imperative to reject α− by being strong and indignant)	*"I'd be behaving like a criminal only worse"* (Would justify their definition of him as α−) Anxiety 8 Anticipatory shame 4 Guilt 5 *"I just sat there – did nothing"* (Moral imperative to avoid being α− by being compliant)	*"I've given in and feel trapped"* (But still rejects α−) Despair 9 Humiliated 9 Hurt 6 Ruminates on "real" self.	Delusions of grandeur (world famous songwriter) *"I'm going to be due a lot of money, soon, as I wrote all these famous songs. All these other people are trying to steal my thunder"* (Substitution of rejected "criminal" self by "real" self by delusions of grandeur. Example of Poor Me paranoia)
Sandra *Mother:* *High EE* Criticism: 2 Hostility: 0 EOI: 3 Positive comments: 7 Warmth 5	*"Mum said 'Nobody's talking about you, why should they?'* *She's being casually dismissive of me. Felt unvalued and selfish"* (defined as α−) Angry 9 Hurt 9 *"Wanted to scream, throw lamp shades etc."* (Existential imperative to reject I and α−)	*"I'd be hurting a very virtuous person"* (Anticipates would be defined as nasty person α− by implication) Anxiety 10 Anticipatory Guilt 10 *"Held my breath and shut up"* (Moral imperative to avoid being a 'nasty person' α− by repressing anger and existential demands)	*"Stuck with her dismissing and not valuing me"* (But rejects 'unvalued and selfish' α−) Frustration 9 Depression 9 Subdued but agitated. Ruminates on valued grandiose self	*"The day will come when I will become the Latter Day Jesus Christ and my lover and I will tour the world doing good deeds"* Communicates with imaginary lover telepathically. Delusional substitution of rejected "unvalued, selfish" self by grandiose self. This substitution probably driven by the existential imperative

Table 13.1 (continued)

Name/Parental EE	Sequence 1	Sequence 2	Sequence 3	Speculative link to symptoms
Nigel *Father:* *high EE* Criticism: 6 Hostility: 0 EOI: 1 Warmth: 3 Positive comments: 0	"Dad assumes I'm looking for a professional job and coping OK. Asks if I am still looking." (Defined as α+) Angry-for-a-second 7 "Want to shout, 'I can't cope. Give us a break!'" (Existential imperative to reject α+ as unfair and demanding)	"If I did that he'd think I was a right waster. Would throw me out the house" (Anticipates being defined as bad, would endorse α–) Anticipated shame 10 "Said nothing. Pretended I was coping." (Moral imperative to avoid α– inhibits any action, conforms to expectations)	"He thinks 'you're a good son'" (α+) but I'm not. He's bound to find out" (α–) (Endorses α–) Depressed 10 Helpless, hopeless. Does nothing. Isolated. Ruminates on what others think of him	Voices saying "You're manure" – amplifying the opinion he felt his Dad would and will have of him from the moral imperative. He generalised this paranoid belief to peers. Negative symptoms such as flattened affect, and avolition could also be a consequence
Cathy *Mother:* *Low EE,* Critical comments: 3 EOI: 1 Warmth: 2 Positive comments: 2	"Mum asked me if I was going to do the dishes as I had said I would, when I got back from posting a letter – accusing me of being lazy and incompetent, always criticising" (α–) Angry 9 Hurt 8 "Want to shout something about how I was going to do it" (Existential imperative to reject α–)	"She would be even more angry and critical" (Would justify α–) Anxious 10 Anticipated shame 10 Behaves appeasingly, due to pressure from moral imperative	"She's treating me like I'm useless and I've allowed it" (Endorses and becomes α–) Feels trapped in this "always being criticised" role) Depressed 8 Frustrated 9 Socially avoidant, hypervigilant of others' conversations	"I can hear people talking about me and being very critical of me. They actually say bad things about me. I became very reclusive" Delusion magnifies perceived critical labelling from mother, driven by moral imperative
Pete *Mother:* *Low EE* EOI: 2 Criticism: 2 Hostility: 0 Warmth: 4 Positive comments: 5	"Mum nags me to do things", "She's a nuisance, it's unnecessary; she treats me like a kid" (α+) Anger 8 "I'd like to just ignore her and walk away, go to the next room" Existential imperative to avoid α+ by escaping scene	"If I did walk away, she wouldn't think I am an ignorant fool, but I would. I'd be worse than I am now, mentally" (He would become α–) Anticipatory guilt 8 "I do what she says" (Moral imperative means Pete feels he has to pretend to agree and tries to agree)	"She treats me like a kid and by going along with I feel that way" (α+) (Pete appears to have lost confidence in own opinions, become dependent on his Mum's definition of him) Depression 8 Social withdrawal. Ruminates about how he would like to be	"I felt like I was much more important than everyone else. I began to hear these voices commenting nicely about everything I did" (Grandiose delusions reflecting unappreciated real self – existential imperative) "Later on the voices started really picking on me" Echoing some perceived criticism in the interactions with his mother, reflecting moral imperative

Matt Did not consent to parents being interviewed	"My Dad had a go at me for finishing with my girlfriend" (First α−) "He thinks I'm useless, worthless" Anger 9 "I wanted to defiantly run away from Dad telling me off" Existential imperative to avoid labelling in the only way he dare	"If I did that he would think I am a complete bastard. The idiot of all time. Nothing goes in". (Second α−). "He'd come after me, give me a whack" Guilt 9 Fear 9 "I can't fight back" Guilt caused by moral imperative means that escape is not an option; he has to accept the label (first α−)	"I can't fight back so he wins the argument. He still thinks I'm a scumbag" – 'Matt hasn't improved". (first α−) (remains caught between anger and the guilt that holds it in) Depressed 10 Ruminates about being powerful and effective	"I assaulted strangers in the street, who were in league with my Dad and hated me" By doing this he appears to have been throwing off Dad's demeaning construction (conspiracy theory is motivated by the moral imperative?)
Bill Mother: Low EE Criticism: 6 Hostility: 0 EOI: 1 Warmth: 0 Positive comments: 1	"My mum is never interested in talking to me. She just watches her soaps. Like I'm a nobody" (First α−) Angry 8 "I want to get really angry with her, make her take notice." Bill wants to be acknowledged (existential imperative)	"She would think, 'Get a grip on yourself. You're showing yourself up, you're showing everybody up'" (Would become α−) Fear 8 "I try to get a grip on myself. I don't say anything" Fears of drawing attention to himself mean that he accepts being ignored	"I can't do anything but be ignored" (Remains a nobody, i.e. remains I) Alone 8 He remains angry about being ignored and ruminates on how he would like to be, and the lonely situation he perceives	"I have these constant voices in my head always criticising everything I do. They really hate me. They have such power and have threatened to kill me if I don't obey them" (Reflects moral imperative, how he feels everyone dislikes him if he draws attention to himself. Flattened affect, social withdrawal. "I sometimes try to reason with them, in fact I'm quite assertive with them" (Reflects existential imperative as he plays the self he would like to be)
Imran Mother: High EE Critical comments: 6 Hostility: 0 EOI: 4 Warmth: 2 Positive comments: 2	"Whenever I do something wrong, my parents never let me forget about it. They treat me as if I'm worth nothing, it's like 'you should be nothing'" (First α−) Anger 9 Suicidal "I want to shout, 'Just stop it can't you see, it'll never happen again'" (Existential imperative wants to reject their α− definition of him by being indignant and asserting he's OK)	"They would be very angry and upset; I would be very ignorant, like I don't know the truth; I should be patient with my parents" (Would become second α−) Guilt 8 "I have to put up with what they say, or else get into even bigger trouble. I have to do what they tell me. I try very, very hard to" (Moral imperative means that he feels unable to assert self and motivates him to work hard at appeasing)	"My test is to get through all this and get through, with God's help. I'm not built to take this amount of torture, though" (Continues to be worth nothing, α+) Depression 10 Anger is still there. Ruminates on criticism and how to win approval	Delusions of reference: "people in the street, on TV, on planes are referring to me. I sometimes feel the Devil is after me, they hate me" Generalisation of perceived incessant criticism from parents: moral imperative "Sometimes I get possessed by something which I think may be the devil" (Existential imperative to assert self even if bad)

1996). If this is the form that anger can take in normal people, it should not be surprising that held-in anger could take the form of uncontrollable thoughts or voices or acting-out behaviour.

In this instance, such thoughts might be a coping strategy, as they are in non-psychotic people. One possibility by which these thoughts might become voices would be if they felt that it wasn't acceptable to think angry thoughts against their parents. Separate studies have shown that clients who heard voices were more likely to think that they ought not to think bad thoughts against their parents (Harrop, 2000; Baker & Morrison, 1998). This is especially pertinent given that many clients are suffering in a state of *objectité*, which entails a feeling of transparency like the other may be aware of and judging a person's thoughts. If it seems that even mild, angry emotions would be followed by strong guilty and anxious thoughts (perhaps self-critical ones like Imran's voices), then extremely angry thoughts could bring about intolerable guilt and anxiety. Yet the imperative is an unstoppable force, hence the only way out for the client might be to attribute responsibility and ownership of the angry thoughts to something external to themselves. Furthermore, if the client's own anger is a cause for shame, then clients might also vacillate from one emotion to the other (one imperative to the other) and back again, from anger to anxiety, in a self-perpetuating manner.

People with obsessive compulsive disorder (OCD) have the common experience where the more they try to repress intrusive thoughts, the more impossible such repression becomes and the more likely the thought is to be intrusive (see Salkovskis & Campbell, 1994). The same principle may apply here – if a client has an angry thought about their mother, they may try to repress it, and this very act of repression may make it worse. Whereas OCD people deal with the guilt (and ownership) by elaborate "rectifying" thought rituals or compulsive behaviours, the clients here do it by attributing the thought to an external voice.

CLIENTS WHO PREFERRED NOT TO TALK ABOUT PARENTS

A sub-group of clients never once spoke remotely critically of their parents; in fact they carefully avoided bringing up any issue involving a parent. Because of this, there are no conflicts from them involving parents, although there are conflicts around other issues. Clients are perfectly within their rights to not want to talk about a personal area, and during interview we took care not to pressure anyone into talking about something they didn't want to. We are within our rights to speculate whether clients avoided parental topics because they chose not to, or were unable to countenance such topics. The reader must decide for themselves but our interpretation is that the majority of this group are on a continuum with the inhibited self-first group. This current group seem to us to be almost completely defined by their moral imperative. The inhibition that comes out of the moral imperative cuts right into the core cognitions that underlie self-construction needs, to such an extent that they are ashamed of even having such thoughts about self-assertion.

To illustrate using one of the previous examples, Alan was very wary at first of expressing any criticism because he feared the interviewer being on the side of his mother. After much engagement he really opened up on these issues, and said how glad he was of the support. Given that the other clients needed such support to bring up parental issues, and that a feature of these parental conflicts was immense guilt and anxiety about ever thinking ill of their parents, it seems likely that there are similar inhibiting fears on the part of the clients who would not talk about parental issues.

It is difficult to report any data on this, because by definition it is a lack of data, but we estimate around 5 out of the 20 clients did not say a word against their parents throughout the interviews, and this probably reflects their behaviour with their parents – they have never said a harsh word to their parents at all. We suspect this reflects an idealised view of their parents. For example, towards the end of our study, clients were asked to name three good points and three bad points of their parents. Of five clients asked, only two could name a single fault their parents had, one of which was leaving the top off the toothpaste. The others were utterly surprised that we should ask such a thing, because their parents were obviously beyond reproach. In the Camberwell Family Interview, none of the parents seemed as perfect as their offspring thought (as indeed the interviewers aren't!). Jack's Dad seemed a very warm man in many respects, and yet when he found Jack drowsy in their kitchen apologising for having just taken an overdose, the first thing he (the father) could think of to say was how selfish Jack was to do this, and how he would never like him again after this, he would always hate him for it. Jack very unhappily told of how he sat in the ambulance, crying because he'd made his Dad hate him, and even eight months later on, his main concern was worrying whether he would ever win back his father's good opinion; indeed this was the only aspect of the whole suicide attempt that he regretted. Jack's dad scored highly on warmth and positive comments in the CFI, and a son's attempted suicide must be unbearably stressful. Jack's Dad made a very understandable human, emotional response to the situation, but Jack did not have a sophisticated enough understanding of his Dad as a fallible human being to understand, and hence was far more hurt than he needed to be by the situation. Jack's primary symptoms were depression and grandiose delusions where he thought he was about to become "The Chosen One".

SELF UNINHIBITED: ANGER EXPRESSERS

Everyone is an anger repressor to some extent, as was found in the comparison study on students mentioned earlier (Huber, 1997), but we think the clients above repress far more, and repress desired actions that most people would usually express. They suffer excruciating guilt and anxiety when they even think of standing up for themselves. However, at the other end of this continuum, there were three clients who had the opposite problem. They appeared to experience no moral imperative whatsoever, and their existential expressivity appeared to know no bounds. However, this is clearly no solution as these clients probably had more severe problems and probably suffered more as a result of their marginalisation from family and peers.

In the following example, Elizabeth acted on her anger, and although her reaction was perhaps extreme, the result for her was a feeling of happiness. However the down-side to such behaviour was that Elizabeth, being generally quite an angry person, was in trouble for beating her 4-year-old daughter.

ELIZABETH

Presentation

Elizabeth was 39 and had been diagnosed as having suffered from schizophrenia since late adolescence. She had been in and out of various hospitals since her first acute episode at 21 and at one point even lived rough on the streets with her child for two years. She left school at 18 and studied art and design at college. She was now in a much better state and hadn't been unwell for ages; she had been married for 13 years. She presented as affable but perhaps rather touchy.

Family Background

We never met Elizabeth's mother so we only have one side of this argument. Elizabeth had a very volatile relationship with her mother; in fact she had cut her parents off to an extent, only having as much contact as she felt happy with. Elizabeth felt this situation worked well for her, and she was very self-assertive, as is seen in her conflict. It is tempting to see this as a blueprint for healthy expression of anger: although she was particularly nasty to her mother – "I wish she was dead, I'd be better off and so would Gill" – the second sheet seems like a much more satisfactory outcome than any of the others. This was one of the few conflicts with parents where the client expressed their anger – and Elizabeth really let rip with everything she felt – and where clients said what they thought. The result was feeling happy (rating of 10), and beliefs of "Mum had to accept that I am a warm and caring person instead of just a machine who does what she's told; I do matter".

Conflict

In her conflict (Figure 13.3), Elizabeth described how her mother wrote her some letters talking about how Gill should be brought up (sequence 1, point A). The letters made her angry (point C) because she felt they were implying that she was no good at anything (point B). Her action of choice was to ring her mother up and tell her exactly what she felt, and this is what she did (sequence 2). Sequence 2 is the final sequence because Elizabeth felt really happy afterwards (point C). "I felt I had really achieved something, I felt a lot better"; "She had to accept I am a warm and caring person" (point B).

Symptoms

One of Elizabeth's main problems was really that she was too angry, too much of the time. Her symptoms were that she was very grandiose, and deluded; she felt she was very special and better than everyone else. She also suffered from paranoia and felt that people were out to get her, although she felt she hadn't really done much wrong ("Poor Me paranoia"; Trower & Chadwick, 1995). She heard a number of different types of voices, some of which were benevolent and others which were malevolent. They were usually voices of people she knew telling her secrets, advising her on what to do, and occasionally barracking her. She also felt she heard God talking and saw signs from him in birds and cars, and on TV. She relied heavily on these directions for most decisions in her life, on a day-to-day basis, in a sense giving up ownership of decisions to these sources.

She described how she felt that her daughter Gill wasn't doing the things that she was supposed to do, and that she felt "I have to do all the work" and "She wasn't doing things quickly enough". She "shouted at Gill, slapped her and ripped things up" (in fact she beat Gill quite badly on a number of occasions and lost custody of her).

DISCUSSION

The small group of clients who fitted the category of being anger expressers were angry to an extent that was problematic. It seems therefore that there are problems with some clients expressing themselves fully, and that some clients may be right to hold in their anger somewhat. These clients were typically poor-me clients, who were sure that they were OK, and that the problem lay in other people (Trower & Chadwick, 1995). In the next

Figure 13.3   Elizabeth's Conflict

Activating Event	Beliefs	Consequences
"Mum wrote me some letters; they made me really angry because I felt Mum and Dad were trying to take over Gill (8-year-old daughter). She was saying that Gill needed bringing up properly"	*Primary* Other-Self: *"She's shown me up in front of my husband. She's saying I'm no good at anything"* Categorise: α− Confidence: 10 Self-Self: *"I am doing a good job. I do all these things"* Actual endorsement: 0 Self-Self potential endorsement: 0 Negativity: 10 Self-Other: *"I wish she were dead. I'd be better off and so would Gill. She's not a very nice person* Categorise: α− Conviction: 10 Negativity: 10 *Secondary* Preferred goal: *To sort her out*	*Emotion* General: Angry Intensity: 10 *Action Impulse* *"I rang her up and really shouted at her, told her how I felt"*
"I put her in her place, told her that she's wrong and I'm right." Describe other's reaction: *"Don't know. I hung up"*	*Primary* Other-Self: *"She had to listen, she accepted it, couldn't ignore me. She accepted I was a warm and caring person instead of just a machine who does things that she's told, does things by mother's power structure"* Categorise: α− Confidence: 10 Self-Self: *"I do matter; I haven't just let her walk all over me"* Actual endorsement: 10 Self-Self potential endorsement: 10 Negativity: 0 Self-Other: *"I've done her a favour, really. Told her the facts of life. It's not just about being middle class. Even her own doctor says so, her conversation is very stupid. She tries controlling everyone, even my husband. She says he's stand-offish"* *Secondary* *"She was OK for a while and then she got all high and mighty, had to be put in her place again"*	*Emotion* General: Happy Specific: *"I felt like I had really achieved something"* Intensity: 10 *Action Impulse*

example, Joel was so prone to blaming others and demanding that others don't ignore him and must validate his grandiose self-presentations that that he became a monstrous tyrant to his family.

JOEL

Presentation

Joel was 35 and had been diagnosed as suffering from schizophrenia since the age of 20. He lost his job as a bus driver at this point when he was first hospitalised, and had been unemployed since. He had been in hospital only once and lived in supervised group hostels for a while. He now lived alone, living within walking distance of his parents. He presented as scruffily dressed, and as very confident and magnanimous.

Family Background

Joel's mother was rated as high EE, and presented as completely exhausted and at the end of her tether from Joel's abusive behaviour. The CFI was virtually a 90-minute list of horrible things he had done when he was being grandiose and abusive (for example, he said hurtful things like "I can't wait 'til you are dead so I can spit on your grave"; he had also threatened to kill her and had assaulted both her and his father on a number of occasions; usually after one of his frequent heavy-drinking sessions). Joel's community nurse corroborated many items of his parents account about his behaviour towards them. On the CFI his mother rated 20 for critical comments, 1 for emotional over-involvement, 2 for warmth and 3 for positive comments. Hostility was rated as 2, because of a rejecting attitude ("I dreaded coming home because I was so scared of him", "For two pins I'd have put a pillow over his face"). His parents blamed the stress Joel caused for his father's quadruple heart bypass (although his father was still a heavy smoker), and his mother's depression, and hearing them relate Joel's tyranny this didn't seem totally unreasonable. The only people that Joel would act in such a derogatory manner with were his Mum, Dad and sister and community nurse; when he met other relatives or strangers he was very quiet, almost too shy to speak. When in the street, or during his times in hospital he would run everywhere to protect himself.

Conflict

In Joel's conflict (Figure 13.4), he put himself in an embarrassing position, where his Mum found out that he had been wearing his young, female cousin's knickers (sequence 1: point A). Joel was upset about this (point C) because he felt "They would think I was a right dirty-minded little prat"

Figure 13.4   Joel's Conflict

Activating Event	Beliefs	Consequences
"I was trying on my cousin's knickers and I tore them; I was scared my Mum would find out"	*Primary* Other-Self: *"They would think I was a right dirty-minded little prat"* Categorise: α Confidence: 10 Self-Self actual endorsement: 0 Self-Self potential endorsement: 10 Negativity: 10 Self-Other: *"They were good people"* Conviction: 10 Negativity: 0 *Secondary* Preferred goal: *"To avoid it all; I shoved them back in the airing cupboard. I went into myself completely"* Action choice: *"I had to say something to explain this, to be able to get on with things"*	*Emotion* General: Guilt, shame Specific: *Total embarrassment, shock* Intensity: 10 *Action Impulse* *"If anything happened to me, it happened there and then. I thought, 'Oh shit what the f . . . am I going to do about this?'. It was almost time for me to go into hospital"*
"I talked to them about it. I was just myself, instead of acting myself. I told Mum about my sexual problem; this was why I was doing it. I think she understood" Describe other's reaction: *"She believed in me, she took it in"*	*Primary* Other-Self: *"She understood me, so Not a prat"* Confidence: 10 Self-Self: *"I told her the truth, that's as much as I could tell them – what I'd done, why I'd done it"* Actual endorsement: Self-Self potential endorsement: Negativity: 3 Self-Other: *"I liked her"* Conviction: 10 Negativity: 0 *Secondary* Preferred goal: *"Carry on as before"*	*Emotion* General: Embarrassed Specific: Relief Intensity: 10 *Action Impulse* *"I could carry on doing what I was doing before"*
"I carried on as I had been doing" Describe other's reaction: *"They put me into hospital after this"*	*Primary* Other-Self: *"They thought I'd gone barmy – ringing up strangers, ripping up clothes, etc"* Categorise: $\alpha-$ Confidence: 10 Self-Self actual: 0 Self-Self potential: Negativity: 10 Self-Other: *"I was angry with them but I knew they'd misunderstood me, so I wasn't really angry with them"* *Secondary:* Failed want goal: *"I wanted the truth brought out. I couldn't stand them thinking something was wrong with me when there wasn't"*	*Emotion* General: *"Upset, oh Jesus Christ, yes"* Specific: Depressed Intensity: 10 *Action Tendency*

(point B), although his actual endorsement of this was 0. He felt confident enough to explain to his parents about the situation, and felt he had told them what the situation was (sequence 2: point A). This made him feel much better and happy (point C) because he felt "She believed in me, she took it in". To Joel's distress, this was the last in a line of odd behaviours and in sequence 3, his parents arranged for Joel to be sectioned. Even when sectioned, Joel felt sure that there wasn't anything wrong with him, and said "I wanted the truth brought out; I couldn't stand them thinking something was wrong with me when there wasn't" (point B). His actual agreement with their impression of him as odd was 0. Even at this stage, he still saw himself as high rank (whereas a bad-me client would have seen themselves as low ranking). He reported some guilt and shame in sequence 2, but this doesn't appear to refer to accepting the label; this appears to have arisen because of the perceived rejection from his Mum and Dad.

Symptoms

Joel was very deluded and would talk for hours about music and science in a way that didn't make sense. He seemed to see his subject matter as being very significant and important. He wrote "books" of philosophy and regarded himself as a prophet. Although he had a high opinion of himself, he also spoke of his parents in a very idealised manner, and to him, at the time of interview, they were the best parents of all time, who had no faults. His speech veered from one topic to another in a way that only made sense to him, and produced many neologisms and clang associations. He also spoke of many reference experiences such as TV and passers-by referring to him.

DISCUSSION

Joel was very egocentric and tended to discount others entirely. His increasing grandiosity had driven people away, and without any feedback from others, there was nothing to temper his grandiosity or structure his thoughts. This conflict shows the power of the existential imperative, in that when the existential imperative expresses itself so unrestrainedly, the moral imperative is completely disregarded. For example, in Figure 13.4, Joel must be ashamed in some sense because otherwise he would not be motivated to do anything about the situation. However, he did not report any self-shame belief and instead simply demanded that everyone else change their way of thinking (a dominant strategy).

Joel's behaviour was eventually modified by a behavioural program in which his rages were ignored until he had to accept certain ground rules, for example, not coming home drunk and abusive. Conflicts that fit with this theme are included in Table 13.2. This group fit the second group mentioned in Chapter 3 in that they seem to have individuated from their parents somewhat, but have lost contact with their peers and are possibly scared by them. Joel was dictatorial to his family but was very shy and withdrawn when anyone else such as wider family came to the house. Only when they had gone would he start being grandiose again. The conflicts in Table 13.2 are typically two-part conflicts because the clients say exactly what they think and repress nothing; in fact the moral imperative seems to have no influence or be almost completely missing. Some of the clients in the previous group of anger-inhibitors may well have originally been anger-expressers but learnt through experience (perhaps through being sectioned like Joel was) to hold themselves in by conforming excessively or totally to the demands of the moral imperative. These conflicts illustrate the difficulty of respecting a client's right to do what they want, and yet wanting to protect the client and others from harm as best they could.

Clients learn a certain pattern of relating to others with their parents that they then transfer into interactions with their peers. Conversely, they also evolve patterns with their peers which they can use with their parents. However, peers are generally less tolerant and more likely to be hurtful than parents, as they have less investment in looking after the client's well-being. Clients who feel inhibited by their parents would be predicted to be even more inhibited by their peers. Similarly, anger-expressing clients would presumably be less tolerated by their peers than their parents. We report conflicts that concern peer interactions in the next chapter.

CHAPTER 14

PEER AND ROMANTIC CONFLICTS

In assessing how clients got on with their peers, it became apparent that few of the clients had many peer friends who were not part of the psychiatric services. Clients without friends were asked about their relationships with their friends in late adolescence, as this was thought to be the time when clients crucially needed their peers' support and theoretically may not have found it. Often they detailed the last interactions they had and the reasons why contact had ceased.

REJECTION BY PEERS/NON-FAMILY OTHERS

Three participants entered the company of strangers, and felt sure that the people there were laughing at them or talking about them. Imran related how he felt even complete strangers hated him when he passed them. Imran showed a very similar pattern of interaction with his peers as he did with his parents, as did most of the other clients in Table 14.1. However, even those clients who showed the same pattern showed some key differences from parental conflicts. For example, clients could usually only suspect what the criticism was, because it was rarely made explicit; sometimes a vague reason was given but even then it was fairly indistinct. It was common for participants to not really know why their peers rejected them (although this might be because they did not want to talk at interview about why they felt they were disliked). The first five conflicts in Table 14.1 show people who were rejected by their friends who were rejected for no apparent reason, or for vague and unlikely reasons. In Cathy's conflict, for example, she felt sure that everyone present knew about her psychiatric history, almost as if they could read it on her face, or as if everyone in the world knew anyway (another example of egocentricity or *objectité*?). Furthermore, the evaluative belief attached to being "one of those ill people" appears to instantly be one of being worthless, an illustration of stigma as a very real and very upsetting entity in Cathy's life. Cathy's immediate impulse was to flee the pub and escape, yet she felt that if she were to do this, the people in the pub judging her so badly would be proved right, and she would be totally trapped in the self of "one of those ill people". So her situation was unbearable, because whatever she did she felt was being used against her by the people there.

Table 14.1 Table Showing Interpretative Summaries of Conflicts Involving Peers or Non-family Others

	Sequence 1	Sequence 2	Sequence 3	Symptom
Bill	"I rang my friend up to ask about a game of football. Someone pretended it was a wrong number. It was my friends and they didn't want to know me" (α−/I) Angry 7 Disappointed "I wanted to say something, let them know what I knew what they were doing" (Existential imperative reflecting hurt, rejected feelings)	"I was scared that if I said anything he'd say he'd found out that I had problems and that he thought a lot worse of me" (Would endorse α−) Anxious 8 "I hung up and took the dog for a walk" Moral imperative means that he has to accept their actions?	"I was left feeling that they didn't want to know me anymore" (Endorses I) Depressed (10) Avoids peer group "Angry at myself for having rung up. I started banging doors a bit, wanted to calm myself down" Angry ruminations and fantasised revenge and justification sequences.	Voices function as a substitute peer group? "Socialises'" with them, argues. Existential imperative to construct substitute group, however having a tendency towards the moral imperative his voices became very hostile and critical; he also suffered a very extreme case of objectité. There was a similar pattern to how he interacted with his Mum. He felt ignored but powerless to do anything about it with his Mum; he feels similarly helpless with his peers
Imran	"People shout while I'm walking down the street – it seems like they're shouting at me. I'm a good-for-nothing, I have to listen to them. I can't do anything right" (α−) Anger 10 Insecure, shock 10 "I want to shout back at them!" Existential imperative	"If I did that, it would be like I had made a fool of myself, I've succumbed, it would be the end of everything, my whole life. They know better than me" (α−) "Like I've made a fool of myself" Guilty 9.5 Do nothing Moral imperative	"I ignore them and say nothing. It's like they're keeping me at bay. I've to be contained – my anger is to be avoided" (α−) Ends up accepting "good-for-nothing" definition Depressed 10 Withdrawing, socially phobic, apathetic	Imran is very socially phobic, withdrawn and anxious. He feels people are out to get him, and that they are trying to tempt him to do bad things (possibly violent). His personal religious beliefs mean that to him, these are trials he has to endure on the way to becoming "pure"

Cathy	"I went into the pub scruffily dressed after badminton – people were look-ing at me" "I thought they were saying 'She's one of those ill people'. They think I'm worthless" (α−)	"If I did leave the pub they would definitely think there was something wrong with me. They'd then think I was worthless" (α−)	"I couldn't leave because that would be proving them right. I couldn't stay, I was stuck"	"I could hear people talking about me, even when I was on holiday in a country where I didn't speak the language. They were saying things about me"
	Anxious 8 "I wanted to flee the pub immediately" Moral imperative?	Anxious 8 "I stayed and talked about work with the person I was with. Monitored others really carefully" Moral imperative	Anxious 8 Obsessively monitoring people's conversations	
Nigel	"My friend looked at me out of the corner of his eye, sneered, looked away and shook his head" "I was wondering what I had done? Perhaps I was looking over-anxious? Perhaps he's angry about a comment I once made? Perhaps they think I'm off my head, weird, pathetic" (αI/α−)	"I didn't say anything but felt that they were being 'holier-than-thou' – trying to put me down" (αI/α−)	"If I did say anything they would just reject me, and tell me to get lost" (α −/αI) "It's like 'you're too pathetic or a nutter to be my friend'" "I would think I wasn't worthy enough to know them" (would endorse α−)	"I felt as paranoid as this quite often, even when I was on my own in public. I felt sure people were talking about me and disliked me" Presented as passive, flat affect, very withdrawn and socially phobic. Occasionally heard a voice saying (in so many words) that he was worthless
	Anxious 10 Shame 10 "Avoided doing anything to make it worse" Kept quiet Moral imperative	Anger 10 Shame 0 "I wanted to say 'what the hell's the matter with you?'" Existential imperative	Anxiety 10 "I sat there for ages without saying anything. I was trying to avoid them rejecting me"	

Table 14.1 *(continued)*

	Sequence 1	Sequence 2	Sequence 3	Symptom
Sandra	"I entered the hall and because I was late the people there were nudging each other, smiling, laughing" "They might be thinking I'm a tart" (α−)	"People interpreted my reaction to the embarrassment as meaning that I was guilty. They are thinking I'm a tart. They don't want to know me" (Rejects α−; experiences I?)	"I can't win; because they think I'm a tart, I give this response, and because of this response, I prove them right and am a tart" (endorses α− or experiences I?)	Sandra avoids her peers, and has an intimate relationship with a special voice character who she constantly converses with, moment by moment. This male voice character will one day arrive in the flesh, bestow special powers upon her and the two of them will travel the country giving lectures, doing good deeds and healing people
	Anxious, 8 Panic, embarrassment, 9 Panic attack, facial grimacing, going red	Anxiety, 10 Wants to escape. Moral imperative	Avoids peers, stays at home	
Pete	"Sometimes when we were playing football I used to get really angry at my friends. They didn't see who I really was, not the real Pete. They saw me as someone ordinary, easy to get on with" (α+)	"If I had shouted something, there would have been a lot of very unhappy people there. They'd have been really angry at me, they'd think I needed a break" (α−) (Would endorse α−)	"They think pretty highly of me but they get on my nerves. It was like playing a role they value, being trapped within that. I hated it" (α+)	Pete used to get angry at his Mum but never dared express it. Here he shows the same pattern with his friends – he gets angry with them but doesn't dare say anything. He so hated conforming that he preferred to talk with his voices than go out with friends
	Angry 9 "I wanted to shout at them" Existential imperative	Guilty 8 Depressed 9 Disappointed in myself "I'd need to apologise a lot" Moral imperative	Loneliness 9 Depression 8 "I didn't go out, lost contact with my friends, spent all my time with my voices instead. Ruminated about letting them know how I felt"	

Elizabeth	"At the start of my illness, I felt that my friends weren't good enough to know me. They were just silly kids. They never insulted me, but just didn't give me enough respect" (α+) Angry 10 "Not so much at the time but later" "I suppose I could have pointed out to them that they should treat me better" Existential imperative	"If I had told them how I felt, they wouldn't have understood I was clever. They might have been hostile" (α−) Depressed 10 "It would just be bringing misery upon myself – it's just not something you do. I'd be like a snail, a tortoise. I'd take refuge in my shell" Moral imperative "I decided I wasn't going to bother with them anymore. They're not good enough"	Doesn't bother with friends Rejects α+ but trapped within it Loneliness 6 Depression 10 Suicidal 8	Elizabeth exploded at her Mum and decided never to have anything to do with her again. Here she doesn't explode at her friends, although she was angry, but she cuts them off just the same. "It might have done them some good; they might have been nicer to me. I also worried that if I let them know I was really clever, they might do it too and also be really clever" Elizabeth heard voices giving important messages from important people which contributed to her being very special. She was too depressed to get up many days. She lived rough on the streets for two years. She was very aggressive to people around her

Not only were these clients rejected for unclear reasons, but they could do nothing; if they did respond to it, then it would be the worse for them. They typically avoided or just kept quiet throughout the incident, hoping not to make things worse. It is interesting how the psychiatric label itself is seen as the thing that their peers hate or reject them for, when the label perhaps partially refers to the sorts of behaviours they show in these cases when they are worried about the label. It is almost as if the client's own fear of madness brings about some of the "mad" behaviours that they are worried about.

As well as being rejected for vague reasons, another group of three clients rejected their friends. Jack was in awe of his friends and preferred not to see them until he was well again (this transpired at interview although he did not want to complete a conflict around it). He was sure they had not thought ill of him, but was worried they might if they knew more about how he was now. He'd rather have them think well of him, and not see them again until such a time when he was better, rather than to have contact with them now and risk them knowing how badly he'd fallen. In the last two conflicts of Table 14.1, the participants grandiosely rejected their friends for not being good enough or recognising the participants' worth. Pete never once said anything to his friends, feeling that it would be enormously traumatic for everyone involved if he did. He preferred to just avoid his friends and not have them know he was so angry with them. Elizabeth also related a conflict in which her friends had not done anything specifically wrong, but she was very angry with them ("not so much at the time, but when I got home"). Again, she would never have dreamt of expressing how she felt to her friends "it would just be bringing misery upon yourself; it's just not something you do".

In summary, some clients commonly felt rejected by their peers, often for reasons that were never expressed. These clients preferred to say or do nothing about the perceived rejection, apparently for fear of making it explicit and thereby somehow more real. Clients felt sure their peers on the whole disliked or rejected them, especially strangers. Another group of clients felt that their friends liked them, but rejected their friends for not being good enough, or acknowledging their grandiosity enough. The end result of peer interactions was nearly always loss of contact and isolation.

ROMANTIC CONFLICTS

The most crucial peer interactions are ones with potential romantic partners, and hence these situations also have the potential to be the most rewarding and also most damaging. Few clients had much experience with the opposite sex, least of all the younger clients in this survey. Hence real-life romantic conflicts were difficult to get. Instead, clients were asked to

Table 14.2 Table Showing Interpretative Summaries of Romantic Conflicts

Imagining how they would feel if an attractive person of the opposite sex smiled at them in public. (These conflicts follow a dierent format to the previous ones, being more exploratory. The first sequence is their initial response to the situation, the second is the imagined best possible outcome, and the third is the imagined typical worst outcome)

	Sequence 1	Best possible outcome	Worst possible outcome
Imran	*"She thinks I'm a load of old rubbish; how could she possibly think I'm normal. I get the feeling that she doesn't fancy me; she really hates me"* (α−)	*"If I did chat her up, she'd give me a wicked eye and then look away, she'd suddenly snap"* (α−) *"I'm too dangerous, lots of stuff in me, rage, guilt"*	*"She was out to tempt me from my family and house and to another life; she's out to ruin me. She sees me as someone to control"* α−
	Anxiety 10 *"Dead Nervous"* *"It's out of the question"*	Relief 10 *"It's all to be avoided. Her being normal, me not being normal, makes me feel low. I'd leave it. Ignore her. Don't smile back"*	Relief 10 *"God has saved me from the day. The lustful part of me is nulled. It's as if I get possessed by an entity that loves every girl in sight. She's out to try to ruin me, make me do bad things"*
Pete	*"She might not find me attractive, I'm not good enough, well-educated, intelligent"*	*"I don't think I would really do anything because if you want to know the truth, I've never really got on with a woman, either physically or whatever"*	
	Anxiety 5 Not happy *"I'd have to speak to her first, see if she was my type"*	Anxious 5 *"If my Mum didn't approve, I'd finish with the girl"*	

Jack	"She thinks I'm interesting, and have a good personality. Good looking" Happy 9 "Smile back. Not go over though. We'd talk and perhaps go somewhere"	"If I did smile back, and get chatting to her or whatever, I'd be worried that I wouldn't know what to do and might hurt her or something; She would really hate me if I had messed it up somehow. She'd think I was a tosser" (α−) Anxiety 7 "I wanted to get away because I might do the wrong thing – just get away without cocking it up"	"I'd do nothing, she'd be disappointed. My mind is filled with ideas about how she'd be the perfect woman" Depression 8 "The truth is that I've never really been out with a girl, I'm not really bothered"
Bill	"She thinks I'm pleasant" "She'd be after a steady relationship" Fear 7 Apprehensive "I'd ask her if she wanted another cup, perhaps get her phone number"	"If I did do anything, she'd get up and walk away" "I'd get a slap in the face. She's just not interested in a relationship" Fear 7 "It would never get this far"	"I couldn't do anything; she ignores me. It's like being kicked in the teeth when you are down" Depressed 8 "I wouldn't ask her out"
Nigel	"She'd think 'What a weirdo!'" "I'd have a full-blown panic attack" Anxiety 10 Shame 10 "I'd want to leave as quickly as possible"	"If I did go up to her and talk to her, she'd react like I was a weirdo. She thinks I'm stupid and weird" Anxiety 8 Embarrassed 8 "I'm going to have a panic attack"	

imagine a hypothetical situation in which there was the possibility of a romantic encounter (only a small number completed this task because this avenue was only explored towards the end of the study). Five male clients completed conflicts around this situation:

> Imagine you are sitting in a public place like a cafe and a pretty girl smiles at you in an encouraging way. How would you feel? What would you expect to happen? What would you like to happen?

As it happened, all five clients had never really had girlfriends, or even been out on a date. As Pete said, "If you want to know the truth, I've never really got on with a woman, either physically or whatever." As the conflicts in this section are more exploratory than in previous sections, they follow a slightly less rigorous REBT format than the previous conflicts. In particular, the second sequence does not "chain" from the first sequence as in previous sections. Instead, the second sequence is the imagined best possible outcome, and the third sequence is the imagined worst possible outcome. For the four older clients, the situation did not contain any positive feelings at all, just anxiety, and fear. All four clients said that they would never make any sort of move on the girl, and would prefer to ignore her (most clients possibly would not have been sitting on their own in a public place).

Table 14.2 lists the five romantic conflicts. The themes running in these conflicts are very similar. Sentiments from one of the youngest clients, Jack (aged 18), probably reflect a common fear of every adolescent starting out with romantic relationships:

> I might not know what to do, I might do the wrong thing and really hurt her or something, She would have really hated me if I had somehow messed it up.

These fears are probably familiar to everyone who has ever been an adolescent, and explored romantic situations for the first time. Jack had never had a girlfriend and admitted that it was something he wanted in principle but not in practice, because he was a little scared of girls. He said he also felt really inadequate and childish around his friends who had got girlfriends. He said he felt he had lost a lot of status with his friends through not having a girlfriend, and it was one more arena within which he was now fairly worthless in their eyes. His friends had all gone to university and successfully made the transition to independent living, whereas Jack was still living at home and if anything had regressed to a more childish, dependent state.

In summary then, those clients who were asked showed a fear of the opposite sex in general, and romantic relationships in particular. Of the small number asked, all were adamant that they would be very anxious about a possible romantic relationship and felt sure that the potential partner really disliked them, no matter what. None had much experience of dating and all saw this as terrifyingly important to them.

DISCUSSION

Methodological Considerations

A feature of the study has been demonstrating that REBT can be used to probe more deeply into what clients are thinking. Much of the detail of the study would not have been found without having a theory-driven reason to probe. The study also shows the benefits of more extensive engagement with the client, and the potential benefits of using real-life situations and interactions with real people. Using hypothetical situations might be less useful given that the subject group is often accused of divorcing reality from fantasy quite often anyway (although fantasy is an important part of the real-life situations here). Similarly, a flavour is given of how research not only needs to respect the differences between clients, but also between the same clients over time – people's symptoms change over time.

The study seems to show that there is much coherence in the thought processes of the clients; the coherence would seem to be there at the time of the interaction, even if recall and reflection on the experience occasionally needed the interviewers REBT help to reach the narrative coherence represented here. Even with the interviewer's questioning, the conflicts are still authentic, and in all places the quotes are genuine client quotes, even if they are abbreviated in places. The study shows very clearly that the client's cognitions are not bizarre and incomprehensible; they are certainly not "empty speech acts".

If anything the many situations covered are surprisingly mundane. The significance of the scenarios is more obvious to the clients themselves, because they cite these situations as being very important to them (although perhaps these situations are only as controversial as they feel comfortable talking about, and they do not want to talk about bigger issues). The assumption that essential roots of the problem can be found in the minutiae of interactions was an important a priori stance of the study ("Life is a filigree of tripwires" Goffman; 1971, p31). Much previous research has looked at instances such as these and seen them as evidence of the wider problem (i.e. the disease or attributional bias) rather than being more directly responsible. This change is something that follows directly from the stance in Chapter 6 where the self was defined as something being constantly created and re-created in interactions. By this definition the self is far less stable and more transient than in other conceptualisations of the self. If the effects of these interactions build up over time and each had a small incremental effect in the same direction, this is consistent with the fact that psychotic delusions generally build up over time. Commonly about 2 years elapses between the first signs and a florid illness (e.g. Beiser *et al.*, 1993).

Another merit of the study was that clients were asked what they would have ideally have wanted to happen or how to act in the situation in very concrete terms. Typically work on "ideal selves" or "future selves" considers client's wishes in the abstract (Markus & Nurius, 1986; Bannister & Fransella, 1966). In this study clients were asked which actions they would like to have taken (a very different sphere of operations from ticking statements about "how I would like to be . . ."). On the whole clients were shown to have wanted to be more assertive, perhaps less down-rank, often just to defend themselves against perceived threats.

Cognitive Behaviour Therapy (CBT) has made great advances in recent years in understanding schizophrenia; current trials are showing it to be an effective treatment alternative (e.g. Haddock & Slade, 1996; Kingdon & Turkington, 1997). CBT practitioners have been successful despite many of them using fragmented, quasi-biological theoretical models, where the psychology is seen as an add-on extra. For example, even the family interventions of the Expressed Emotion paradigms do not have any one explicit mechanistic model, and hence work in a "we don't know why it works but it does" manner. Such work originated from behaviour therapy as applied to learning disabilities, and as behavioural approaches are specifically devoid of the concept of self, it is not surprising that the resultant treatments do not include any stated convincing theory of "the person", despite the repeated calls for such a paradigm mentioned earlier (Chadwick, Birchwood & Trower, 1996).

SECTION SUMMARY

To summarise the main findings from this study:

- Participants had crippling fears about what would happen if they acted the way they really wanted. These fears were often catastrophic and out of proportion.

- The majority of participants inhibited their anger and moderated their aggressive impulses to the point of seeming to show no overt annoyance at all. We speculated that this would lead normal people to ruminate angrily, and hence rumination was proposed as a mechanism to produce uncontrollable automatic thoughts. Such thoughts would be a cause for great guilt and shame in our participants, because of the same beliefs that caused them to repress anger in the first place. We speculated that this would lead them to experience automatic thoughts as voices.

- Existential and Moral imperatives were cast as the prime movers behind many of the symptoms. Evidence was presented for this in the tables in Chapter 13 and the current chapter. The data concerning the two types of imperative illustrated that a large proportion of the symptoms are concerned with themes

    . . .which invariably reflect the patient's concern about his or her position in the social universe. (Sims, 1988)

Many of the supposed symptoms of schizophrenia can be seen as meaningful and purposeful behaviour when the full situation is known – for example social withdrawal and the lethargy and depression of negative symptoms make more sense in the context of the entrapment sequence demonstrated here.

- There appeared to be two themes of psychotic thought in this study. They depended on which side of the existential–moral equilibrium the balance has shifted to. For the inhibited self group, the balance had shifted almost entirely to the moral imperative side. Their moral imperative-influenced symptoms were about being disliked and useless, and they felt compelled to accept threats to self-construction that they perceived from the people in their life. The other smaller group, the anger expressers, seemed to be ruled mostly by the existential imperative. Although this group got to pursue their grandiose needs, in the long term their behaviour was self-defeating because it annoyed other people and therefore separated them from others. This group was usually the most overtly disturbed of the two. A simplistic conclusion from the moral imperative group would be that all clients should be encouraged to express themselves more. However the anger expresser group need almost the opposite sort of encouragement as they need to give moral goals precedence and be more considerate. In both cases, therapy aimed at training in external rather than internal attention focus, and development of better theory of mind skills, would be recommended, and is discussed in Section Four.

- Our study showed a third theme of psychosis in a third group which had *both* imperatives to excess. Some of the clients in the first group showed strong existential symptoms, and hence had both grandiose existential themes, but also self-hating moral delusions. Here the two imperatives appeared to clash violently with each other to produce terrible conflict within the person themselves, oscillating wildly even as they completely isolated themselves in an attempt to find peace.

- Finally, peer conflicts seemed to follow different patterns to conflicts with parents, especially situations involving potential romantic partners. Clients seemed to see peer conflicts as more intimidating, almost taking the perspective that it was not worth arguing with peers, it was easier to just not see them (in many cases ever again).

SECTION FOUR

WHAT CAN BE DONE? THERAPEUTIC IDEAS

Our aim so far in this book has been to provide a broad range of people – from professionals, to people who have had a psychotic episode themselves – with a clear picture of psychosis in late adolescence and early adulthood. We have tried to paint a background landscape to represent the various stakeholders' views and painted over any biological supremacy view for a more balanced composition. In the foreground we have outlined our view that the problem commonly emerges from blocked adolescent development which thwarts the need – so pressing at this stage in the lifespan – to construct an authentic Self. Much of the detail in this picture came from the drama of real people's lives, to show evidence of these blocks and traps in action. Now we address another big question: What can be done about it?

The first issue we address is the general problem of blocked adolescence which we outlined in Section One. Here, we presented the argument that young people who have a psychosis have not grown out of the stage of adolescent egocentricity (a term which does not mean selfish, but rather refers to an internal- rather than external-focused mode). We argued that adolescents are typically self-focused (and often very self-conscious and critical of themselves) because they have not developed a detailed understanding of other people (and of themselves!). This is normally only a transitory problem, as they develop a more external focus (and with it de-idealise other people, perhaps also refining their own natural grandiosity). This sort of psychological development is an important step towards being able to attach to peers and perhaps leave the parental nest. However, when a person gets stuck in this stage – particularly when their egocentrism and idealism pushes them towards losing contact with their peers and becoming really isolated – that person is vulnerable to the kinds of self-construction threats – emptiness or alienation – that we discussed in Sections Two and Three. So what can be done about it?

In Chapter 15 we consider ways to kick-start the developmental process to a more external focus. We describe our externally-focused "character-based" training, designed to enhance understanding of other people and their traits, quirks and emotional complexities. These techniques are aimed both at taking people's attention off themselves, and helping them focus on others, to build objective and realistic pictures of others (and of themselves) that will be vital to healthy self-construction.

The second issue we address is the problem of blocked self-construction that emerged in our research into the relationships of participants reported in Section Three.

In Chapter 16 we develop some proposals for tackling the beliefs we have found to underpin problems with the two imperatives described in Sections Two and Three – the existential and the moral. We summarise the relevant points from those sections, and then work through specific examples of each type of emotional episode, and outline some interventions for each. This chapter is aimed more for practitioners, though it should be of interest to people themselves and their relatives.

The third set of issues we address are the symptoms of psychosis and the associated beliefs, emotions and behaviours. We suggest that symptoms of psychosis can be understood within our model, and the beliefs people have about the symptoms make them vulnerable to the threats to self-construction. In Chapter 17 we describe a range of practical, self-help methods for coping with some of the more immediate and distressing symptoms themselves.

A fourth issue is one that is outside the scope of this book, and that is the issue concerned with the social environment – can it be changed in a way that people can be facilitated in their self-construction goals? The practical task is to provide, or at least facilitate, the conditions that will enable the vulnerable person to construct his authentic self in relative psychological safety. Most of us construct ourselves (i.e. present our "selves" to affirming others) in the form of social roles. Hence, in a sense, a person *is* his roles in life, and without any roles he is (in a very real sense) not any thing. Many of our young clients are in this position of not having many or any roles and feeling they are not any thing. Alternatively they feel trapped in negative "roles" such as "unemployed yob" or "drop out", made infinitely worse by the stigmatising "role" of "a schizophrenic". So at the same time as helping them dismantle the cognitive self-focused beliefs that trap them in a self-perception of either emptiness and alienation, or engulfment and shame, (and in both cases not in the world), we need to provide them with the social role possibilities where they can become a real person.

Not all services provide such enabling environments, but there are exciting new developments under way. Services for the earliest stages of psychosis – the new Early Intervention Services – are striving to provide just such environments and opportunities in the UK and Australia and elsewhere, and are described in recent publications (McGorry & Jackson, 1999; Birchwood, Fowler & Jackson, 2000). The UK government has recently committed large sums of money to set up 50 new Early Intervention Teams, focusing mainly on age-appropriate services for young adults. Scandinavian countries have also pioneered excellent Early Intervention and identification projects (e.g. TIPS project; Larsen *et al.*, 2000).

Services for later stages of psychosis, aimed at rehabilitating people back into ordinary life as far as possible, are also being pioneered in the United States. Such initiatives (developed by Larry Davidson and others) have the specific aim of helping clients to develop a sense of self and self-efficacy, often after many years of deprivation and external control (Davidson, in press). What all these services are partly trying to set up are role-creating (and hence self-creating) opportunities in employment, education and social groups of various kinds.

CHAPTER 15

"CHARACTER-BASED" TRAINING

DE-IDEALISING, EGOCENTRICITY AND THEORY OF MIND

> A traveller climbs a hill and can see a new town on the horizon. He asks an old man who appears to have come from the town: "I've just come from the town over the way; what are the people in this new town I see like?" The old man looks at him and asks "What were the people in your town over the way like?". "Awful", the traveller said, "the town was full of rogues and liars and thieves." "That's what the new town will be like for you then", said the old man. (Adapted from Watzlawick, 1990)

What Watzlawick's story illustrates is that people come to new situations with expectations about how others will operate. All of us think we know what other people are like – their beliefs, attitudes and so on. This was a key concept in Section One: we each have a "theory of [other people's] minds". For basic interactions most of the time most people are not too far off the mark (notwithstanding racial and other prejudices). In Chapter 3, we showed that these empathic abilities are thought to develop over adolescence, and that with them comes greater social skill, and the psychological independence to outgrow the family environment. However, when people become chronically and habitually internally focused – as we believe young people can be "stuck" with the egocentricity of youth – they don't attend to others and the outside world. If they don't attend, they won't develop a theory of other people's minds; instead they assume they know what others think – *other people think what they think*. Given the importance of other people in the self-construction process, this leaves them extremely vulnerable to threats to self-construction mentioned in Sections Two and Three.

By learning to be externally focused rather than internally focused, young adults discover that other people on the whole *don't* think what they think, and they learn instead that there is a rich world of alternative perspectives out there. Such a shift entails learning about other people's characters, differences and quirks; in a sense acquiring a "worldliness" (Hogarty & Flesher, 1999). For example, a development might be learning to deal with moral ambiguities and perhaps such dual-meaning situations such as "spin". Perhaps in the context of Watzlawick's story, it could mean learning to differentiate between genuine rogues and well-intentioned people; as Yalom points out (below), if we look closely at other people (or if we were privy to their intimate confidences), we might find that other people persist in being much more complicated and emotional than we might otherwise have assumed. Such a shift in focus is, we believe fundamental to developing beyond egocentrism, idealisation and black and white thinking, and is certainly a learnable skill. This is not only our view, but is right at the cutting edge of recent developments in cognitive therapy, as we shall discuss later.

> What have I learnt about mankind? Two things: People are much more unhappy than one thinks. And then the fundamental fact that there is no such thing as a grown up person. (Malraux's priest in Yalom, 1980, p13)

SHIFTING FOCUS

It may be the case that moving the person's focus outwards to the external world is a major part of what happens implicitly in effective psychological therapies. We think this is a valuable framework to structure part of the therapy process and aid understanding. For example, take the case of a man in therapy for issues to do with having a physically abusive parent. A typical route for therapy would be to look very closely at how the client understood the abuse at the time, when they were a child, and to try to come to a more objective understanding from the perspective of adulthood. As a child, the client may have seen their parent as someone superior and powerful, who knew a lot, who understood what was right and wrong, and whose opinions were generally agreed with by most adults. From an adult perspective, the client might come to alter this perception of their parent to see them as someone who wasn't particularly wise, who was often wrong and misguided, perhaps very moody or drank a lot. They might also come to see that most people didn't hold the same views as their parent, and that they themselves don't agree with the views the parent had then. In making this change, the parent moves from someone big, important and powerful, to someone much smaller, rather unimportant and perhaps even rather unhappy – in other words, very ordinary!

Someone with a more developed understanding of others is probably better off in lots of ways. For example, a popular Chinese proverb says:

> If a man is told 10 times a day that he is no good, he will come to believe it.

However, if a man is told this 10 times a day by the same person, and no-one else is saying it, they will possibly come to really dislike this one person. If they manage to mentally marginalise their assailant's viewpoint, the constant criticism might make no difference at all to their self-image;

their assailant might become just the annoyance who criticises at every possible opportunity, whom nobody else agrees with (possibly many people dislike). From this perspective they may be able to grant themselves permission to answer back or avoid the assailant, even if the assailant is trying to enforce rules about how rude the target is if he doesn't listen and respect them, or spend lots of time with them. The target may even come to understand why the assailant insists on criticising (e.g. lack of social skills, sour disposition, jealousy, own unmet needs) and thus perhaps even find some good will towards them. If the target's attention was constantly directed towards themselves, they might be so self-aware (*internally focused*) that they would never become aware of the assailant's uncharitable tendencies (*externally focused*). In this instance they could take on board the other's criticisms completely as if they were facts, attributing all the negativity to their own failings; this could lead the target to get very depressed. Figure 15.1 attempts to represent this graphically.

Figure 15.2 attempts to show diagrammatically how a person who is not

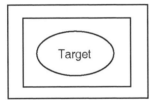 

Target's cognitions about self
"I'm too inconsiderate"
"I'm useless at this"
"I'm stupid"
"I should listen to them"

Target's cognitions about other
"They are wise and good"
"Everybody agrees with them"

Figure 15.1a Taking a Critical Person's Opinions Onboard Completely

Target's cognitions about self
"I'm OK, not that bad"

Target's cognitions about other
"They are habitually critical"
"They are wrong"
"I don't agree with them"

Figure 15.1b Getting to Grips with Another Person's Character so as to See Criticism as Part of their Character Rather Than Their Own

very good at understanding other people's motivations and perspectives could easily become incapacitated by attributing everything to themselves. Empirical evidence shows that people who are depressed tend to attribute bad occurrences to their failings, for example they are responsible for all bad things, and not able to do anything right (Beck, 1983).

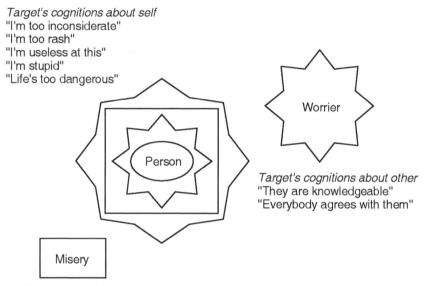

Target's cognitions about self
"I'm too inconsiderate"
"I'm too rash"
"I'm useless at this"
"I'm stupid"
"Life's too dangerous"

Worrier

Person

Target's cognitions about other
"They are knowledgeable"
"Everybody agrees with them"

Misery

Target's cognitions about other
"They are wise and good"

Figure 15.2a   A Person Attributing a Lot to Themselves

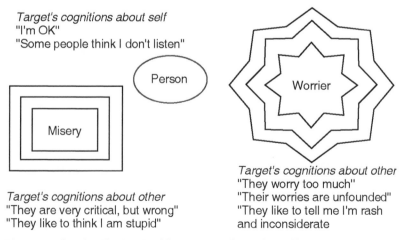

Target's cognitions about self
"I'm OK"
"Some people think I don't listen"

Person

Worrier

Misery

Target's cognitions about other
"They are very critical, but wrong"
"They like to think I am stupid"

Target's cognitions about other
"They worry too much"
"Their worries are unfounded"
"They like to tell me I'm rash and inconsiderate

Figure 15.2b   Attributing Problems Away from the Self

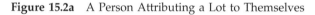

Of course the diagrams here are over-simplifications; life does not easily reduce down to either being critical or worrying too much; there are many more characteristics, particularly positive characteristics such as discretion and caring. This is approaching the realm of literature, theatre and life-experience. It has been said that at 35 you can re-watch all the drama you watched at 18 because its meaning to you will have changed to quite a large extent in light of the life-experiences you have had since. However, traits such as being critical and worrying can be difficult to be consciously aware of for many people, particularly if the assailant is contradicting their behaviour with words which insist they are altruistic.

Having shown that one of the things that really changes during therapy is the client's view of other people (and their view of self), the question remains of how a therapy can really focus in on these views. With some notable exceptions, individual therapies place the primary focus on a person understanding themselves, their beliefs, feelings and needs; that is they have a clear "introspective" emphasis. This is important, but without including an "exterospective" understanding of others and their power to block, it could remain incomplete, and even slightly immature! To work on a person's negative beliefs about themselves in a vacuum, if they are constantly being put down by others, is not fair (and in fairness to therapies, this is not generally what therapists do). There are a number of potential problems in looking at relationships, such as previously docile people becoming aggressive and difficult, or paranoid ideas becoming fixed onto family members; this is a fraught area and it would be foolish to go there incautiously; a particular worry would be if a therapeutic style was used that seemed to encourage the person to rubbish other people rather than understand them. However, if it is genuinely believed that the problems are predominantly in the life arena, then these issues cannot be skirted, however difficult. Their difficulty reflects their central importance.

For example, one approach in Cognitive-Behavioural Therapy for psychosis is to challenge the power of the voices (see Chapter 17). The essence is to help the client to de-idealise the voices, for example, re-evaluating whether the voices do in fact know everything, and whether they do have great power over the client. Clients are usually better off when they decide that voices have limited control and only share the same knowledge that they themselves have. In effect, this is a process of moving the client's attention onto the other, in this case the voice-character. The client refines their knowledge of how the voice-character works. At first they assume the voice knows everything – in the same way children assume their parents know everything (and there is work showing that people relate to the voice-characters in the same ways as they relate to real people in their lives; Birchwood *et al.*, 2000b).

MOVING ATTENTION ONTO THE OTHER: DE-IDEALISATION

In the same way therapy can challenge the power of the voices, it is a small step to a therapy which recommends challenging the actual or perceived power of real people. Some are in awe of their idealised parents and feel controlled and overwhelmed by them. Of course, there are also some people with a psychosis who are already very emancipated from their parents and in fact terrorise them quite badly (as we saw in Chapter 13); perhaps if they had a better understanding of their parent and their feelings these people would be more sympathetic towards their family.

A good place to start would be with a number of questions about the parents to prompt new lines of thought, aimed at looking at parents as being real people rather than idealised cartoons. In our experience, many people who have had a psychotic episode are slightly nonplussed when they are asked about their parents' or other people's personalities. Partly this might be understandable because they might have expected their psychology research sessions to be purely about them, particularly if they have bought into the medical model. Partly it might be an understandable reluctance to involve parents or to defend them from what they anticipate could be an attack on them. A further proportion do not dare say anything about their parents (see Chapter 13). In many cases, we feel that many people who have had a psychotic episode are astonished that their parent could even be of relevance. Many we asked felt very confidently that their parents didn't get things wrong, didn't really worry about things, didn't have hopes and aspirations for themselves. There was a sense in which they didn't really *know* their parents *as people*. Where the person is wondering about the relevance of working on their understanding of their parents, perhaps a good place to start is the influence their parents have had on them, the standards and opinions we all inherit from our parents.

For example: "What rules for life do you think you have adopted from your parents?"

Naturally, it is not for anyone to tell anyone with a psychosis what to think of their families. But they might benefit from putting in place the structures and processes that will help them assimilate and understand their experiences of them. What traits, little facets of their parent's characters have they picked up?

For example, here are some questions they might like to try:

- Do your parents ever get things wrong? Are they ever grumpy, for example when tired?

- Are they morning people or evening people (or both?)

- What are their goals in life?

- How do they like to be seen?

- What are the things they pride themselves on? What are the things they are ashamed of?

- What was their best moment/worst moment?

- How do they get on with their friends? How do they get on with each other? What sort of things do they argue about? How were their first dating experiences? How do they cope with their partner flirting? Do they get jealous?

- What do they worry about? How did they cope with parenthood?

- How do they cope with getting old? How do they relate to death? Have they lost many important people? How did they cope with these losses?

- How do they feel about you becoming independent and leaving home?

- How do they feel about you being unwell? How do they cope? What aspects of your illness affect the parent most?

- What do they worry about on your behalf? What did they worry about when you were younger?

These are the kinds of questions we believe are not asked by those who are frozen in a self-focused rather than other-focused frame of mind. These are the kind of questions which can help a young person to deepen their understanding of their parent and really get to know them. They may have a bias towards seeing their parent as either bad or good; it may be important to move towards mixing these up, to get a more balanced picture.

To make the process more entertaining, it might be useful for them to imagine they were a reporter writing their Dad's biography, or someone else's child trying to get a feel for what their Dad is like. Here are some further prompts:

- How did you Mum/Dad act when they were your age? Were they happy? Did they ever feel unpopular?/ unintelligent?/a failure?

(In these areas the aim is to direct them to dwell on comparisons with themselves; many parents are understandably reluctant to talk about less heroic aspects of their lives, but it may help people with a psychosis to feel less miserable and useless to know that their parents have struggled with similar issues to the ones they are confronted by).

- How did your parents get on with their parents? (i.e. their grandparents;

this is another valuable source of information about the parents' beliefs, again allowing comparisons with their own life). If the parent often argued with their parents, or if they didn't argue and regret it, this could give valuable insights and normalisation. The current generation of clients are going to have grandparents from a culture that is just post-Victorian; hence the grandparents' parenting styles will probably have been a lot more strict than modern-day.

People generally think their parents (and people we are attached to) are special, and people who have had a psychosis seem to particularly idealise their parents.

For example: One client said that he saw his family's house as being an oasis of special-ness in the world, almost like a spaceship, the most perfect and ideal house there was.

When people idealise their parents in this way, they may assume them to be perfect role models and feel pressured to follow in their footsteps. Whether the parent's way of living is really ideal might be a useful topic for discussion. This sort of conversation could also instigate a fresh dialogue and sharing of experiences between parents and offspring: "In what ways is it good to be different from your folks?" It may be natural to feel a version of the special regard and attachment to your own home illustrated above, particularly when you are younger, but it is useful to develop the intellectual understanding that other people also have homes that are just as important to them.

The paradox between one's own family seeming particularly special and unique and the rather crushing intellectual realisation that yours is just one family out of millions is common to everyone and is something everyone needs to work out for themselves. Similarly, it might be useful to consider that other people have parents, and that friends' families may seem equally ideal to them. For example, different families have different hobbies and political views.

DE-IDEALISING BY CONSIDERING CONSENSUS AND RIGHTNESS

Some of the main aspects of learning about others considered above are to do with consensus, uniqueness and power/worthiness; in effect, separating out a parent's views from everyone else's. The force of a person's argument can be strengthened by appearing to have lots of other authorities behind them who agree with them. As children, there is a tendency to see parents as knowing everything and having standards that are typical of everyone.

For many aspects of life this may be true, but part of the individuation process of adolescence is to test this consensus and perhaps realise there are alternate viewpoints. It is therefore quite a therapeutic theme for therapy to ask: "Who agrees with your parents? Who disagrees? Have they ever felt differently themselves/are they perhaps in a peculiar mood? Even if a few people agree with them, do you agree with them? Even if everyone agrees with them, what do you yourself think?"

In the same way as clients gain from a greater understanding that there is more than one perspective, an important understanding is that there is more than one right or wrong. Moral values are very dependent on the agenda of the person choosing the label. Almost any behaviour or role can be "spun" as good or bad depending on the painter's perspective. Some people are better than others at spinning the situation, and by so doing, creating a social reality in which they own all the right-ness and worthiness. Clients can benefit from playing around with moral weightings and definitions of situations, perhaps exchanging adjectives to cast things differently. Look at the following example.

interest vs suffocating	firmness vs coldness	loyalty vs sycophancy
honesty vs cruelty	protecting vs controlling	loving vs babyish
concern vs gloating	self-assertion vs selfishness	independence vs remoteness
helping vs intruding	hurt vs self-indulgent	obedience vs compliance
duty vs boringness	grown-up vs disrespectful	helping vs patronising
caring vs nagging	confidence vs arrogance	

It is almost a question of clients just having the confidence to align themselves with a set of adjectives which suits them, even if they are different to those that other people might use. Good adjectives align that person with a laudable role and help in the process of constructing a worthwhile self.

DE-IDEALISING PUBLIC FIGURES

Pablo: I read your article. I must thank you for how well you portray me; too well, I think. Furthermore, it seems you portray yourself pretty well, too. The first thing a revolutionary who writes history has to do is stick to the truth like a finger inside a glove. You did that, but it was a boxing glove, and that's cheating. (Ernesto "Che" Guevara, 1963)

A side-effect of the way the media works nowadays is to turn ordinary people into mythical people. People who were essentially human – albeit with many good qualities and some exceptional achievements behind them – get turned into a brand, where everything they have ever done appears to have been perfect and wise, and they are retrospectively seen to have embodied particular virtues. Brands embody only the positive virtues and impressive associations, because they are meant to be aspirational, and often meant to sell products. For example, John Lennon is now seen internationally to embody lots of positive qualities such as integrity, peace-loving and independence. One of the authors (CH) has a relative who went to art college with John Lennon when they were both teenagers, and John as a teenager was reportedly far from the worthy brand he was later portrayed as. In fact he was always disrupting lessons, showing off, and had a particularly caustic attitude; according to *this* source, he wasn't at all popular!

It's natural for a young person surrounded by these superhuman ideals to want to live up to them and pull themselves up from their self-perceived low social rank, even to compete with them; unfortunately it's not possible because even the famous people themselves were never as laudable as the brands they later became associated with. Young adults feeling bad about themselves because they don't compare very well to the brand of, say, John Lennon, should feel assured that neither would John himself, most of the way through his life (and he probably wouldn't have wanted to). We suggested earlier that some people who hear voices see the voice as an idealised mentor figure, and that they might get some emotional support from feeling they are attached to such a character. If a person with a psychosis is fixated on a voice-character or indeed anybody else, it may be useful for them to find out as much of the reality of that character as they can. It might be instructive for clients to research their own favourite idealised famous person to look for weaknesses in them, the parts where they are seen as human and fallible.

Useful questions that might focus people on media celebrities might be:

- Why do people want to be interviewed in papers? Are there any aspects of themselves they might hold back? What flaws, faults and moods might they have?

FINDING AND DE-IDEALISING PEERS

Parents are relatively easy to work on because they are (usually) physically available to the client. However, one theme of this book has been that the problems with peers are as significant, if not more so, than problems with parents. This presents difficulties because many people with a psychosis have lost contact with their peer group and would probably need to make contact with them again to make great developments in their understandings of them. All the individuation in the world isn't going to help if the client has no access to friends. Being stuck with their parents all day is at the very least an unhelpful situation for a young person's vital self-construction development, and probably an unpleasant and difficult experience for both parties to boot. It would seem from previous chapters that such a situation has a lot of potential to eventually become quite acrimonious. Parents are a good place to learn some basics and try things out in a relatively safe manner, but these skills are of most use in that they can be transferred to the peer arena where the real process of self-construction has to take place. The peer group is also a vital source of normalisation with regards to how other people behave with their parents.

However, there is a danger that someone who has been excessively self-conscious, who idealises their parents (or who is not aware of the complexities of their parents' experience) will have a similar problem with peers – they may idealise them as well. It is quite likely that they will have similar unrealistic and "legendary" views of their peers as well as their parents. For example, they may feel like their friends are all better adjusted or more important than them. Again there are lots of questions that might be useful here, many of which are similar to those used previously (people whose social circle is somewhat limited might have to think back to friends that they used to have, and how they used to act):

- How did your friends get on with their parents? What things did they fall out on? What things did they value about their parents?

- Did your friends ever feel unloved? Unhappy? Psychotic? Unpopular? Unintelligent? Successful?

- How did your friends feel they were seen by their friends? By you?

- What goals did they have?

- How did they cope with peer-pressure? How did they cope with their first dating experiences? How did they find being at school? Leaving school? How did they keep in touch with people?

- Did they have any unusual beliefs? Who did they look up to? Who were they scared of? What sort of things would they feel guilty about?

- How did they see themselves in relation to others? How do they feel about you now? Were they ever selfish? Were they ever unfair or spiteful? Were they ever grandiose or egocentric?

There are a lot of questions here, and almost too many things for anyone to ever answer or be aware of (it is almost quite creepy for anyone to want to know all this!). The important thing is to get their locus of awareness off themselves and onto others, and start the process of observation. It helps to understand peers a bit more, which should be more conducive to having better relations with them, and being able to be more reciprocal with them. For people with a psychosis it would mean they were less scared of their peers, more likely to see their peers' strengths and weaknesses as humans, and less likely to incorporate them into their delusions and problems. It should illustrate to them that they are not the only people to have unhappinesses, rejections and problems, that these are universal and part of life. It will also help them discern character traits that they might not have noticed before e.g. one friend always makes them feel small, and also picks on everyone else; another friend is the group leader and yet is not a god or a "brand", but quite human and flawed really.

- People with a psychosis might also benefit from a fresh look at key events with friends, such as fallings out or particular embarrassments (such as in Section Three, Chapter 14). Can they see where their friends were coming from, retrospectively? Does having been in the wrong stay with them forever? What do they think their friends would say their own key events were?

- Do/did their friends act differently when they are around other friends to how they are on a one-to-one basis? Do they act differently when they are around their own parents/the client's parents?

- How do their friends react to being seen unfavourably? Can their friends recover from their own mistakes in a way that they themselves haven't been able to so far?

ROMANTIC RELATIONSHIPS

Romantic relationships are a particularly important focus, but possibly also the most difficult to work with (as we saw in Chapter 14). A client may want to go straight into dating, as dating is something most young people will normally want to do. It can be done, but it might possibly be better to see dating as the culmination of a longer and broader re-socialisation process that includes learning to decentre. A good strategy might be to start by getting used to coping in a job or voluntary work, and getting used to the frequent interpersonal contact that entails, putting themselves in the "external focus" frame of mind. They probably need to get re-acquainted with making and retaining friends and going out, learning to understand other people, and through understanding to trust others, and being trusted in return. Generally they can feel reassured that they are worthy of friendship! From this position, they are better placed to pursue romance, because friends may be able to help them meet potential romantic partners, and can be a source of contact and support through the early dating manoeuvres. Then if the relationship doesn't work, the friend can look after the client and reassure them it is not the end of the world, perhaps help the client to understand what happened, and particularly any role their own behaviour had in any problems. Perhaps even more useful as a decentring exercise is for the client to learn to play this role for the friend, since this requires acquiring and practising good "theory of mind" skills; it would take the focus of attention onto the other, and helps to build interpersonal bonds. Either way, from the perspective of attachment theory, it is easier to explore from a secure base of friends, and clients are less likely to be devastated if it goes wrong because they still have an attachment base.

In addition to the importance of securing peer support, the client will almost certainly need specific help with decentring, hinted at above. No group of people is probably more in need of de-idealisation than potential romantic partners. Many people are so self-conscious in a dating situation that any understanding of romantic partners starts and ends with the most negative parts of their own self-image, as was apparent in Chapter 14. It is not an accident that potential or desired romantic partners are so often incorporated into delusions.

Again, similar questions apply here to aid the process of de-idealising and building a realistic picture of the other person.

- What fallibilities, as well as strengths, does the romantic partner have?

- What dating experiences have they had so far? How do they get on with people in general? How do they get on with teachers/bosses? With friends? How do they behave around their parents?

- What things do they pride themselves on?

- What worries do they have about potential relationships? What things would you want to improve about them? What are their likes and dislikes?

- Do they ever make mistakes? Can they ever be moody or unpredictable or childish?

- Are they different at different times of day? What sort of things interest them about you, and what sort of things bore them?

- How do they behave in arguments? What sort of compromises will they make? What sort of things make them jealous? How do they feel about punctuality? Cleanliness? What are their ambitions?

A very effective way of getting such information appropriately is to include them as part of a valuable social skills strategy – the use of listening skills. Being a good listener is the least demanding of the conversational skills; it ensures they are focused on the other and not self-focused, and shows in an overt way an attitude of warmth and interest which will nearly always be positively responded to. Hence they are vital in the early stages of friendship formation. Good listening skills are fully described in Trower, Bryant and Argyle (1978), and include:

> 1. Watching the the other person, including their body language; listening carefully to the verbal content but also the so-called paralinguistic cues (voice volume, pitch and intonation patterns) that give added meaning.
> 2. Using good "attending behaviour" such as being the right distance away (neither too close or far), body and head being turned to the other, and an open posture (arms not closed protectively across the body). They can also maintain eye contact (avoiding looking at the ground or 'through' the other), have a positive facial expression (particularly avoiding having a blank face) and be responsive to the other's dialogue, particularly using posture and gestures which are responsive to what the other says.
> 3. Opening the conversation with a general greeting-type question and then encouraging the other to talk by a combination of open and closed questions, paraphrasing the content of what is said, reflecting the feeling being overtly or covertly expressed, and giving lots of small listener cues like head nods, and "mhmm"s.
> 4. The use of an overall strategy of reciprocal self-disclosure (basically, "tell me a bit about yourself and I'll tell you a bit about myself", "tell me a little more and I will reciprocate"). All these skills are designed to be rewarding to the speaker, and of course the more the other speaks and gets relaxed and comfortable, the less self-conscious the client becomes, until the client feels able to start contributing speaking parts to the conversation.

Sometimes people applying social skills can place so much emphasis on what the other wants that they overvalue and idealise the other – clients may need to be careful not to do this. They may need reminding that their needs and ideas are just as important as the person they are listening to!

INITIATING AGENCY, A SENSE OF SELF: EXISTENTIAL IMPERATIVE

In this chapter so far, we have argued that understanding and building a picture of others is a vital route to:

(a)   overcoming egocentricity, and

(b)   getting attention externally rather than internally focused.

A number of suggestions have been made as to how people's attentions can be directed towards important people in their lives, with particular regard to moral interpretations and consensus. Yet in earlier sections we considered that people with a psychosis get stuck in this normal process of de-idealisation, in many cases because it is too threatening or difficult for them. At this point then, we need to consider whether the de-idealisation we are urging in this chapter will still be very threatening for them. We should predict that many people with a psychosis will find it very difficult to discuss other people's behaviours, because they do not feel that they have a right to an opinion on other people's behaviour. This could be admirable in a way, because people have a right to privacy. However, as we saw in Section Three, many people later said they wanted to talk about people but just didn't dare to because it made them feel guilty, or afraid of retribution. Many felt sure that anything they said would go straight back to the other party, because they couldn't conceive of other people not being in league with these other parties, and therefore not disclosing that they had been "disloyal". A further group felt their parents would instantly know if they had been talked about (cognitions of omniscience/mind-reading/thought broadcast). For people who dare not discuss their parents, the rules about whether it is disrespectful to talk about parents need to be discussed. Many clients need a lot of reassurances along the lines of "it is natural to be annoyed or upset with your parents sometimes; it is a normal part of being a son/daughter", or "just because you are annoyed with one part of your friend doesn't mean you are annoyed with all the good parts of them; you can't like everything about someone or they wouldn't be human, just an act". They may need reassurances that other people are sometimes annoyed with their parents. It might be useful to ask them if their friends (present day or when they were at school) ever moaned about their parents. The adolescence literature can also be useful here, as can pop songs that talk about classic adolescence issues such as being misunderstood and not getting on with parents.

People who are prone to alienation/engulfment experiences, and excessively vulnerable to moral pressure, will not only find it nerve-wracking to discuss people, but will have difficulty even holding onto their own perspective and sense of agency about social judgements. In our studies, many people were more adept at learning other people's values and opinions, and found it hard to have their own opinions. We propose that building a sense of self might be a furtive and difficult experience for some clients prone to alienation experiences, as it might feel like an unbearably rebellious act, to throw off an alien role imposed on them. There may well be reasons why they've felt compelled to adopt imposed roles, reasons to do with feeling threatened if they dare have their own views.

For this reason, forming a sense of self might be something they have to do quietly and in secret. To help them to actually hold on to their own perspective they may need to write things down, or else they might forget them, possibly because it negates or refines some other strongly-held conviction or assumption in the family story. A notebook (suitably hidden from prying eyes at all times) can provide a memory of what might otherwise be difficult to hold in mind. In other words, until these new ideas can be fully internalised into a complex and detailed mental representation of the other person, the notebook can act as that representation. Where a person with a psychosis feels uncomfortable with something, or angry or upset about something, or pleased with something, they can look at the people involved more closely. They are looking for connections, patterns, traits, habits *in other people*, clarifying the boundary between themselves and the others, trying to learn the patterns of the important people in their lives, trying to understand them. Without this, other people will always be relative strangers to them.

Some people with a psychosis may have problems because they are imagining a catastrophe that could occur if they were deemed disobedient, if their attachment to their parents was threatened. For example, in Chapter 13, Alan felt he would be sacrificed to the Devil if he displeased his parents. Many people with a psychosis felt they would be thrown out of the house if they weren't very careful. People who hear voices driven by the need to affiliate (discussed earlier as the "moral imperative") may be being constantly warned that they shouldn't misbehave even slightly. If the voice-character is telling the individual that they can't remotely rebel, and that there are likely to be terrible consequences if they do, that person will naturally find it very distressing to be led down the path of questioning their parents. This will have to be addressed before any real de-idealisation can start; we look more closely at this sort of issue in the next chapter.

Some people we worked with had very intimidating parents who appeared to literally not tolerate there being differences between themselves and their offspring, and could be very punitive if they perceived such independence. In these cases, it is probably important to address the consequences of individuation, perhaps in a family therapy context, or perhaps by having the client live away from but accessible to the parental home while the groundwork for individuation is prepared.

SUMMARY

This chapter has suggested a number of routes for therapeutic work to focus on. If people with a psychosis are prone to *"objectité"* (see Section Two, Chapter 10), and to having only a limited, idealistic notion of how other people work, then it will be useful to get their attention off themselves, and to start to improve their understanding of others. A "character-based" training, built on understanding other people's characters, was described towards this goal. This should help diminish egocentricity and perhaps grandiosity, in the same way that similar learning is thought to help adolescents develop their interpersonal skills and negotiate the adult world. It will also help people learn to deal with threats to self-construction.

In previous chapters, we noted that many clients seemed to be plagued by crippling amounts of guilt and shame about self-expression – what we called "a rampant moral imperative". To help with this, we discussed later how to help people allow themselves to be reasonably "rebellious", since what some parents might label "rebellious", an impartial observer might label reasonable "assertiveness". We also pointed out the catastrophes many suspect might happen probably won't. A person trying to start off their own "rebellion" – i.e. reasonable assertion – (after a lot of experience feeling they are not allowed to) might need to do it clandestinely at first, to get used to the experience at a level which doesn't involve anyone's actual reaction.

The suggestions in this chapter cover how a client can develop the vital strategy of being outward rather than self-focused, and how he can use this strategy to learn about others, and to develop new and improved relationships. What happens if a person is too preoccupied with and trapped within psychotic phenomena to use these methods? Sometimes, psychotic symptoms appear to take on a life of their own – voices literally seem like real people and can seem to irrevocably block the sort of changes we are advocating. Some of the well-established techniques for combating symptoms such as voices and delusions are described and discussed in Chapter 17.

First, in Chapter 16, we look more closely at ways in which self-construction blocks can be tackled therapeutically, in terms of the specific cognitive beliefs and feelings behind the twin imperatives.

OVERCOMING INTERPERSONAL BLOCKS TO SELF-CONSTRUCTION

We begin this chapter with a summary of the problem of blocked self-construction in psychosis, to which we gave detailed attention in Sections Two and Three. We then describe our proposals for therapeutic intervention for this problem. These particular proposals are geared to therapists who already have a background of skills, and are designed for therapist–client work. Individuals themselves and their close relatives should also find this chapter of interest, but in the final chapter (Chapter 17) we outline more general practical techniques that may be more directly useful.

SUMMARY OF THE PROBLEM OF BLOCKED SELF-CONSTRUCTION

Successful relationships and a healthy sense of self are usually achieved when individuals enable each other, within the boundaries of social rules, roles and rankings, to meet their self-construction needs. As we suggested in Chapter 8, people usually achieve a workable (if imperfect) balance by compromising between their own existential needs and their moral duty to others – the wanting to be recognised and valued *by* others, and the duty to give recognition and value *to* others. Resolvable difficulties arise when the balance is disturbed, such as when a person's existential needs are suppressed because of pressure to meet social and moral duties to others. Such problems are commonly either resolved or the inequalities are tolerated because of discussion, persuasion and a general give-and-take in everyday life.

Our existential drive and our sense of moral duty to others are of course healthy, indeed essential aspects of human nature and experience – life as we know it would hardly be conceivable without them, and certainly healthy self-construction would be an impossibility. Our aim is not to change these needs and duties in any way, but rather to work on enabling them to be normally expressed and self-construction to be achieved. Our focus in therapy therefore is on those severe blocks to self-construction which arise when one or the other or both individuals in a relationship escalate their existential needs and/or duties into absolute imperatives, in the form of demands and "musts" (we draw specifically here on REBT theory, particularly the notion of the unhelpfulness of a demanding philosophy of life. However, we take complete responsibility for the adaptations to this notion in the present chapter, the theoretical basis of which is described in Trower, 2003).

Probably the most common problem is where the existential imperative (the *demand* for recognition, respect, love) and the moral imperative (the moral *demand* of duty to the other) are in conflict. The conflict is between my existential imperative/your moral imperative to pursue my wants/your oughts, and your existential imperative/my moral imperative to pursue your wants/my oughts. In such a scenario there is no compromise and no balance, and there has to be a winner and a loser, the winner usually being the person higher in social rank terms (Gilbert, Price & Allan, 1995). This gives rise to one of two problems – the moral imperative problem and the existential imperative problem.

In the moral imperative problem, let us suppose that I – the loser in the conflict – give way to you, the winner ["You" and "the Other" may be individual (mother, father, sibling, spouse, care worker) or an individual group with a common approach to the client (parents, family, care team)]. You achieve this by using the moral imperative to persuade or even coerce me into believing that I *must* (imperatively) do what I ought (which may be to be a person who subserves your existential needs), and must not do what I want (which is to promote my existential needs). In this illustration, you as the other(s) use (unconsciously or deliberately) the moral imperative to try to produce two effects: enforcing my alienation (being constructed by the other) and blocking my self-construction. It enforces alienation by the threat that, if I don't conform to the moral imperative, I will be labelled as morally bad, i.e. reconstructed as totally bad in my very being. Either way I end up in a state of *objectité* – becoming a social object, which has been taken control of by the other. People who commonly experience the alienation threat (the Alienated Self – see Chapter 10, page 83) commonly try to cope with that threat by avoidance of and escape from those (usually up-rank powerful others) who use or appear to use such controlling strategies. (It is no coincidence that many people with a psychosis often sleep in really late and stay up later at night.) If they cannot, or believe they cannot avoid or escape from the Other, they will either succumb, maybe in depression and defeat, or on rare occasion, angrily lash out (Gilbert, 1992).

As the above description shows, the existential imperative problem is precisely the opposite of the moral imperative problem. In this case the person escalates his existential need into an imperative, and the person then *must* have certain specific Others affirm and value his self-presentations. On the face of it, it doesn't seem like a problem so long as I, pursuing my existential imperative, successfully achieve my demand to have you and others subserve my existential needs. However it can become a problem, in two ways.

Firstly, in an extreme case, you and others will learn to avoid and get away from me because of the aversiveness of the alienating experiences. This reaction of others is a problem often faced by the Insecure Self (Chapter 9) – those characteristically disposed to the existential imperative and who may, through an underlying insecurity, try to use the moral imperative to pressurise others to give them what they need, but only succeed in alienating others. However, when you and others are more powerful than me, you may turn the tables on me and force me into compliance.

Our research, reviewed in Section Three, showed that most of our clients fell prey to the moral imperative trap and became blocked. However, even these clients, usually oppressed by others through the moral imperative will, perhaps following long periods of angry rumination, periodically reach a "breaking point" and demand others validate their presented selves. This is because the existential need, though oppressed, never dies. The more it is repressed, the more it is likely to surface at some point as a compelling demand, perhaps aggressively expressed. However, they will then invariably experience the full force of the other's moral imperative, see themselves as extremely bad, and return to an even more oppressed style, maybe to ruminate and build again to a later "outburst", thus perpetuating an unfortunate cycle.

OVERCOMING BLOCKS TO SELF-CONSTRUCTION

Our focus in the next section is to explore potential therapeutic solutions, by using mainly Cognitive Behaviour Therapy (CBT) methods and our method of micro-analysis (as described in Chapter 12). We adopt the specific theme of blocks to self-construction, and divide the subsections into the moral imperative problem, the existential imperative problem and the interaction of the two. We have assumed therapy will be conducted one-to-one, but ideally it should be conducted with the two or more key people involved in these episodes.

First, some general comments on assessment and formulation in preparation for this type of intervention.

ASSESSMENT AND FORMULATION

As in any type of CBT, as with many other forms of therapy, it is essential to negotiate a clear assessment and formulation of the problem that the client understands, agrees with and that feels insightful for him/her. In addition to this, the formulation can provide a blueprint or guide for implementing changes, and to this end can be continually modified as therapy progresses and new, alternative beliefs and behaviours are targeted. It is useful to carry out traditional assessments – history-taking, questionnaire assessment, identification of positive and negative symptoms and other background information. However, our own focus means that the key assessment and formulation tasks will be concentrated on specific emotional episodes, especially conflicts, where self-construction issues are prominent. This can be done by means of our situation-specific structured ABC interview, as we have outlined in Section Three. It can also be done by videotaped role-play simulations of interpersonal emotional episodes, and the assessment and formulation then carried out by "video-aided recall", that is identification of events, beliefs and emotional and behavioural responses using video feedback as a prompt, and our ABC format as a guiding structure. (A procedure of this kind is given in Trower, Casey & Dryden, 1998.)

We have illustrated the application of our theory in the assessment and formulation of self-construction problems described in Section Three, and the reader is referred to this section for more detailed guidance on how to complete the ABC analyses. The assessment and formulation is structured in terms of *ABC sequences of cognitive-emotional episodes* and the further sequencing of these episodes in complex chains. Specifically:

an

Activating Event (A)

triggers

Beliefs (B)

and these in turn give rise to emotional and behavioural

Consequences (C).

These episodes are linked to second, third or more episodes in a complex chain. It is within these episodes and complex chains of episodes that the problems of blocked self-construction lie.

We turn first to those that underlie the moral imperative problem.

TACKLING THE MORAL IMPERATIVE PROBLEM

We have already mentioned that, in civilised society, it is each individual's moral *duty* to the other that he should give the other respect as a *self*, just as the other's moral duty to him is that she reciprocally respect him as a self. These and associated moral rules are inherent in all social relationships

(Harré, 1979), and underlie our extensive rules of etiquette in everyday life. Of course such rules get broken, and respect and valuing are often withheld or withdrawn if the person being judged is seen to be breaking the rules. But we don't expect perfection in the real world and such incursions are tolerated on the whole. However, the moral *imperative* (as we have seen) makes no allowances. The moral imperative rule says:

> To be a morally good person I *must* comply, with the consequence that when I comply, as I must, I am good, and when I don't comply, as I must not, I am bad.

A whole series of unhelpful beliefs follow from this fundamental rule. The moral imperative *demands* that I give respect, but respect in this definition means that I *must* comply with the other's wishes, that it is *imperative* that I subordinate myself to him/her (Gilbert, 1992), that it is my absolute moral duty to do. Consequently, if I don't, I risk being condemned as a totally bad (as in wicked) person in my very being i.e. having a bad self. Woe betide the subordinate who doesn't pay this kind of respect to Vito Corleone (in the film *The Godfather*)!

In the following pages we present intervention strategies firstly for tackling the cognitive-emotional episodes relevant to the moral imperative problem, secondly for tackling those episodes relevant to the existential imperative, and lastly to show how they interact to form a trap, and how this formulation can help guide intervention. We use cases to illustrate the process.

THE "BAD ME" ANXIETY EPISODE

The "bad me" anxiety episode is the cognitive-emotional episode most closely associated with the actual blocking of self-construction because it is characterised by behavioural avoidance, i.e. avoidance of presenting the true self for fear of being labelled "bad". It is also the key episode in bringing out the moral imperative, and may be one of the main mechanisms underlying social anxiety (Gilbert & Trower, 2001). This whole episode is characteristically a visualisation played out in the client's mind of what he predicts would happen if he asserted himself (as we saw in Chapter 13).

In this episode A (the activating event) is the client's imagined assertion of self; B is the belief that the other would negatively evaluate him as a person if he did this (Other-to-Self or 'O-S'), and that she would be right (Self to Self or 'S-S'). He believes she would be right because he would have acted against the moral must, e.g. he must be compliant but wasn't. We then get anxiety at C (the Consequence) that results from the anticipation of the O-S, and the avoidant action, namely avoiding negative assertion and instead behaving compliantly. An example is that of David's second sequence, where David imagines that if he refused, his Mum would call him a bad person and he would believe it. He would then draw the moral imperative rule "I must do as she says" and consequently, due to the extreme anxiety this anticipation evokes, he ends up doing as he is told.

The two key beliefs to be challenged here are the two beliefs that underpin the moral imperative, namely a demand that I should behave the way the other wants (the must belief) and the condemnation of self as thoroughly bad if I don't (the self-devaluation belief, O-S, S-S). When the person is blocked by the moral imperative in the way described above our task is to dismantle these two underpinning beliefs.

Different therapies approach this in different ways. In Rational Emotive Behaviour Therapy (REBT) the aim is to not only to challenge and give up these "unhelpful" beliefs but also to replace them – with an alternative preferential belief (i.e. to freely choose what is preferable) to replace "the must", and a self-accepting belief to replace the self-devaluation.

Challenging the Self-devaluing ("I'm bad") Belief

Imagine you spontaneously want to act in a certain way – e.g. be assertive, ask for something, refuse a request – but you're afraid you'll be accused of being a bad person if you do (especially if you're rather vulnerable to such accusations and rather inclined to believe they are true). You therefore decide you must not do what you want at all but what the other wants.

How do we challenge and change the "I'm bad" belief? The first task is to dismantle the components of the belief. This type of belief is often made up of two components, namely what the other thinks of you (O-S) and what you think of yourself (S-S). It only works as a self-devaluing belief if it is:

(1)   already one of your core beliefs (e.g. "I'm bad"; S-S)

(2)   you recognise and value the other's beliefs about you as credible ("My Mum thinks I'm bad and she knows"; O-S)

(3)   there is a match between your own and the other's beliefs about you – a fusion of O-S and S-S in S-O-S or image-of-self-in-the-eyes-of-the-other (e.g. "people can see I'm a bad person").

We challenge (1) by using traditional REBT and other CBT methods, by, for example, *empirical disputing* (Dryden, 1995; Chadwick, Birchwood and Trower, 1996). Before commencing such challenging it is always essential to check and make clear that the client is making a total, not a partial, self-evaluation. Key questions then are:

• Even assuming the worst, how does acting badly make you a totally bad person and not just a fallible person who sometimes does bad things?

• How does one bad act make the whole of you bad?

• What can you do to prove you cannot be a totally bad person?

Such questioning needs to be in the context of a comprehensive CBT intervention, where such loosening of unhelpful beliefs and considering helpful alternatives forms the insight stage, but is followed by behavioural testing of beliefs as hypotheses, implementing the new beliefs into future emotional episodes, and acting in ways consistent with the new beliefs and against the unhelpful beliefs.

We challenge (2) by questioning the credibility of the other's beliefs. Sometimes clients so idealise their parents (and voices) that they invest in them power to be all-knowing such that whatever they assert is true almost by definition. Some probes to question this assumption are:

• If she called you a porcupine, would you be one? Just asserting something doesn't make it true. What counts as evidence?

• Is she a fallible person? Does she make mistakes? Does she have special powers to know the truth? What's the evidence for that?

Such questions are designed to "normalise" and de-idealise the other (see Chapter 15, which is a detailed account of how this can be done).

We challenge (3) in two ways. The first way is most appropriate when it seems the client is projecting his own view of himself onto the other, and then looking back at himself as if through the other's eyes. In effect this is producing a single "image-of-self-in-the-eyes-of-the-other" (or what is often called the "observer perspective"). As we said earlier, this happens because clients often fuse the two perspectives – what they think (S-S) is what the other thinks. This way there is always (the illusion of) a perfect match between what the other thinks of me and what I think of me. This image of self can be so vivid and so strong a "felt sense" that it takes on a compelling reality for the client, and "becomes" the evidence that is almost literally staring them in the face. Our aim therefore is to dismantle this fusion of the other's belief and the client's own belief.

The first task is to help the client become aware of the following, quite complex idea: by being so self-focused they are building a picture of themselves from their subjective feelings and not objective facts. They then assume this is how others see them, when in fact it is only their own opinions "projected" onto others. The next task is to obtain realistic information about how they really appear to the other by, for example, comparing their image of self to a video replay of them in an actual social situation. Detailed guidance on this approach is given by Wells (2000) and Clark (2001).

We said we challenge (3) in two ways, and have just described the first. The second way is more appropriate when it seems the client may be right that others view him negatively, and with some justification, i.e. he has acted badly. The way we challenge the "I'm bad" belief in these circumstances is a variant of the way we challenged (1), namely where it is already one of the client's core beliefs. We would help the client to challenge that core belief and embrace an alternative, self-valuing belief. This alternative can take the form of an unconditional acceptance of self as a periodically mistake-making, badly behaving fallible human who also does things wrong and does things right/does good things too. This alternative view of self is one of the main aims of Rational Emotive Behaviour Therapy (Dryden, 1995). When this is successfully achieved, it helps the client to act the way he wants to act in the knowledge that, even if it turns out he was wrong to act that way, he will always unconditionally accept himself (new belief) despite the other's attempt to redefine him as a bad person.

The "bad me" belief may well have an Other-to-Self (O-S) origin; a close relative may have actually, or been perceived to have been critical, and implanted the belief in the client's head when he was little and growing up. Such a pattern may have continued over long periods in the family context. However, having developed an observer perspective, the client may now come to believe that *everyone* thinks he is bad.

Bad Me or Poor Me?

Of course clients may not necessarily develop a "bad me" belief, even in the circumstances just described. Some will defend against such a perceived judgment by projecting the badness back into the accuser, seeing themselves as persecuted and innocent, and developing instead a *"poor me"* belief. Some may go backwards and forwards from one to the other, sometimes viewing the self as bad, sometimes viewing the other as bad. Interventions for these alternative patterns are described elsewhere, e.g. Chadwick, Birchwood & Trower (1996). Our focus here is on the main underlying mechanism of self-construction blocks and the therapeutic principles that can be used to disrupt that mechanism.

Challenging the Moral Must

One of the traditional REBT ways of disputing any "must" is to ask the rhetorical question:

• Where is the evidence you must? Prove you must.

The question is rhetorical in the sense that there is no conceivable evidence that ordinary fallible human beings absolutely must behave in given ways. Certainly we have moral conventions about what we *should* do and it is right that we try to aspire to them and expect others to do so. However it is not even possible for fallible humans to guarantee they will perfectly conform to their musts even if they wanted to (Ellis, 1994).

Therapy aims to help the client challenge and give up the "must" and replace it with a preference, albeit a very strong one; if it's a moral issue, for example "try my hardest to do" in place of "must do".

However, the next step is to help the client see the link between his must and his self-devaluing belief – in other words to gain insight into the full moral imperative, namely that "I absolutely must comply in order to be a good person, and if I fail to comply I will be a bad person". The client will possibly be relieved to see that this statement is no kind of fact, that it is a rule with no conceivable evidence for it, that he alone maintains, and one that sets an impossible target. Once the client can see that he alone is responsible for maintaining the rule and that there are no grounds for it, he will have the liberating insight that he can, in principle, give it up. If appropriate, he can replace the moral imperative with a moral preference of something like:

> If I should comply I will try to do so but if I fail, it at worst means I acted badly but never means I am a bad person.

This alternative moral-preference schema should enable the client to carry out the next stage of therapy, which is to put into practice his new beliefs, and act self-assertively. He might do this by assertively (but not aggressively) refusing to comply, without being blocked by fear of global self-devaluation but at most experiencing healthy concern at having acted badly if, at worst, he gets it wrong.

We have assumed so far that the client will return to the environment in which his feelings of being criticised originally developed, but of course the client will have taken his moral-imperative beliefs into new relationships. He may have assumed that others will be critical of him if he asserts himself, and may have characteristically blocked his self-assertion; thus he will never disconfirm his others-will-be-critical-of-me expectation. His new self-assertive behaviour will break that vicious cycle.

Real-life Practice and Attention-Switching

The work on dislodging moral-imperative beliefs is essential but not enough to bring about change. The client then, of course, has to implement his new thinking in new behaviour. Therapist and client now need to agree "*in vivo*" (real-life) social tasks, where the client goes back into situations where previously he was blocked. Here again we use the ABC episode structure. Inevitably Mum or someone will ask David to do more chores, and before responding David can deploy his new thinking and responding. It is crucial to prepare David, perhaps in ABC role-play simulations, to implement his new thinking and respond at exactly the right moment.

How do we ensure the client chooses the right moment to implement the change? A clue comes from the fact that the moral-imperative block comes into operation with an actual or imagined critical comment or look from the other – the A. This immediately evokes in the client an attention switch, from external to internal. At that moment the client switches into the perspective of image-of-self-through-the-eyes-of-the-other (S-O-S or *"observer perspective"*). Simultaneously the person experiences anxiety or fear or panic. In other words, you have the sense of the other person looking at you critically, so, for example, when the other person turns their gaze of wrath and disapproval on you, as they utter the condemning words, you immediately become self-focused. At this point you are in the observer perspective, in other words you are now seeing yourself through the eyes of the other, and this explains why the effect of the other is so powerful. As the existentialists say, "I am as the other sees me".

So the intervention here is

(a)   not only to implement the new belief and behaviour, but also

(b)   to get the person to switch from an internal to an external focus.

In this way the client switches to a self-to-other (S-O) perspective and can begin to see the other now, not only what she is really communicating, but also to see, in the longer term, what she is like as a person, that she is not so powerful and perfect but quite human and fallible. So, for example, David might begin the process of building a realistic picture of his Mum, not so much domineering as defensive, not a powerful figure but rather a somewhat fragile middle-aged woman.

Such interventions are best when thoroughly prepared and rehearsed in imagination or in role-play, before being carried out in real life. This is important because the effect described above is so emotionally and experientially powerful and automatic. Video feedback can be used to practise attention-switching, belief-implementation and behaviour-rehearsal. Post mortem simulations can also be carried out, to analyse what went right and what went wrong with the *in vivo*/in situ assignment, and improvements again practised ready for the next occasion.

THE "BAD ME" DEPRESSION EPISODE

The "Bad Me" depression episode comes about when the client doesn't avoid behaving the way he wants to behave as in the "bad me anxiety episode", but actually does carry out his self-assertive behaviour in reality and derives the conclusion he is indeed a bad person. In practice we often found that, given the strength of the repressed anger, if clients did overcome their inhibitions, they actually acted in an inappropriate and overly aggressive way, thus seeming to give ample evidence for the "bad me" evaluations.

In the "Bad Me" depression episode, A is the client's self-assertion or aggression and the other's actual response; B is the other's actual or presumed negative evaluation of him as a person (O-S), and his belief that she would be right (Self to Self or S-S) because he has acted against the moral must, e.g. he must be compliant, and he wasn't. Below is another example from David, where he did assert himself with his mother:

A Activating Event	B Belief	C Consequence
David refuses to make tea and says "piss off". His mother says, "Aren't you a nasty little sod?!"	*She hates me. She thinks I'm bad. She's right I am bad. This is awful. I knew I had to do what she wanted and I didn't.*	Depression, shame Withdraws, hides, behaves defeated

This episode shows how individuals learn to anxiously anticipate responses from the other that they perceive to be devaluing if they do not conform to the moral must. David learned to develop his "bad me anxiety episode" from episodes such as the one above. In future he visualised exactly this type of outcome, and learned to usually avoid it happening again.

The therapy for deconstructing the beliefs driving the depression episode is almost identical to that which we outlined in the anxiety episode (see page 172) – principally by identifying, challenging and replacing the two beliefs that underpin the moral imperative, namely the negative self-evaluation (as bad) and the moral must, and the real-life practice and attention-switching.

However, there is one crucial additional factor. By behaving according to the "bad me" label (i.e. when it functions as a kind of behaviour-guiding cognitive schema) a person in effect constructs the self consistent with the critical label, thereby "proving" the label is true. Thus David actually constructs his self and creates the reality of "bad" person (shame behaviour e.g. hiding, head down) recognised as such by himself and others. In effect, David creates the very evidence that is used by his self and others to justify the "bad me" label – "he knows he is a bad person – just look at him!" This fact adds enormously to the significance of the principle of acting against the dysfunctional belief (in this case the "bad me" belief) and in accordance with the alternative functional belief (the self-accepting "fallible me" belief). Having worked hard at the "insight" that he is not the former but the latter, the client has compelling reasons to commit himself to the even harder work of putting his new belief into action.

Where the behavioural focus of the real-life task in the anxiety episode was self-assertion at point C, the behavioural task in the depression episode switches to presentation of self at point C not as ashamed (which validates the "I'm bad" belief), but as "I'm OK", or at worst "I'm-OK-even-if-I-behaved-badly" (which validates the unconditional self-acceptance belief).

Such a presentation attitude is hard to convey in words! But behaviourally it involves replacing shame behaviour, gaze avoidance, head down, hiding, etc, with perhaps a frank and sincere apology but delivered non-defensively with good eye contact, head up, facing the other, etc. The presentation does, of course, need to be skilfully done, since its validity will depend on how convincing it is. We cannot over-emphasise the importance of this part of the intervention, for here is where the client truly reconstructs himself, in the spirit emphasised throughout the book. In achieving this task the client

(a)   disconfirms the old belief and confirms the new

(b)   achieves this not only in his own eyes but that of the other, and

(c)   interrupts a negative cycle of interpersonal behaviour.

TACKLING THE EXISTENTIAL IMPERATIVE PROBLEM

One of the main themes of this book is that everyone has an "existential need" to construct a self, to be the "author" as it were of their own, authentic self, and that this involves presenting the self to others and having others recognise, accept and validate the self as presented. People rarely achieve all their existential constructions and get thwarted frequently, but in the real world we all accommodate to this in the give-and-take of everyday life. However, the existential *imperative* (just like the moral *imperative*) allows for no such accommodation. The existential imperative rule is

> To be a real (significant) person I must present myself absolutely well and you (others) absolutely *must* recognise and value (admire, respect, like, love etc) that/me. The consequences of failing to conform to the existential imperative are dire – if you don't affirm me in the way I want (as you must) I am of no worth and you are bad.

The problem with the existential imperative is that it flies in the face of reality; for example, only rarely will people guarantee to affirm us in the way demanded (except possibly in a dictatorship) and so the dire consequences will inevitably follow, giving rise to rage and/or depression as we saw in Chapter 13. Whereas the moral imperative can give rise to a "bad me" belief (because this is concerned with a moral theme), the existential imperative gives rise to an "empty self" belief, defined in existential terms as an experience of emptiness and not really existing. (There is no term in English that captures precisely the essence of the existentialist concept of non-being or nothingness, which Sartre describes as *le néant*. In ordinary French it is close to "ennui" – tedium, weariness, exhaustion, disillusion. It is revealed in isolation and loneliness, when a person is abandoned and without others and feels like a nonentity. We use the term "empty self" here to mean non-being). The aim of therapy again is to identify, challenge and replace the key beliefs, namely the existential must and the associated "worthless me" belief.

The Empty Self: Hurt and Angry Episode

The angry episode is one form that the existential imperative can take when the other breaks the must rule.

A	B	C
Brian approaches Dad who says, *"Not now, son"*	*He thinks I'm a waste of space* (O-S). *Poor me. He's a bastard* (S-O) *He mustn't treat me like this – I'll make him sorry*	Hurt, Angry Goes with prostitute

In this example Brian approaches his father for self-affirmation. Brian admires his father greatly and has put him on a pedestal, partly because, coincidentally, he actually is a nationally famous person. His father, however, appears indifferent and pre-occupied, barely looking up as Brian enters the room. Brian is deeply hurt and humiliated by this, and characterises his self as "poor me". Given a history of such reported treatment by his father, Brian has now reached the point where he is applying the existential-imperative rule – his father must now at last give him attention or he will, in effect, be making Brian completely worthless and of no consequence. However, Dad is not responding and it is at this point that Brian's hurt and humiliation provokes anger, even rage. Brian feels his father would be a bastard for doing that, and this enrages him. Unfortunately, his father's behaviour communicates to Brian that he indeed thinks he is a nonentity – a waste of space. Brian angrily tries to discredit this (O-S) definition by going straight to a S-O definition of his father as a bad person (bastard). Brian then proceeds to construct himself in a way that will diminish his father by carrying out a behaviour that he knows will maximise his (father's) embarrassment. Such a response follows from the existential imperative absolutely, simply because it *demands* affirmation from the other, and the demand gets translated into such behaviour.

An REBT approach here would be to challenge the two beliefs that drive the existential imperative. One challenge would be aimed at the must. As discussed earlier, the aim would be to help the client discover that there is no possible evidence that others *must* affirm and value us, and indeed if there were, such a compulsion would reduce others to automatons and their "affirmation" would become meaningless. It only works if freely given, and a necessary part of the other's choice is that she may withhold it. The second challenge is aimed at the belief that drives the demand – the belief that only this person X (Dad in Brian's case) can affirm him (Brian) and that his indifference annihilates him.

However, the most effective intervention comes from understanding the interesting and complex way that the two beliefs relate. They work powerfully together in the form of the fusion of the O-S and S-S in the image-of-self-in-the-eyes-of-the-other or observer perspective discussed earlier. The existential position is that a person exists through the eyes of the other. So long as the other looks at and recognises me (my self-presentation) I am constructed, but when the other is indifferent and I am unrecognised I become an "empty self". A person then comes to believe he *must* be recognised by the other in order to *be*. For this threat to work:

(1)   a person believes he is nothing without person X's recognition (S-S)

(2)   the other withholds recognition (O-S)

(1) and (2) are fused in the observer perspective, and the person is locked into an apparent self-construction reality where he is dependent on this one person for his existence.

As with the moral imperative, we separate out the two components for the client and then challenge each.

First (1), we show that, far from nothing, the client has intrinsic worth, namely intrinsic personal qualities and potentialities and social skills that he can produce whenever he wants to for whomever he wants. The client can prove this in a behavioural experiment, for example, by initiating a similar request with someone else – a family member or friend.

Second (2), person X can only recognise or *withhold* recognition – he does not *give* the actual qualities and potentialities – these are intrinsic to the client (point i). In addition to this, person X is only one of many who can give or withhold recognition – if he decides not to, then many others will be able to take his place, and recognise the client's self-presentations. These considerations not only enable the client to reject the empty self-belief, but enable him to re-evaluate the other more realistically, as much less of a threat, and someone who no longer needs to evoke such hostility and aggression. Also, techniques in Chapter 15 should help them understand the other's motivations better – rather than Brian's father thinking Brian is worthless, maybe he is simply preoccupied with worries and doubts of his own. Such a shift in Brian's perspective may also help him overcome anxiety about meeting more people, since he will be able to see them, too, in the round, and not see them as negatively focusing on him. The more Brian gets exposed to this "social reality", the more he will consolidate his new thinking.

At this point, the therapist can help the client put his new beliefs, as hypotheses, to the test – if he has intrinsic worth, than he only needs to present himself to others in his life to test this. He will at the same time demonstrate that person X is strictly limited in her power to construct him. As with the moral imperative, the new thinking and behaving can be rehearsed in role-play with video feedback, in preparation for actual interactions with different people.

The Empty Self: Depression Episode

The empty-self depression episode comes about when the client gives into the implication they perceive from the other, that they are a nonentity, an empty self of no significance. In this episode, A is the other's behaviour; B is the perceived meaning that he is worth nothing and the client's endorsement of this via the existential rule; C is the resultant depression and the behaviour pattern that actually enacts the state of being an empty self.

A	B	C
Brian approaches Dad who says, "Not now, son"	*He thinks I'm a waste of space* (O-S). *He's right* (O-S). *To be anybody he must value me and he doesn't.*	Depressed Withdraws. Isolates self, loses all motivation. Behaves as if he is nothing

Therapy for the empty-self depressive episode is similar to the empty-self anger episode. One of the main differences is that the behaviour at C creates a reality of "being nothing", thus seeming to validate the "empty self" belief. Attention therefore needs to be given to getting the client to rehearse an alternative behavioural response to such indifferent treatment from significant others, a presentation which conveys a message in line with the new belief: "I have intrinsic worth and there are plenty of others that will recognise it and value me."

This behaviour pattern will also be much more likely to actually elicit such valuing responses from others, whereas the "I'm nothing" behaviour pattern will not, and will only maintain the vicious cycle of belief reinforces behaviour reinforces belief.

TACKLING THE MORAL-EXISTENTIAL IMPERATIVE CONFLICT

We have seen how the moral must can block self-construction by evoking high anxiety and avoidance strategies, and how the existential must can, when thwarted, give rise to extreme anger and aggression with equally destructive effects on selves. In the first case the therapist works on the anxiety and avoidance (by challenging the moral-imperative beliefs) in order to unblock the block to self-construction. In the second case she works on the anger and aggression (via the existential imperative beliefs) in order to moderate the existential drive. We now turn to the interaction of the two musts in producing an entrapment in which the client experiences depression and defeat, and gives up, temporarily at least, trying to construct a self. We suggested earlier (Chapter 11) how this entrapment can also give rise to psychotic symptoms. The therapeutic principles we have discussed in the preceding sections on the moral and existential imperatives can be used strategically to tackle the complex entrapping chains that occur when the two imperatives operate together.

If we look at the full three-sequence interaction between David and his mum we can see how the two imperatives come together in the third episode to produce a depressive entrapment.

A	B	C
"Go and fetch me a cup of tea"	She's giving me an order. She's treating me like a worthless shit (O-S). How dare she! (S-O) I *mustn't* let myself be treated like this	Anger (10) Action Impulse: *"Refuse to do it and tell her to get lost"*
Imagines he refuses to do it, and tells her to get lost	If I do that she will tell me I'm bad. (O-S) I will "feel" (experience myself) as a bad person (S-S). That would be awful I *must* avoid that. I *must* do as she bids. I couldn't stand that	Anxiety Does as he is bid
Goes and fetches her a cup of tea	By carrying out her order I am allowing myself to be treated like a worthless shit. That's what I am (S-S).This is awful I *mustn't* do this (because it makes me worthless). I *must* do it (because it would otherwise make me bad). I am trapped	Depression Paralysis?

In this example, the first episode (discussed above) reveals the existential imperative, the thwarting of the self and the anger and aggressive impulse that results. However, this episode is already a complex episode, in that Mum (on David's report) is not just indifferent but is actually using the moral imperative to thwart David's existential needs, and even to coerce him into constructing an alien self. The second episode (also discussed earlier) reveals the moral imperative, the inhibition of the self by anxiety and avoidance, and was extensively analysed earlier. In the third sequence the two imperatives come together again, two musts which demand opposite actions: one not to act compliantly (and therefore fulfil the existential imperative and against the moral imperative), the other to do the reverse. Often the client will act compliantly, and therefore repress his existential needs, but become depressed and withdrawn and lose motivation.

The therapist will have preferably already have prepared the ground in the way suggested in the last two subsections, by helping the client to identify, challenge and replace the moral imperative and existential imperative beliefs. If successful, this will have toned down the two musts and the associated devaluing beliefs, and enabled the client to choose between preferences. Now the therapist can bring the whole formulation together for the client so that he can more easily see the choices he can make. The choice the therapist will encourage the client to make at this point will be to pursue his existential needs, to assert himself but to moderate his self-presentations to accommodate the needs of others.

When one or the other imperatives predominate it is reasonable that therapist and client agree to work on that one. However, when both are salient, then the therapist should attempt to work on both in parallel as far as is practicable, since otherwise there may develop an imbalance between the two.

We pointed out at the beginning of this chapter that most people reach a workable balance between their existential needs and their duty to others, and this is a goal of therapy. There is a danger that, working on the moral and not the existential imperative may disturb the balance in a potentially dangerous way. The problem may arise that the existential imperative, untempered by a moral sense of responsibility for the other's needs, may result in unbridled anger and aggression with at least the oppressive consequences that we saw in a minority of clients in Section Three.

APPLYING THE METHOD TO OVERT SYMPTOMS OF PSYCHOSIS

In this chapter our examples of moral and existential imperative blocks are common, everyday conflicts which can happen in many families, not just where there is a problem of psychosis. Nonetheless these examples were taken from our cases, and were real conflicts involving clients with psychoses. In Sections Two and Three we discussed how we think these conflicts can lead to self-construction blocks and in turn to symptoms of psychosis. However, our method can sometimes be directly applied to symptoms. For example, clients can have conflicts with their voices in much the same way that they have with significant others in their lives. For example, voices often command clients to behave in certain ways, and clients can be highly anxious about resisting such commands for fear of being criticised and labelled as bad, with the consequence that clients will at least do something to appease the voice or even carry out the command. Such interactions as these can be analysed using the ABC format and construed in terms of the moral imperative. In addition to voices, our method can be applied to delusions. For example in one type of paranoia the client believes others are conspiring to harm him because of something bad he has done and he believes he deserves to be punished. Here the person may be seeing himself through the eyes of others as totally bad, and by behaving in an avoidant and fearful way, goes from a "bad me" image to a "bad me" construction.

In the next chapter we describe a range of less technical but practical, self-help methods for symptoms and problems specific to psychosis.

EXPLORING THE METHOD WITH THE STIGMA OF MENTAL ILLNESS

The moral imperative principle may be applied when the client is depressed by the stigma of mental illness, which often happens after discharge and "insight" returns (Birchwood et al., 2000a). It is particularly appropriate when the client equates a compulsory hospitalisation with punishment for being bad in some way, and may be extremely anxious about being hospitalised again. This can be an entrapping situation of the moral-existential imperative conflict type, where the client is fearful of asserting himself and instead conforms to a restrictive regime designed by the mental-health services, but does so feeling depressed and defeated. This path can lead, we believe, to social withdrawal and negative symptoms. The path we recommend is to unblock the person's existential drive and to provide services which facilitate the pursuit of an authentic self.

CHAPTER 17

OVERCOMING SYMPTOMS

In this chapter we suggest practical, self-help ways for a troubled person to deal with the actual experiences of psychosis, as sometimes these can get in the way of them helping themselves at the interpersonal and relationships level. We describe a number of techniques which can help people overcome any entrapments (particularly from voices) which can block their development and recovery.

GETTING THE RIGHT AMOUNT OF SPACE

A useful way to think about the two threats to self-construction (insecurity and alienation) is to view them representing the ends of a continuum (as in Figure 17.1). Threats to self are extreme versions of common, everyday experiences, and modulating our own position on this continuum is something we all do all of the time (for example, balancing our levels of exhaustion against our need for stimulation). If we are too overwhelmed by work, we have a quiet night in, or perhaps arrange a holiday. If we are bored or lonely, we phone some friends and arrange a night out. All of us have an equilibrium that we are constantly attending to (as best we can, given the pressure of work and family commitments).

Throughout this book, we have proposed that people with a psychosis have difficulty keeping their equilibrium, and modulating their own levels of arousal. We have proposed that they have experiences at the extreme ends of the continuum in Figure 17.1: some not only feel overwhelmed, they feel imposed upon and alienated absolutely from their lives, even their own bodies. Others feel so isolated that they have a need to invent people to relate to who aren't really there. It would seem that people with a psychosis need help moving back to the comfortable zone circled at the middle of Figure 17.1. Where people with a psychosis are overwhelmed and alienated, they might like help to get some space, to get attention off themselves and onto others, and particularly to get respite from the onslaught that voices can often represent. At the start of this chapter, we focus on ways they can do that. Where they are

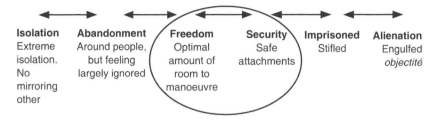

Figure 17.1 Illustration of How All of Us Modulate our own Arousal to Keep an Equilibrium, and How this Process can go to Extremes in Psychosis
We thank our colleague Carol Shillito-Clarke for helping us develop this model

extremely isolated, we look at ways they can lessen their isolation, and therefore lessen the need for voice-relationships and what might be seen as a delusional need for others to be interested in them. We particularly focus on the need to build peer relationships and to reintegrate people back into meaningful peer-interactionary roles.

WHY DO VOICES COME ABOUT?

In previous chapters, we suggested many voices come about for either isolation or alienation reasons; we also argued that although some start because of isolation reasons, many still end up as alienating. How can voices start as a result of isolation? From the point of view of the voice-hearer, voices are a kind of bodiless people. In the same way that people seek out others for security and to feel valued, so people who have had a psychosis can seek out voices for much the same reason. When feeling lonely and empty they can "court" their voices, and have conversations with them. Psychologists Paul Chadwick and Max Birchwood (1994) showed that, just like some people, some voices are benevolent and respond positively to the client. However sometimes they are (or turn over time) quite nasty and become "malevolent". Then they criticise the person, give them dangerous commands or misleading advice, and can, in the end, seem to become completely engulfing. In other words, like people, voices can make the voice-hearer feel, on the positive side, valued, but on the negative side either inherently bad or worthless and empty. Having arisen because of self-construction threats and needs, they go on to present significant threats to self-construction themselves.

With the origin of these kinds of voices in mind, it might seem problematic to work to reduce contact with voices which come about from isolation – after all, if the voices reflect a need to have somebody to relate to, stopping the person relating to one voice will probably lead to another voice or reference-experience starting. Better solutions would be to increase the amount of social contact, particularly peer contact, and this is discussed later in the chapter. However, as we mentioned in the previous paragraph, sometimes voices which start for good reasons get out of hand, and end up absorbing the person's attention in a negative way – opportunities for rewarding interaction in the real world may be hindered because these emergency psychological measures are still in place.

Whatever their origins, voices often become very intrusive and upsetting. For example, some of the most common voices are "commentators", which make wry and often hurtful comments about everything the person does. Such voices can be incredibly alienating, and it can seem like there is nowhere to hide from them. One of the things people who hear them say most often to professionals is "Can I make them stop/go away?"

Relief from Alienation: Are Voices Bodiless People?

People who hear voices usually try to make sense of the experience and have hypotheses about the voice's identity. For example, people often feel they have a good idea whose voice it is, and what that person's motives are. Voices often seem to know a lot about the voice-hearer, and this can make people feel sure that the voice knows everything there is to know about everything – after all, the voice seems to know everything that they know (it is often useful to prompt them to think if there are any other reasons why this might be the case, i.e. the voice comes from them). The way voices know everything can often make people think their voices must be really powerful, and people can be quite scared of them. Sometimes, voices appear to dislike being talked or thought about, and issue threats against the hearer; this is important to bear in mind if someone is trying to engage the person in therapeutic contact (Chadwick, Birchwood & Trower, 1996).

Benevolent voices appear to just offer support and help, perhaps being secretly on the hearer's side against other people. Malevolent voices seem to criticise the hearer all the time. Malevolent voices say things which shock or hurt the voice-hearer, and perhaps want to get the voice-hearer into trouble. Voice-hearers wonder how much control voices have over them; as we mentioned some voices threaten all sorts of dire consequences for disobedience, and listeners can feel compelled to be controlled by them. For many it can feel like a constant battle between them and their voices, and understandably they feel exhausted and depressed a lot of the time. What is encouraging is that many people spend large amounts of their time successfully resisting what their voices want them to do, which gives a glimpse of the strengths the person actually has. Many of the following coping strategies come from sources such as Tarrier et al. (1988) and Chadwick, Birchwood and Trower (1996).

CAN VOICES BE CONTROLLED?

A good first step is for voice-hearers to have a think about when and where voices are at their worst. People generally vary as to when their voices are worst. For example, many people hear voices mostly at night when they are trying to get to sleep. Others hear them when they are on their own, others when they are with people. For some, the voices they hear are worst first thing in the morning, for others when watching TV at night. Often, people who hear voices haven't really thought too closely about which situations trigger voices most, and they can find it surprising that there are clear patterns in voice-activity.

Once someone has realised that some situations trigger voices more than others, the next step is to try to manipulate situations to see if voices can be made more or less frequent. For example, if someone always heard voices when they are on their own, that person could seek out some company, perhaps a parent or a friend, and see if this makes the voices come on less. If altering the situation varies the occurrence of the voice, this might be the first indication that the voice-hearer does actually have some control over the voice.

Having found patterns in when voices appear, the next step is to try to alter the way the voice-hearer responds, to see if this can have any effect.

RESTRICTING TIME GIVEN TO VOICES

If the voice-hearer responds by engaging their voice(s), they usually find that voices have an insatiable appetite for time. A listener can be engaged for hours and hours, if they allow their voices to engage them. A better response might be to set aside a time when the voice-hearer will listen to the voices, otherwise to ignore them, or distract themselves from them. For example, voices could be "granted" five minutes every morning when they will be listened to properly, and the rest of the time they will not be engaged with (although not consciously avoided, as that can make voices occur more frequently, as we shall see later). A person who decides to ignore the voice in this way, rather than talk back to them, and get involved in a debate with them, will often find this helps decrease voice activity.

SWITCHING ATTENTION

Ignoring voices sounds easy, but can actually be quite difficult. People who hear voices might find it easier to ignore if they deliberately change the focus of their attention to something else such as a book or magazine or TV. With an effort of will, some people can force themselves to think about this new topic, and let the voice natter on in the background. In this situation, it is important that they don't interact with the voice, perhaps by answering it back, or thinking about what the voice appears to be saying. The idea is to not listen to the voice at all. This is hard at first, but gets easier with practice.

A more systematic method of attention training entails the person:

- learning to listen alternately to three different sounds in the room rather than the voice, e.g. a clock ticking, a radio etc

- then, the person learns to pay attention to three distant sounds, e.g. traffic, wind etc

- then they learn to switch with increasing rapidity from one sound to another

Finally, and after some training, the person tries to be aware of all the sounds simultaneously (Wells, 2000).

Another approach that some people prefer is for the hearer to try to empty their mind completely. Again, this means not interacting with the voice, not answering them back. Some people feel it is possible to mentally "turn down the volume" of the voice or voices. This way they can slowly reduce the noise from the voice until it is just a dull murmur in the background, or perhaps even not there at all. A similar technique called "mindfulness meditation" involves the person being trained in a number of systematic steps to be able to focus their minds, such as allowing disturbing thoughts to enter and exit from their minds, and to float through their minds, without emotionally engaging with them (Segal, Williams & Teasdale, 2002) – just "watch" them float through!

DON'T FEAR THE VOICES

Experts disagree whether it is best to try to consciously stop thoughts, and also voices. It does seem that one of the strange things about the way our minds work is that if we try to consciously suppress a thought, it actually comes back stronger and more intrusive. (Perhaps you may want to try this to prove it to yourself – pick a thought and try as hard as you can not to think it! Do you find it comes back stronger?) For this reason we are not suggesting that people concentrate on trying to actively stop their thoughts or voices. We are suggesting that they try not to engage them and to direct their attention elsewhere, leaving their voices to carry on without being listened to. It is likely that each person needs to experiment with distraction for themselves, to see whether distraction works for them or not and whether avoidance makes things worse or not. For example, it might be that distraction is a useful technique in the short term (for example, if there is a situation that the person really wants to be able to concentrate on), but as a longer-term strategy it might be counter-productive.

PHYSICAL DISTRACTION

The options above can need quite an effort of will. Sometimes, attending to something else can be helped by physically disrupting the ability to listen to voices. For example, talking over the voices can be useful, as can speaking or perhaps singing to themselves just under their breath. Others have found that using a walkman or putting music on in the background can help, or wearing earplugs.

INCREASING ACTIVITY LEVELS

Alternatively, physical distraction can be taken to the next stage, and the voice-hearer can get involved in something more active such as jogging, playing football or swimming. This can be useful not only as a distraction technique, but also to change mood. It is more difficult for a person to listen to voices when they are so occupied, and these activities will often make people feel better anyway. Similarly, if voices are quieter when the hearer is in the company of other people, it might be a good idea for them to actively seek out other people when the voices are hard to bear.

MOOD CHANGING

Some voice-hearing can be improved by ignoring them or by the person who hears them trying to distract themselves. For other people, voices may be linked to the mood they are in. They might get more critical voices when they are feeling worse about themselves. They might hear fewer voices, or perhaps also hear positive voices when they are feeling good about themselves. If this is the case, a useful strategy for them might be to do something which will change their mood, typically by doing something nice they enjoy such as having a bath, going for a walk somewhere quiet or watching something funny on TV (presuming they feel OK to watch TV).

SELF-ESTEEM BUILDING AND POSITIVE
SELF-STATEMENTS

A good way for a person to lift their mood is to tell themselves realistically good things that they believe about themselves, for example, reassuring that they are OK, and have done their best. This might be especially important when voices might be giving them a different message. For example, when a voice says "You're no good", the client can use a realistically positive retort, such as "Everybody's fallible; so what?". Finding positive statements that feel convincing may take some practice, but they are useful because these statements can really make them feel better about themselves and make the hurtful things voices say seem less upsetting (and may also make voices less active). Self-esteem can be started by making lists of all the good things about themselves, for example, things they have done well, the people who like them, all the things they don't get wrong in a day. People who don't have many items in their positive list can be asked what sorts of things they could realistically do which might be worthy of going in that positive list (these should be short term, achievable things rather than the long-term things that people with a psychosis often beat themselves up for already, such as not having a job or a relationship.) It might be useful for them to consider what other people do to count themselves as worthwhile – would this be enough for them? Often, people discount things about themselves that others would be proud of – they discount past achievements or convince themselves that people who like them actually don't really like them, or just don't count. Voice-hearers might want to write a few of these types of statement down and display them in prominent places around the house (depending how they feel about other people seeing this sort of thing). For example, "I am a good person who deserves good things" or "I don't have to listen to these voices" could be displayed on the bedroom cabinet.

GETTING SOME SPACE: MORE RELIEF FROM ALIENATION

Some of the worst alienation experiences come from voices, and so we have looked first at how to work with voices to feel better about life. Other alienation experiences seem to work in relation to real people, and we look next at how to alter the parameters of interactions so as to make them more comfortable. Finally, we look at techniques that many people use that help them relax, and to find a bit of mental space, before going on to look at ways to combat the other extreme in Figure 17.1, isolation.

CONTROLLING THE PARAMETERS OF INTERACTIONS

In Chapter 13, people prone to alienation and engulfing experiences seemed to hold strong beliefs about how they *ought* to relate to other people, and also to their voices; often these rules seemed to be quite demanding, and weighted heavily against that person, resulting in them feeling alienated.

For example, it wasn't unusual for a client to feel they had no right to defend themselves even if they felt the other person was putting them down, because they obeyed rules such as, "I shouldn't answer back to my parent, I should be respectful", or made assumptions like "Other people know everything, I don't know anything" or "Others have rights/I have no rights". These cognitions appeared to leave them feeling powerless and defenceless; in the absence of them being able to verbalise a more favourable perspective, they had to remain constructed by the other in a particularly bad light. If they also hold rules about having to stay and listen while other people go on about their mistakes or duties, they not only can't disagree, but have to sit and endure the point being hammered home to them over and over. In this situation, rules about the syntax of the situation work to entrap them, namely "I must sit and listen if that's what they want". In these situations, a first goal might be to assert their right to politely leave the situation. For example, they might want to retreat to their room, perhaps, or just change the subject/stop talking to the other person. They might also be surprised how the other person does not take the offence they imagined they would at this. Alternatively, they may need help to cope with negative or critical responses such as being accused of being ill-mannered by "walking out"; coping with such a response is something that many people with a psychosis find very difficult and cognitive therapy may be used to help here.

Prompts might follow the lines of:

- Why is it so awful to change the subject? Would you be offended if they wanted to talk about something else?

- Do you have a right to an opinion about whether you want to carry on this conversation or not? If they think you are rude, do you agree that you are rude? Would anybody disagree with them? Does this one disagreement cancel out all the positive interactions you have had with this person?

- How long do you think it will take for them to get used to the idea that you are allowed to end conversations when you want to?

For some people with a psychosis, being able to leave situations might be the first step to feeling able to hold different opinions and ideas to others; in other words throwing off the alien self they feel is imposed on them by the other. Once they are used to the amount of being "different to the other" entailed in taking control of the situation enough to end it, they might like to work on holding other different opinions and perhaps even having disagreements with others. It would probably be best to start this process on some topic which is not too emotional for either party, just some abstract topic on which they can have an eccentric but harmless position. Being able to tolerate the discomfort that this brings about may be the first step to being able to tolerate difference on more important issues, and hence gaining the right to some psychological independence. At the point where they feel up to holding different opinions on some more substantial topics, they might like to be reminded of some of the typical issues that people argue with their parents about, and which represent classic independence issues. Good examples are: times of coming or goings, tidiness of room/flat, lifestyle choices, self-care such as food-shopping and cooking, hygiene, washing clothes, buying things for self like CDs or clothes, choice of friends or romantic partners. These are issues on which many people argue with their families, and eventually get a lot of control over and independence through.

People who are not used to having a stance of their own on these issues may find the process of being different a very guilty experience, the result of an overdeveloped sense of the moral imperative! It is important that they learn to live with any guilt, and keep telling themselves that they are not hurting anyone by wanting control over their own life, and that difference on these one or two issues does not mean rejection of the other person as a whole, both past and future. The de-idealisation exercises in Chapter 15 should help them feel that the person/people they want psychological space from are not perfect or ideal; in fact they are just human (perhaps lovably so). They might also worry that there will be catastrophic consequences for wanting such independence, such as being thrown out of the house; it may be important to address how realistic and likely these predictions are. Contact with a supportive peer who can validate a viewpoint that is different to the parent's might be important here. To get control over these parameters while being able to deal with any guilt and fear of catastrophe would be a great step towards throwing off any alien self, throwing off the feeling that parts of their life are imposed on them by others.

RELAXATION

Many people with a psychosis can feel very overwhelmed by events, and find it hard to relax; they constantly feel stressed out. Learning to relax is a useful skill; it means that one can at least feel less exhausted. Figure 17.2 provides a guided imagery story that might help here. Part of the story involves imagining a world whose guiding principle is that "everything goes right for them; everything goes as they want it". In essence, it is a world where the existential imperative can run riot, people can get *all* their existential needs met. Here they can imagine themselves to be as accomplished, as rich, as popular as they want, unfettered by excessive moral imperative concerns. They also don't have to worry about their attachment needs being met, because in this perfect world people respond as they want them to. If they feel that sharing the details of this positive

Figure 17.2   Guided Imagery: Positive Place

Imagine you are walking in the countryside on a nice day, on your own. You can feel the sun shining on you, feel the breeze and smell the flowers by the side of the path. You can see mountains ahead of you. You walk on for a bit, enjoying the scenery and the sensations, the subtle noises of the birds, and the feel of the path beneath your feet. By and by, the path begins to turn upwards, and you climb upwards with it, getting a little bit higher. You get to an area where there are fewer trees, and the air is a little bit colder, perhaps with the hint of snow in it. You turn around and look behind you, where you have come from: you can see the path leading down into the valley, and you can just make out people down there, looking very small, like ants. Where you are is really peaceful and you can still hear birds singing and bees humming.

You continue up the path, and it starts to get a bit colder still, although not unpleasantly cold. The first sign of snow appears on the ground, and you realise you are above the snowline now. You carry on. Finally you get to a huge secluded field, covered in snow. The snow has not been touched at all, apparently not for weeks. You feel sure you are in a place that really is safe and secret. You wade through the snow to the other side of the field, making little footprints. When you get to the other side, you feel sure you can find your way back.

At the other side of the field is a little mountain lake, with a path around it. You walk along the path a little way, admiring the colour of the water. At one point there is a wall between the path and the lake, and you realise that you can get to the other side of the wall if you climb down the banks of the lake a bit. There's a little ledge where you can sit behind the wall, perfectly safe. You climb down, and edge along the wall until you can't see the path – and anyone on the path couldn't see you (not that there's anyone on the path). It is a nice place to sit and watch the lake, think your thoughts. Just as you sit down, you realise there's a little door in the back of the wall, and feeling brave, you test it to see if it is open. It is! You go in. Inside it is like a little cave, still full of light, even though it would appear to be underneath the path at the side of the lake. There's fine sand on the floor. At the other end of this rather well-lit cave, there's another door – and this one has your name on it. You open it!

Inside you find a room that is everything you want it to be. It can have any decoration you want it to have. It has as many gadgets and gizmos as you want – any stereo, TV, collection of videos, CDs, computer games. There's a beautiful view out of the window of whatever you want to look at. It can have whatever furniture, whatever decoration you want. It can have whatever books you want (a massive library, perhaps). The room can be for just you on your own, or it can have other people in, anyone, or animals or anything. Nobody else need ever see this room, or ever have an opinion about it. You don't ever have to discuss it with anyone. It is just full of whatever you want it to be full of, and its content can change as you feel like it, so it can be full of different things or have different colour schemes as you see fit at any moment. This is your special room and the more detail you can notice about it the better. What do you notice about the room? What does it smell like? How warm or cold is it? What noises can you hear? How does it feel?

You can stay in the room for as long as you want. When you feel like it, you can leave the room, and lock it with a special key you've found in the room. You also take with you a special device that lets you and only you return to your room instantly whenever you feel like it, without the effort of climbing up to it. You move out through the cave, out by the lake, up the banks, along the path, and across the snow-field back to the path. From there you make your way home. You can go back to your special room whenever you want.

world for them would compromise it in some way – perhaps they might feel others disapprove of what they want there, or that their positive world is not as good as someone else's, or how someone else might expect their positive world to be, then it is better that they do not share or discuss this world. It is important this positive world is there solely for there own needs, not any alien needs imposed on them. Building themselves a scenario where things turn out right is useful for a group of people who often can't even conceive of things going well for them.

It must be said though that building oneself a little positive mental space is only a security zone to fall back on. This "positive world" is no substitute for the real world and the real and tangible rewards the real world can bring. In the next section we look at ways to help very isolated people build a social network, to ease themselves back into more frequent social interactions, particularly with peers.

EASING BACK INTO SOCIAL INTERACTIONS

> You can hold yourself back from the suffering in this world; that is your right, and you are amply allowed to do so. But perhaps this holding back is the only suffering you have the power to do something about. (Franz Kafka, 1931)

As extreme isolation appears to play an important part in bringing about psychotic problems, part of recovery is going to be getting used to being around people on a regular basis again. As the quote from Kafka illustrates, the misery of isolation may be worse in the long term than the pain of having to reintegrate socially. An increasingly important part of proper rehabilitation is the work placement or some sort of scheme that involves greatly improving the amount of social contact people have (Davidson *et al.*, 2000; Mueser, Salyers & Mueser, 2001). However, people who have had a psychosis who are used to being on their own a lot may find it overwhelming to go straight back into environments where they have to meet a lot of new people. New audiences represent one of the toughest tasks in self-construction, because the person can't be sure how people will react to them. What advice can be given to people who are feeling quite socially phobic as they start to go back into more frequent social interactions?

It would seem to be important for them to maintain their own equilibrium where possible. This might mean taking more time away from the new situation at first, so they can ease themselves in as gently as possible. A work placement scheme which gradually increases the amount of time they spend on placement from perhaps two days to a week initially to three or four later on, may have a better chance of succeeding into a long-term, five-day week placement.

The converse of this is that the more experience they have of the people they work with, the quicker they will get to know them, get to know their traits, characters, habits and foibles. The sooner they feel they understand their workmates, the easier they will find it to fit in with them and to cope with the job. Perhaps they can remember another situation where they started not knowing anyone and eventually made friends, for example, at school. The logic of this means that they should push themselves quite hard to spend more rather than less time with their new workmates (without overdoing it and making themselves feel so overwhelmed that they can't cope and perhaps even become unwell).

It might be useful if they can find one person at the placement who they can feel particularly close to and supported by. This mentor may help ease the difficulty of starting a new placement. It is also useful to bear in mind that the first few weeks of any new job are nearly always the most difficult, for anyone; but after a few weeks we do get to know people, and start to get familiar with them. It is useful to be aware that everyone finds new jobs uncomfortable and difficult at first and this difficulty does not mean they are mad or different. Things will get easier.

People starting a work-placement scheme may need reassuring that their new colleagues are not excessively interested in them, nor will they be overly critical of them; chances are their new colleagues will barely notice them! In a work situation people are often too busy to spend much time thinking about newcomers, or even make time to chat to new people; this does not mean they have been offended, or don't like the newcomer – just that they are probably just busy with their own work. Alternatively, if work colleagues do appear to have a negative attitude towards them, it might help them to be reminded that these people do not really know them and are therefore in no position to judge. It might be useful to remind someone who has a history of feeling that people do not like them that they might often jump to conclusions and should perhaps suspend these judgements for a while, until they have firmer evidence.

It may also be useful to remind them of the benefits of having a job, such as money and status; how their job will make them feel in terms of self-image, and how they will feel others will regard them.

ORIGINAL EVIDENCE FOR BELIEFS

When people get really isolated, they can develop some ideas which other people might see as unusual. It has been shown that people with a psychosis have a style of "jumping to conclusions" in ambiguous situations (Garety & Freeman, 1999; Rector & Beck, 2002). This phenomenon, we suggested earlier, could be a consequence of, or at least exacerbated by, the state of *objectité*, since this state can cause such severe disruption to normal objective processing. Clients sometimes come to see as gospel truth something that may not be quite so clear-cut. In these instances, if they hold beliefs which they acknowledge other people may find unusual, it might be useful for them to revisit the original situation where they first made decisions behind those beliefs. They might find that, with the benefit of time, there are alternative ways of looking at the situations.

For example: Bob had been very hurt when he tried to ring a friend and instead got a voice he didn't recognise telling him he had got the wrong number. Bob felt sure that his friend had asked someone else to answer the phone to pretend it was a wrong number, because he felt his friends hated him. With a bit of reflection, Bob began to wonder whether he hadn't in fact actually got a wrong number, and that he had just misinterpreted his original "evidence" that his friends hated him.

Similarly, Phil had decided people in his neighbourhood were watching him, because there always seemed to be a couple of cars in the road near his house that he could see from his bedroom window. With a bit of reflection, Phil realised that the space where they parked was in fact right by the entrance for a large field where people used to come to walk their dogs – hence they weren't watching Phil at all. Phil also felt people in cars passing him on the street where watching him, because they seemed to keep looking at him. After chatting about this, he realised that they were looking at him because he was staring at them! He was so worried they were looking at him, that he himself appeared to take an excessive interest in them, so naturally, they looked back!

It can take a lot for a person with a psychosis to re-examine some of the most upsetting moments in their life, to see if there is a more positive interpretation of events. Their negative interpretations are often primed by emotional reasons, such as the existential and moral imperatives, and thus they project interpretations that fit with how they feel about themselves.

BEHAVIOURAL TESTS

Sometimes, people are unsure whether their interpretation of things is accurate, and in these situations it can be useful for them to think of ways in which they can test their ideas.

For example: Alisha felt sure the TV could predict the future and was actually giving her messages about what was going to happen. She decided to test whether this was actually true by writing down the TV's predictions, as she understood them at the time. A few days later she returned to the predictions to see how many of them had come true. Much to her surprise, she began to feel less convinced that TV could accurately predict things.

RELAPSE PREVENTION AND PLANNING

Having a period of being unwell (feeling more psychotic) is often upsetting and frightening for people with a psychosis. There is also evidence that each time a person becomes unwell, their chances of being unwell in the future increase slightly (Birchwood, McGorry & Jackson, 1997); it is better for people to spend as little time frankly unwell as possible. Many find it difficult to know when they are getting unwell until after the event, and because of this are too late to take preventative steps such as taking some time out to relax, being with family/friends or talking to their community nurse. In this situation it can be useful for people to take time out to look at how they feel when they start to become unwell, and also to plan what to do if they do get unwell. Most people with a psychosis have their own "relapse signature", their own idiosyncratic signs which first indicate they are losing it. For some this may be becoming more withdrawn, feeling more like everyone is out to get them. For others, it may be feeling very manic, and having far too much energy for everything, perhaps taking more risks than normal. There are lists of such "early signs" which people can use. Typically, a person would fill in such a list every week, and see how their score is doing. If their score increases, this suggests they may need to take action to stop themselves becoming more unwell. This action can be planned in advance and tailored to that person's individual needs: some people may want to talk to their community nurse for advice or support, others may want to get friends or family involved, or again perhaps want to talk to their psychiatrist about getting their medication altered. Having a detailed plan about what to do when they are becoming unwell helps many people feel less panicky about the situation, and worry less about it happening.

LOW-POINTS

When unpleasant experiences happen, such as being sectioned, people often have a point at which things seemed unbearably bad, as if nothing could ever be the same again (Grey, Holmes & Brewin, 2001). Memories of these "oh shit" moments can be particularly vivid and upsetting.

For example: Rawle related how he was held down by four staff members and forcibly injected with medication. For him, this was the ultimate humiliation from which he could never recover or be forgiven. In self-construction terms, these "hotspots" seem to be interpreted as being so bad that they will always taint any future self-constructions. These moments seem inescapable, and seem to cancel out good things from before them.

If people can go over these experiences in their minds, they can re-evaluate things in the calm light of day, and see whether things really were as bad as they thought at that time. Rawle managed to reassess his being injected as something he could put behind him: unfortunate but not a judgement on his character as a whole or his ability to have friends or be a worthwhile person. Often, in times of crisis like this, people can't quite take everything in, and there may be value in going back and trying to remember exactly what happened.

SAFETY-SEEKING BEHAVIOURS

Many people with a psychosis become slightly superstitious, in that they develop rituals that are designed to stop bad things from happening (Morrison, 2001). For example, Gary had a few favourite mental sayings that he would repeat to himself in his mind when he felt threatened by something; Laetitia had a habit of hiding in her room when anything might possibly go wrong. These safety-seeking behaviours can be useful because they make people feel reassured that something horrible isn't going to happen. Unfortunately, they also convince people that they need to take these preventative steps to avert a catastrophe. Sometimes the person can feel addicted to their safety routine, and they feel they have to complete their routine to feel safe, even though there is no real threat. Because they never try to cope without their safety routine, they never test whether they need the routine or not. Safety-seeking behaviours can trap people into fears they don't need to be scared of. The way around this is for them to cut back on the safety-seeking behaviour as much as they dare at a time, perhaps just reciting half their mental rituals or spending half as much time in their room. Cutting back gradually in a way they feel comfortable with is a good controlled way for them to check whether they really need the ritual or not. (They themselves have to feel in control of this process, as it will not work if someone else forces them to do it.)

CONCLUSION

There are lots of coping strategies and therapeutic ideas that can help with some of the more upsetting psychotic experiences. Some of these are simply aimed at showing the person they can get some control over the symptom, such as some of the techniques regarding voices. Others are aimed at some of the fundamental beliefs about themselves and others, such as self-esteem and key events in the past. These strategies can be used to take the pressure off people who are suffering particularly strong psychotic symptoms, freeing them up to look at some of the life issues mentioned in Chapters 15 and 16.

SECTION SUMMARY

This section has offered a number of "therapeutic ideas", some practical ideas for people themselves and their relatives (Chapters 15 and 17) and some mainly for therapists working one to one with people with or recovering from psychosis (Chapter 16). These have included:

- Techniques to help people move from an internal to external focus, and in the process restart a developmental process involving de-idealising parents and differentiating themselves from others. These techniques should foster a greater understanding of others, as a key part of psychological development.

- Ways of de-idealising peers and potential romantic partners.

- Ways of overcoming beliefs that may have blocked this process previously, such as an overactive sense of duty that might come from the moral imperative.

- Ideas designed to temper unbearably pressing beliefs about needing recognition (i.e. existential imperative).

- Ways of freeing the client from entrapment within moral-existential imperative conflicts.

- Techniques to help people keep their equilibrium between experiences of being overwhelmed and alienated. For example, to help them assert their rights to be different and to withdraw when they need to.

- Strategies that can help reduce the activity and impact of voices, and techniques aimed at raising self-esteem.

- Ways of reassessing the origins and situations that might have contributed to the original formation of key beliefs, especially if there is a chance the person may have "jumped to conclusions" on limited and inaccurate evidence.

- Strategies aimed at monitoring well-being objectively and helping people to know when to seek help.

- Advice on how to re-establish regular contact with others, so as to have the opportunities for self-construction that such interactions bring.

CONCLUDING REMARKS

We have put forward a cognitive-developmental account of psychosis at late adolescence; we hope that this account will encourage those that have the condition to be optimistic about their ability to live and work with it. A developmental psychological account is also compatible with the most recent biological accounts (e.g. Feinberg, 1997; Keshavan & Hogarty, 1999) which see any biological differences between psychotic and non-psychotic people as arriving at the time of late adolescence; this convergence of perspectives is virtually unprecedented in many decades of competing biological and psychological research. Our developmental approach seems to us to herald the return of "the person" into psychological models, with consideration of self-construction issues being long overdue in this area.

A cognitive-developmental model should engender optimism because it would seem to indicate (and we would like to think) that the problem of psychosis is not intractable as it may have seemed to be. Perhaps this optimistic note is the best note on which to end this book!

APPENDIX 1

THE SELF AND OTHER SCALE

The Self and Other Scale is designed to show the extent to which a person might be vulnerable to the two types of threat to self-construction that we discussed in Section Two, Chapters 9 and 10. The first seven questions measure a person's anxiety about other people who are important to them being indifferent and excluding them. The remaining seven questions measure a person's anxiety about other people being over-intrusive and taking control. In Section Four of the book we discuss what can be done about such vulnerabilities.

The scale has been scientifically evaluated and is acceptably psychometrically robust, as reported in two articles (Dagnan, Trower and Gilbert, 2002; Dexter-Smith, Trower, Oyebode & Dagnan, in press).

If you would like to fill in the scale, we suggest the following steps:

- First read and think about each statement carefully.
- Second circle the appropriate number that indicates how *frequently* you have these thoughts.
- Third, tick the number that represents how strongly you agree or disagree with (i.e. *endorse*) the statement.
- Fourth, add up the total for each subscale, and divide by seven (the number of items) to get the mean score).

Frequency Score:

1 = almost never; 2 = rarely; 3 = sometimes; 4 = often; 5 = very often

Endorsement Score:

1 = strongly disagree; 2 = slightly disagree; 3 = unsure; 4 = slightly agree; 5 = strongly agree

Insecurity Items	
1. Having a secure relationship helps me feel I exist.	1 2 3 4 5
2. When I am alone I feel the need to contact someone.	1 2 3 4 5
3. I have to be close to someone to have a sense of who I am.	1 2 3 4 5
4. I am nothing without certain special other people.	1 2 3 4 5
5. Sometimes when I am alone I have a strong feeling I am not real.	1 2 3 4 5
6. If I am not getting the right attention it's like I am not there.	1 2 3 4 5
7. Special people are vital to my sense of being a person.	1 2 3 4 5
Alienation Items	
8. I dread being under someone else's control.	1 2 3 4 5
9. I have to get away from other people in order to have a sense of who I am.	1 2 3 4 5
10. If I am getting too much attention it can feel like I am being taken over.	1 2 3 4 5
11. I would hate certain people to know the real me.	1 2 3 4 5
12. Often I wish people would give me space to be myself.	1 2 3 4 5
13. Sometimes I only feel like me when I am on my own.	1 2 3 4 5
14. I can feel suffocated if I am too close to someone.	1 2 3 4 5

Reproduced with permission from *Journal of Rational-Emotive and Cognitive-Behavior Therapy* ©Kluwer Academic/Plenum Publishers.

You may be interested to compare your score with others. We have one set of norms for Birmingham University students aged between 18 and 21. For the frequency version of the scale the insecurity sub-scale had a mean score of 20.1 (SD = 5.2) and the alienation sub-scale had a mean score of 19.7 (SD = 5.4). For the endorsement version the insecurity sub-scale had a mean score of 17.5 (SD =5.1) and the alienation sub-scale had a mean score of 19.9 (SD = 5.8). We obtained a set of norms for a much wider age range (16 to 75) but only for the frequency version of the scale. These norms were: insecurity sub-scale 16.9 (SD 5.6) and alienation subscale 19.0, SD 5.1).

REFERENCES

Akbarian, S., Kim, J.J., Potkin, S.G., Hagman, J.O., Tafazzoli, A., Bunney, W.E. & Jones, E.G. (1995). Gene expression for glutamic acid decarboxylase is reduced without loss of neurons in prefrontal cortex of schizophrenics. *Archives of General Psychiatry* **52**, 258–266.

Akbarian, S., Vinuela, A., Kim, J.J., Potkin, S.G., Bunney, W.E. & Jones, E.G. (1993). Distorted distibution of nicotinamide-adenine dinucleotide phosphate-diphorase neurons in temporal lobe of schizophrenics implies anomalous cortical development. *Archives of General Psychiatry* **50**, 178–187.

Altorfer, A., Goldstein, M.J., Miklowitz, D.J. & Neuterlein, K.H. (1992). Stress-indicative patterns of nonverbal behaviour – their role in family-interaction. *British Journal of Psychiatry* **161** (s18), 103–113.

American Psychiatric Association (1994). *Diagnostic and statistical manual of mental disorders: DSM-IV – 4th ed.* Washington DC: American Psychiatric Association.

Arkowitz, H., Hinton, R., Perl, J. & Himadi, W. (1978). Treatment strategies for dating anxiety in college men based on real-life practice. *Counselling Psychologist* **7**, 41–46.

Asken, M.J., Schwartz, R.C. (1998). Heading the ball in soccer: what's the risk of brain injury? *The Physician and Sports Medicine* **26** (11), 100–103.

Baker, C. & Morrison, A.P. (1998). Metacognition, intrusive thoughts and auditory hallucinations. *Psychological Medicine* **28**, 1199–1208.

Bannister, D. & Fransella, F. (1966). A grid test of schizophrenic thought disorder. *British Journal of Social and Clinical Psychology* **5**, 95–102.

Barham, P. (1993). *Schizophrenia and human value.* London: Free Association Books.

Barker, G. (1951). *The dead seagull.* New York: Farrar, Strauss and Young.

Barnes, M. & Burke, J. (1973). *Two accounts of a journey through madness.* Harmondsworth: Penguin.

Baxter, D. & Appleby, L. (1999). Case register study of suicide risk in mental disorders. *British Journal of Psychiatry* **175**, 322–326.

Bebbington, P. & Kuipers, L. (1994). The predictive utility of expressed emotion in schizophrenia – an aggregate analysis. *Psychological Medicine* **24**, 707–718.

Beck, A. (1976). *Cognitive therapy and the emotional disorders.* New York: International Universities Press.

Beck, A.T. (1983). Cognitive therapy of depression: New perspectives. In P.J. Clayton & J.E. Barrett (eds) *Treatment of depression: Old controversies and new approaches.* New York: Raven Press.

Beiser, M., Erickson, D., Fleing, J.A.E. & Iacono, W.G. (1993). Establishing the onset of psychotic illness. *American Journal of Psychiatry* **150**, 1237–1243.

Bentall, R. P. (1990). *Reconstructing schizophrenia.* London: Routledge.

Bentall, R.P., Haddock, G. & Slade, P.D. (1994). Cognitive-behavioural therapy for persistent auditory hallucinations: from theory to therapy. *Behaviour Therapy* **25**, 51–66.

Bentall, R.P., Jackson, H.F. & Pilgrim, D. (1988). Abandoning the concept of "schizophrenia": Some implications of validity arguments for psychological research into psychotic phenomena. *British Journal of Clinical Psychology* **27**, 303–324.

Bentall, R.P., Kinderman, P. & Kaney, S. (1994). Self, attributional processes and abnormal beliefs: towards a model of persecutory delusions. *Behaviour Research and Therapy* **32**, 331–341.

Berndt, T.J. (1979). Developmental changes in conformity to peers and parents. *Developmental Psychology* **15**, 608–616.

Bezirganian, S., Cohen, P. & Brook, J.S. (1993). The impact of mother-child interaction on the development of borderline personality disorder. *American Journal of Psychiatry* **150**, 1836–1842.

Birchwood, M. & Tarrier, N. (1992). *Innovations in the psychological management of schizophrenia; assesment, treatment and services.* Chichester: Wiley.

Birchwood, M., Fowler, D. & Jackson, C. (2000). *Early Intervention in psychosis: A guide to concepts, evidence and interventions.* Chichester, UK: Wiley.

Birchwood, M., Iqbal, Z., Chadwick, P. & Trower, P. (2000a). Cognitive approach to depression and suicidal thinking in psychosis. *British Journal of Psychiatry* **177**, 516–521.

Birchwood, M., Mason, R., MacMillan, F. & Healy, J. (1993). Depression, demoralisation and control over psychotic illness: a comparison of depressed and non-depressed patients with a chronic psychosis. *Psychological Medicine* **23**, 387–395.

Birchwood, M., McGorry, P.D. & Jackson, H. (1997). Early intervention in schizophrenia (Editorial). *British Journal of Psychiatry* **170**, 2–5.

Birchwood, M., Meaden, A., Trower, P., Gilbert, P. & Plaistow, J. (2000b). The power and omnipotence of voices: subordination and entrapment by voices and significant others. *Psychological Medicine* **30**, 337–344.

Blatt, S.J. & Homann, E. (1992). Parent–child interaction in the aetiology of dependent and self-critical depression. *Clinical Psychology Review* **12**, 47–91.

Bleuler, E. (1911). *Dementia praecox or the group of schizophrenias.* (Translated in 1950.) New York: International Universities Press.

Blos, P. (1962). *On adolescence.* London: Collier-Macmillan.

Booth, A., Shelly, G., Mazur, A., Tharp, G. & Kittok, R. (1989). Testosterone, and winning and losing in human competition. *Human Behaviour* **23**, 556–571.

Bowlby, J. (1969). *Attachment and loss: Vol 1 Attachment.* New York: Basic Books.

Boyle, M. (1990). *Schizophrenia – a scientific delusion?* London: Routledge.

Breggin, P.R. (1993). *Toxic psychiatry: drugs and electroconvulsive therapy: the truth and the better alternatives.* London: Harper Collins.

Brentano, F. (1995/1874). *Psychology from an empirical standpoint.* London: Routledge.

Brookes-Gunn, J. & Warren, M. (1985). The effects of delayed menarche in different contexts: dance and nondance students. *Journal of Youth and Adolescence* **11**, 285–300.

Brown, G.W. & Birley, J.L.T. (1968). Crisis and life-changes and the onset of schizophrenia. *Journal of Health and Social Behaviour* **9**, 203–214.

Chadwick, P. & Birchwood, M. (1994). The omnipotence of voices: a cognitive approach to auditory hallucinations. *British Journal of Psychiatry* **164**, 190–201.

Chadwick, P.D.J. & Birchwood, M.J. (1995). The omnipotence of voices II: The beliefs about voices questionnaire. *British Journal of Psychiatry* **166**, 11–19.

Chadwick, P.J., Birchwood, M. & Trower, P. (1996). *Cognitive therapy for delusions, voices and paranoia.* Chichester: Wiley.

Chadwick, P., Trower, P. & Dagnan, D. (1999). Measuring negative person evaluations: the Evaluative Beliefs Scale. *Cognitive Therapy and Research* **23**, 549–559.

Ciompi, L. (1980). The natural history of schizophrenia in the long term. *British Journal of Psychiatry* **136**, 421–436.

Ciompi, L. (1981). The social outcome of schizophrenia. In J.K. Wing, P. Kielholtz & W.M. Zinn (Eds) *Rehabilitation of patients with schizophrenia and depression.* Bern: Hans Huber.

Clark, D.M. (2001). A cognitive perspective on social phobia. In W.R. Crozier & L.E. Alden (Eds) *International handbook of social anxiety: Concepts, research and interventions relating to the self and shyness*. Chichester: Wiley.

Coleman, J.C. (1974). *Relationships in adolescence*. London: Routledge and Kegan Paul.

Coleman, J.C. (1979). *The school years*. London: Methuen.

Coleman, J.C. & Hendry, L. (1990). *The nature of adolescence* (2nd Ed). London: Routledge.

Cooley, C.H. (1922). *Human nature and the social order*. New York: Scribner's. (Originally published in 1902.)

Corcoran, R., Cahill, C. & Frith, C.D. (1997). The appreciation of visual jokes in people with schizophrenia: a study of 'mentalizing' ability. *Schizophrenia Research* **24**, 319–327.

Crow, T.J. (1994). Prenatal exposure to influenza as a cause of schizophrenia: there are inconsistencies and contradictions in the evidence. *British Journal of Psychiatry* **164**, 588–592.

Crow, T.J., Macmillan, J.F., Johnson, A.L. & Johnstone, E.C. (1986). The Northwick Park study of first episodes of schizophrenia II: A controlled trial of prophylactic neuroleptic treatment. *British Journal of Psychiatry* **148**, 120–127.

Cutting, J. (1987). The phenomenology of acute organic psychosis: Comparison with acute schizophrenia. *British Journal of Psychiatry* **151**, 324–332.

Dagnan, D., Trower, P. & Gilbert, P. (2002). Measuring vulnerability to threats to self-construction: The Self and Other Scale. *Psychology and Psychotherapy: Theory, Research and Practice* **75**, 279–293.

Davidson, L. (in press). *Living outside mental illness: Qualitative studies of recovery from schizophrenia*. New York: New York University Press.

Davidson, L. & Strauss, J.S. (1992). Sense of self in recovery from severe mental illness. *British Journal of Medical Psychology* **65**, 131–145.

Davidson, L., Stayner, D.A., Chinman, M.J., Lambert, S. & Sledge, W.H. (2000). Preventing relapse and readmission in psychosis: using patients' subjective experience in designing clinical interventions. In B. V. Martindale, A. Bateman, M. Crowe and F. Margison (Eds) *Psychosis: Psychological approaches and their effectiveness*. London: Gaskell.

Davison, K. (1983). Schizophrenia-like psychoses associated with organic cerebral disorders: A review. *Psychiatric Developments* **1**, 1–34.

Davison, K. & Bagley, C.R. (1969). Schizophrenia-like psychoses associated with organic disorders of the Central Nervous System: A review of the literature. In R.N. Herrington (Ed) Current problems in neuropsychiatry: schizophrenia, epilepsy and the temporal lobe. *British Journal of Psychiatry* (special publication no. 4).

Dexter-Smith, S., Trower, P., Oyebode, J. & Dagan, D. (in press). The self and other scale. *Journal of Rational-Emotive and Cognitive-Behavior Therapy*.

Dryden, W. (1990). *Rational emotive counselling in action*. London: Sage

Dryden, W. (1995). *Brief rational emotive behaviour therapy*. (Wiley series in brief therapy and counselling). Chichester: Wiley.

Duval, S. & Wicklund, R.A. (1972). *A theory of objective self-awareness*. London: Academic Press.

Edwards, E. & Potter, J. (1992). *Discursive psychology: Inquiries in social construction*. London: Sage.

Egeland, B., Pianta, R. & O'Brian, M.A. (1993). Maternal Intrusiveness in infancy and child maltreatment in early school years. *Development and Psychopathology* **5**, 359–370.

Elkind, D. (1967). Strategic interactions in early adolescence In W. Damon (Ed) *Social and personality development: Essays on the growth of the child*. New York: Norton.

Elkind, D. (1979). Imaginary audience behaviour in children and adolescents. *Developmental Psychology* **15**, 13–44.

Elkind, D. & Bowen, R. (1979). Imaginary audience behaviour in children and adolescents. *Developmental Psychology* **15**, 38–44.

Ellis, A. (1994). *Reason and emotion in psychotherapy.* (Revised and expanded edition.) New York: Birch Lane Press.

Enright, R., Lapsley, D. & Shukla, D. (1979). Adolescent egocentrism in early and late adolescence. *Adolescence* **14**, 687–695.

Enright, R., Shukla, D. & Lapsley, D. (1980). Adolescent egocentrism–sociocentrism and self-consciousness. *Journal of Youth and Adolescence* **9**, 101–116.

Estroff, S.E. (1989). Self, identity, and subjective experiences of schizophrenia: in search of the subject. *Schizophrenia Bulletin* **15**, 189–198.

Evans, S. & Hodges, J.K. (1984). Reproductive status of adult daughters in family groups of common marmosets. *Folia Primatologica* **42**, 127–133.

Feinberg, I. (1997). Schizophrenia as an emergent disorder of late brain maturation. In M.S. Keshavan & R.M. Murray (Eds) *Neurodevelopment and adult psychopathology.* Cambridge: Cambridge University Press.

Frith, C.D. (1979). Consciousness, information-processing and schizophrenia. *British Journal of Psychiatry* **134**, 225–235.

Frith, C.D. (1992). *The cognitive neuropsychology of schizophrenia.* Hillsdale, New Jersey: Lawrence Erlbaum Associates.

Garety, P.A. & Freeman, D. (1999). Cognitive approaches to delusions: A critical review of theories and evidence. *British Journal of Clinical Psychology* **38**, 113–154.

Garron, D.C. (1973). Huntington's chorea and schizophrenia. In A. Barbeau, T.N. Chase, and A. Aulson (Eds) *Advances in neurology* (729–734). New York: Raven Press.

Gilbert, P. (1992). *The evolution of powerlessness.* Hove, UK: Erlbaum.

Gilbert, P. (1993). Defence and safety: their role in social behaviour and psychopathology. *British Journal of Medical Psychology* **32**, 131–153.

Gilbert, P. & Trower, P. (2001). Evolution and process in social anxiety. In W.R. Crozier and L.E. Alden (Eds) *International handbook of social anxiety: Concepts, research and interventions relating to the self and shyness.* Chichester: Wiley.

Gilbert, P., Price, J. & Allan, S. (1995). Social comparison, social attractiveness and evolution: How might they be related? *New Ideas in Psychology* **13**, 149–165.

Goffman, E. (1959). *The presentation of self in everyday life.* Harmondsworth: Penguin.

Goffman, E. (1971). *The presentation of self in everyday life* (2nd edition). Harmondsworth: Penguin.

Gollwitzer, P.M. & Wicklund, R.A. (1985). Self-symbolising and the neglect of others' perspectives. *Journal of Personality and Social Psychology* **48**, 702–715.

Goodman, S.H. & Brumley, H.E. (1990). Schizophrenic and depressed mothers – relational deficits in parenting. *Developmental Psychology* **26**, 21–39.

Gray, J.A. (1993). Consciousness, schizophrenia and scientific theory. In *Experimental and theoretical studies of consciousness* (Ciba foundation symposium 174), 263–281. Chichester: Wiley.

Gray, J.A., Feldon, J., Rawlins, J.N.P., Hemsley, D.R. & Smith, A.D. (1991). The neuropsychology of schizophrenia. *Behavioural Brain Sciences* **14**, 1–20.

Grey, N., Holmes, E. & Brewin, C.R. (2001). Peritraumatic emotional "hotspots" in memory. *Behavioural and Cognitive Psychotherapy* **29**, 367–372.

Guevara, E. (1963). Letter to Pablo Gonzales. In *Episodes of the Cuban revolutionary war 1956–58.* (English translation published 1996). New York: Pathfinder Press.

Gunnel, D., Lopatatzidis, A., Dorling, D., Wehner, H., Southall, H. & Frankel, S.

(1999). Suicide and unemployment in young people – analysis of trends in England and Wales, 1921–1995. *British Journal of Psychiatry* **175**, 263–270.

Haddock, G. & Slade, P.D. (1996). *Cognitive behavioural interventions with psychotic disorders*. London: Routledge.

Haddock, G., Wolfenden, M., Lowens, I., Tarrier, N. & Bentall, R.P. (1995). Effect of emotional salience on thought-disorder in patients with schizophrenia. *British Journal of Psychiatry* **167**, 618–620.

Häfner, H., Maurer, K., Löffler, W. & Riecher-Rössler, A. (1993a). The influence of age and sex on the onset and course of schizophrenia. *British Journal of Psychiatry* **162**, 80–87.

Häfner, H., Reicher-Rössler, A., An Der Heiden, W., Maurer, K., Fätkenheuer, B. & Löffler, W. (1993b). Generating and testing a causal explanation of the gender difference in age at first onset of schizophrenia. *Psychological Medicine* **23**, 925–940.

Harré, R. (1979). *Social being: a theory for social psychology*. Oxford: Blackwell.

Harré, R. (1986). *Varieties of realism: a rationale for the natural sciences*. Oxford: Blackwell.

Harré, R. & Gillet, G. (1994). *The discursive mind*. London: Sage.

Harré, R. & Secord, P.F. (1972). *The explanation of social behaviour*. Oxford: Blackwell.

Harrison, P.J. (1999). The neuropathology of schizophrenia: a critical review of the data and their interpretation. *Brain* **122**, 593–624.

Harrop, C.E. (2000). *Schizophrenia: adolescent development and self-construction*. Unpublished PhD manuscript, University of Birmingham, UK.

Harrop, C.E. (2002). The development of schizophrenia at late adolescence. *Current Psychiatry Reports* **4**, 293–298.

Harrop, C.E. & Trower, P. (2001). Why does schizophrenia develop at late adolescence? *Clinical Psychology Review* **21**, 241–266.

Harrop, C.E., Trower, P. & Mitchell, I.J. (1996). Does the biology go around the symptoms? A Copernican shift in schizophrenia paradigms. *Clinical Psychology Review* **16**, 641–659.

Hashemi, A.H. & Cochrane, R. (1999). Expressed emotion and schizophrenia: a review of studies across cultures. *International Review of Psychiatry* **11**, 219–224.

Hemsley, D.R. (1987). An experimental psychological model for schizophrenia. In H. Häfner, W.F. Gattaz and W. Janzarik (Eds) *Schizophrenia, concepts, vulnerability and intervention*. Heidelberg: Springer.

Hendry, L.B. (1983). *Growing up and going out*. Aberdeen: Aberdeen University Press.

Higgins, E.T. (1987). Self-discrepency: A theory relating self and affect. *Psychological Review* **94**, 319–340.

Hingley, S.M. (1992). Psychological theories of delusional thinking: In search of integration. *British Journal of Medical Psychology* **65**, 347–356.

Hogarty, G.E. & Flesher, S. (1999). Developmental theory for a Cognitive Enhancement Therapy of schizophrenia. *Schizophrenia Bulletin* **25**, 677–692.

Hope, D.A., Gansler, D.A. & Heimberg, R.G. (1989). Attentional focus and causal attributions in social phobia – Implications from social psychology. *Clinical Psychology Review* **9**, 49–60.

Horney, K. (1950). *Neurosis and human growth*. New York: Norton.

Huber, J. (1997). *The effect of threats to self-construction in high and low Expressed Emotion environments*. Unpublished dissertation: University of Birmingham.

Hunter, J.A. (1991). A comparison of the psychosocial maladjustment of adult males and females sexually molested as children. *Journal of Interpersonal Violence* **6**, 205–217.

Ingram, R.E. (1990). Self-focused attention in clinical disorders: review and a conceptual model. *Psychological Bulletin* **107**, 156–176.

Inhelder, B. & Piaget, J. (1958). *The growth of logical thinking from childhood and adolescence.* New York: Basic Books.

Iversen, S.D. (1995). Interactions between excitatory amino acids and dopamine systems in the forebrain: implications for schizophrenia and Parkinson's disease. *Behavioural Pharmacology* **6**, 478–491.

Jablensky, A. (1997). The 100-year epidemiology of schizophrenia. *Schizophrenia Research* **28**, 111–125.

Jablensky, A. & Cole, S.W. (1997). Is the earlier age of onset of schizophrenia in males a confounded finding? *British Journal of Psychiatry* **170**, 234–240.

Jackson, H.F. (1990). Are there biological markers for schizophrenia? In R. Bentall (Ed) *Reconstructing schizophrenia.* London: Routledge.

Jackson, H.J., McGorry, P.D. & McKenzie, D. (1994). The reliability of DSM-III prodromal symptoms in the first episode psychotic patients. *Acta Psychiatrica Scandinavica* **90**, 375–378.

James, W. (1891). *The principles of psychology* (Volume 1). London: McMillan.

Jernigan, T.I., Zatz, I.M., Moses, J.A. & Cardellins, J.P. (1982). Computed tomography in schizophrenics and normal volunteers: I Fluid Volume. *Archives of General Psychiatry* **39**, 771–773.

Johnstone, E.C., Crow, T.J., Frith, C.D., Husband, J. & Kreel, L. (1976). Cerebral ventricle size and cognitive impairment in schizophrenia. *Lancet* **ii**, 924–926.

Kafka, F. (1931). *The Burrow (Der Bau).* English translation published 1992 in *Metamorphosis and other stories.* Minerva: London.

Kandel, E.R., Schwartz, J.H. & Jessel, T.M. (1989). *Principles of neural science* (3rd edition). New York: Elsevier.

Keshavan, M.S. & Hogarty, G.E. (1999). Brain maturation process and delayed onset in schizophrenia. *Development and Psychopathology* **11**, 525–543.

Keshavan, M.S., Haas, G.L., Kahn, C.E. (1998). Superior temporal gyrus and the course of early schizophrenia: progressive, static or reversible? *Journal of Psychiatric Research* **32**, 161–167.

Kingdon, D.G. & Turkington, D. (1997). Cognitive behaviour therapy of schizophrenia; integration and collaboration. In C. Mace & F. Margerison (Eds) *The Psychotherapy of psychosis.* London: Gaskell.

Kohut, H. (1972). Thoughts on narcissism and narcissistic rage. *Psychoanalytic Study of the Child* **27**, 360–400.

Kohut, H. (1977). *The restoration of the self.* New York: International Universities Press.

Kotrla, K.J., Sater, A.K. & Weinberger, D.R. (1997). Neuropathology, neurodevelopment and schizophrenia. In M.S. Keshavan & R.M. Murray (Eds) *Neurodevelopment and adult psychopathology.* Cambridge, UK: Cambridge University Press.

Kraepelin, E. (1896). *Psychiatrie* (5th edition). Leipzig: Barth.

Kroger, J. (1996). *Identity in adolescence: the balance between self and other.* London: Routledge.

Laing, R.D. (1965). *The divided self: an existential study in sanity and madness.* London: Penguin.

Laing, R.D. (1969). *Knots.* London: Penguin.

Lamborn, S.D., Mounts, N.S., Steinberg, L.D. & Dornbusch, S.M. (1991). Patterns of competence and adjustment among adolescents from authoritative, authoritarian, indulgent and neglectful families. *Child Development* **62**, 1049–1065.

Lapsley, D.K. & Murphy, M.N. (1985). Another look at the theoretical assumptions of adolescent egocentrism. *Developmental Review* **5**, 201–217.

Lapsley, D.K., Milstead, M., Quintana, S.M., Flannery, D. & Buss, R.B. (1986).

Adolescent egocentrism and formal operations: tests of a theoretical assumption. *Developmental Psychology* **22**, 800–807.

Larsen, T.K., Johannessen, J.O., McGlashan, T., Hroneland, M., Mardal, S. & Vaglum, P. (2000). Can duration of untreated psychosis be reduced? In M. Birchwood, D. Fowler & C. Jackson (Eds) *Early Intervention in psychosis: A guide to concepts, evidence and interventions.* Chichester: Wiley.

Lawrie, S.M., Whalley, H.C., Abukmeil, S.S., Kestelman, J.N., Miller, P., Best, J.J.K., Owens, D.G.C. & Johnstone, E.C. (2002). Temporal lobe volume changes in people at high risk of schizophrenia with psychotic symptoms. *British Journal of Psychiatry* **181**, 138–143.

Lazarus, A.A. (1992). Clinical and therapeutic effectiveness. In J. Zeig (Ed) *The evolution of psychotherapy.* New York: Bruner-Mazel.

Leary, M.R. (1995). *Self-presentation: Impression management and interpersonal behavior.* Madison, Wisconsin: Brown and Benchmark.

Leff, J.P. & Vaughn, C.E. (1985). *Expressed Emotion in families.* New York: Guilford Press.

Levin, D. (1992). *Theories of the self.* Washington: Hemisphere.

Lewis, C.S. (1961). *A grief observed.* London: Faber & Faber.

Loebel, A.D., Lieberman, J.A., Alvir, J.M.J., Mayerhoff, D.I., Geisler, S.H. & Szmanski, S.R. (1992). Duration of psychosis and outcome in first episode schizophrenia. *American Journal of Psychiatry* **149**, 1183–1188.

Maher, B.A. (1974). Delusional thinking and perceptual disorder. *Journal of Individual Psychology* **30**, 98–113.

Markus, H. & Nurius, P. (1986). Possible selves. *American Psychologist* **41**, 954–969.

Marshall, R. (1990). The genetics of schizophrenia; axiom or hypothesis? In R. Bentall (Ed) *Reconstructing schizophrenia.* London: Routledge.

Maslow, A.H. (1954). *Motivation and personality.* New York: Harper.

Masterson, J.F. (1989). *The search for the real self.* New York: Free Press.

Mazur, A. & Lamb, T.A. (1980). Testosterone, status and mood in human males. *Hormones and Behaviour* **14**, 236–246.

McCulloch, G. (1994). *Using Sartre: An analytical introduction to early Sartrean themes.* London: Routledge.

McGorry, P.D. & Jackson, H.J. (1999). *The recognition and management of early psychosis: a preventative approach.* New York: Cambridge University Press.

McGorry, P.D., Chanen, A., McCarthy, E., Vanriel, R., McKenzie, D. & Singh, B.H. (1991). Post traumatic stress disorder following recent onset psychosis – an unrecognised postpsychotic syndrome. *Journal of Nervous and Mental Disease* **179**, 253–258.

McGorry, P.D., Edwards, J. & Pennell, K. (1999). Sharpening the focus: early intervention in the real world. In P.D. McGorry & H.J. Jackson (Eds) *The recognition and management of early psychosis: A preventative approach.* New York: Cambridge University Press.

McGorry, P.D., McFarlane, C., Patton, G.C., Bell, R., Hibbert, M.E., Jackson, H.J. & Bowes, G. (1995). The prevalence of prodromal features of schizophrenia in adolescence: a preliminary survey. *Acta Psychiatrica Scandinavica* **92**, 241–249.

McGuire, T.G. (1991). Measuring the economic costs of schizophrenia. *Schizophrenia Bulletin* **17**, 375–388.

Mead, G.H. (1934). *Mind, self and society.* Chicago: University of Chicago Press.

Mischel, T. (1975). *Human action.* New York: Academic Press.

Mitchell, I.J., Cooper, A.J., Brown, G.D.A. & Waters, C.M. (1995). Apoptosis of neurons in the vestibular nuclei of adult mice results from prolonged change in the external environment. *Neuroscience Letters* **198**, 153–156.

Mitchell, I.J., Cooper, A.J., Griffiths, M.R. & Barber, D.J. (1998). Phencyclidine and corticosteroids induce apoptosis of a subpopulation of striatal neurons: A neural substrate for psychosis? *Neuroscience* **84**, 489–501.

Mitchell, I.J., Lawson, S., Moser, B., Laidlaw, S.M., Cooper, A.J., Walkinshaw, G. & Waters, C.M. (1994). Glutamate-induced apoptosis results in a loss of striatal neurons in the Parkinsonian rat. *Neuroscience* **63**, 1–5.

Mitchell, P., Robinson, E.J., Isaacs, J.E. & Nye, R.M. (1996). Contamination in reasoning about false belief: an instance of realist bias in adults but not children. *Cognition* **59**, 1–21.

Mollon, P. (1993). *The fragile self: The structure of narcissistic disturbance.* London: Whurr Publishers.

Montemayor, R. & Hansom, E. (1985). A naturalistic view of conflict between adolescents and their parents and siblings. *Journal of Early Adolescence* **5**, 23–30.

Morf, C.C. & Rhodewalt, F. (1993). Narcissism and self-evaluation maintenance: Explorations in object relations. *Personality and Social Psychology Bulletin* **19**, 668–676.

Morrison, A.P. (2001). The interpretation of intrusions in psychosis: an integrative cognitive approach to hallucinations and delusions. *Behavioural and Cognitive Psychotherapy* **29**, 257–276.

Morrissey, S. (1984). *Heaven knows I'm miserable now* [Recorded by The Smiths]. On Hatful of Hollow [CD]. London: Warner Chappell Music.

Morrissey, S. (1986). *There is a light that never goes out* [Recorded by the Smiths] On The Queen is Dead [CD]. London: Warner Chappell Music.

Mueser, K.T., Salyers, M.P., Mueser, P.R. (2001). A prospective analysis of work in schizophrenia. *Schizophrenia Bulletin* **27**, 281–296.

Nuechterlein, K.H. (1987). Vulnerability models for schizophrenia: state of the art. In H. Hafner, W.F. Gattaz & W. Janarzik (Eds) *Search for the causes of schizophrenia.* Berlin: Springer.

Nyback, H., Wiesel, F.A., Bergren, B.M. & Hindmarsh, T. (1982). Computed tomography of the brain in patients with acute psychosis and in healthy volunteers. *Acta Psychiatrica Scandinavica* **65**, 403–411.

Pam, A. (1990). A critique of the scientific status of biological psychiatry. *Acta Psychiatrica Scandinavica Supp* **362**, 82, 1–36.

Peters, E.R., Joseph, S.A. & Garety, P.A. (1999). Measurement of delusional ideation in the normal population: introducing the PDI. *Schizophrenia Bulletin* **25**, 553–576.

Phillips, L.J., Velakoulis, D., Pantelis, C., Wood, S., Yeaun, H.P., Yung, A.R., Desmond, P., Brewer, W. & McGorry, P. (2002). Non-reduction of hippocampal volume is associated with higher risk of psychosis. *Schizophrenia Research* **58**, 145–158.

Rector, N.A. & Beck, A.T. (2002). A clinical review of cognitive therapy for schizophrenia. *Current Psychiatry Reports* **4**, 284–292.

Reed, D. (1977). *Anna.* London: Penguin.

Reicher-Rössler, A., Häfner, H., Staumbaum, M., Maurer, K. & Schmidt, R. (1994). Can estradiol modulate schizophrenic symptomatology? *Schizophrenia Bulletin* **20**, 203–214.

Roberts, G.W. & Bruton, C.J. (1990). Notes from the graveyard: schizophrenia and neuropathology. *Neuropathology and Applied Neurobiology* **16**, 3–16.

Roger, D. & Najarian, B. (1989). The construction and validation of a new scale for measuring emotional control. *Personality and Individual Differences* **10**, 845–853.

Roger, D. & Schapals, T. (1996). Repression – sensitisation and emotion control. *Current Psychology: Developmental, Learning, Personality and Social* **15**, 30–37.

Rogers, C.R. (1967). *On becoming a person: a therapist's view of psychotherapy* (2nd ed). London: Constable.

Romme, M.A.J., Honig, A., Noorthoorn, E.O. & Escher, D. (1992) MAC: Coping with hearing voices: an emancipatory approach. *British Journal of Psychiatry* **161**, 99–103.

Rose, S. (1984). Disordered molecules and diseased minds. *Journal of Psychiatric Research* **18**, 351–359.

Rose, S., Kamin, L.T. & Lewontin, R.C. (1984). *Not in our genes.* London: Penguin.

Rosenberg, M. (1979). *Conceiving the self.* New York: Basic Books.

Russell, B. (1930). *The conquest of happiness.* London: Unwin Hyman Ltd.

Rutter, M., Graham, P., Chadwick, O. & Yule, W. (1976). Adolescent turmoil: fact or fiction. *Journal of Child Psychology and Psychiatry* **17**, 35–56.

Ryan, R.M. & Lynch, J.H. (1989). Emotional autonomy versus detachment: Revisiting the vicissitudes of adolescence and young adulthood. *Child Development* **60**, 340–356.

Salkovskis, P.M. & Campbell, P. (1994). Thought suppression induces intrusion in naturally-occurring negative intrusive thoughts. *Behaviour Research and Therapy* **32**, 1–8.

Sapolsky, R. (2000). The possiblity of neurotoxicity in the hippocampus in major depression: a primer of neuron death. *Biological Psychiatry* **48**, 755–765.

Sapolsky, R.M., Uno, H., Rebert, C.S. & Finch, C.E. (1990). Hippocampal damage associated with prolonged glucocorticoid exposure in primates. *Journal of Neuroscience* **10**, 2897–2902.

Sarbin, T.R. & Mancuso, J.C. (1980). *Schizophrenia: medical diagnosis or moral verdict?* New York: Pergamon.

Sartorius, N., Jablensky, A., Korten, A., Ernberg, G., Anker, M., Cooper, J.E. & Day, R. (1986). Early manifestations and first-contact incidences of schizophrenia in different cultures. *Psychological Medicine* **16**, 909–928.

Sartre, J.-P. (1943/1957). *Being and nothingness.* London: Methuen.

Sartre, J.-P. (1962). *The reprieve.* Harmondsworth, Middlesex: Penguin.

Schlenker, B.R. (1980). *Impression management: The self-concept, social identity, and interpersonal relations.* Monterey, California: Brooks/Cole.

Schultz, S.C., Koller, M.M., Kishore, P.R., Hamer, R.M., Gehl, J.J. & Friedel, R.O. (1983). Ventricular enlargement in teenage patients with schizophrenia spectrum disorder. *American Journal of Psychiatry* **140**, 1592–1596.

Seeman, P., Lee, T., Chau-Wong, T. & Wong, K. (1976). Antipsychotic drug doses and neuroleptic/dopamine receptors. *Nature* **261**, 717–718.

Segal, Z.V., Williams, J.M.G. & Teasdale, J.D. (2002). *A new approach to preventing relapse.* New York: Guilford.

Shelton, R.C. & Weinberger, D.R. (1986). X-ray computerised tomography studies in schizophrenia: A review and synthesis. In H.A. Nasrallah & D.R. Weinberger (Eds) *The neurology of schizophrenia*, pp 207–250. Amsterdam: Elsevier Science Publishers.

Silverberg, S.B. & Steinberg, L. (1987). Adolescent autonomy, parent adolescent conflict, and parental well-being. *Journal of Youth and Adolescence* **16**, 293–312.

Sims, A. (1988). *Symptoms in the mind.* London: Baillière Tindall.

Slade, P.D. & Bentall, R.P. (1988). *Sensory deception: a scientific analysis of hallucination.* London: Croom Helm.

Slater, E. & Beard, A.W. (1963). The schizophrenia-like psychoses of epilepsy: Discussion and conclusions. *British Journal of Psychiatry* **109**, 143–150.

Sloviter, R.J., Valiquette, G., Abrams, G.M., Ronk, E.C., Sollas, A.I., Paul, L.A. & Neubort, S.L. (1989). Selective loss of hippocampal granule cells in the mature rat brain after adrenalectomy. *Science* **243**, 535–538.

Smetana, J.G. (1989). Adolescents and parents reasoning about actual family conflict. *Child Development* **60**, 1052–1067.

Smith, J., Birchwood, M., Cochrane, R. & George, S. (1993). The need for care of high and low expressed emotion families. *Social Psychiatry and Psychiatric Epidemiology* **281**, 11–16.

Snyder, C.R., Higgins, R.L. & Stucky, R.J. (1983). *Excuses: masquerades in search of grace.* New York: Wiley.

Steinberg, L. (1981). Transformations in family relations at puberty. *Developmental Psychology* **17**, 833–840.

Steinberg, L. (1988). Reciprocal relation between parent child distance and pubertal maturation. *Developmental Psychology* **24**, 122–128.

Steinberg, L. & Silverberg, S. (1986). The vicissitudes of autonomy in early adolescence. *Child Development* **57**, 841–851.

Steinberg, L.D. (1987). The impact of puberty on family relations: effects of pubertal status and pubertal timing. *Developmental Psychology* **23**, 451–460.

Stevens, R. (1996). (Ed) *Understanding the self.* London: Sage in association with the Open University.

Strauss, J.S. & Carpenter, W.T. (1977). Prediction of outcome in schizophrenia. *Archives of General Psychiatry* **30**, 429–434.

Szasz, T.S. (1974). *The myth of mental illness.* New York: Harper & Rowe.

Szasz, T.S. (1987). *Insanity; the idea and its consequences.* New York: Wiley.

Tarrier, N., Barrowclough, C., Porceddu, K. & Watts, S. (1988). The assessment of psychophysiological reactivity to the expressed emotion of the relatives of schizophrenic patients. *British Journal of Psychiatry* **152**, 618–624.

Taylor, P.J. & Gunn, J. (1999). Homicides by people with mental illness: myth and reality. *British Journal of Psychiatry* **174**, 9–14.

Taylor, R., Ward, A. & Newburn, T. (1995). *The day of the Hillsborough disaster: a narrative account.* Liverpool: Liverpool University Press.

Thierry, A.M., Tassin, J.P., Blanc, G. & Glowinski, J. (1976). Selective activation of the mesocortical DA system by stress. *Nature* **263**, 242–244.

Thomas, E.J. (1968). Role theory, personality and the individual. In E. Borgetta and W. Lambert (Eds) *Handbook of personality theory and research.* Chicago: Rand McNally.

Trower, P. (1984). A radical critique and reformulation: from organism to agent. In P. Trower (Ed) *Radical approaches to social-skills training.* Beckenham, Kent: Croom Helm.

Trower, P. (2003) Theoretical developments in REBT as applied to schizophrenia. In W. Dryden (Ed.), *Rational Emotive Behaviour Therapy: Theoretical developments.* London: Brunner-Routledge.

Trower, P. & Chadwick, P. (1995). Pathways to the defence of the self: A theory of two types of paranoia. *Clinical Psychology, Science and Practice* **2**, 263–278.

Trower, P. & Gilbert, P. (1989). New theoretical conceptions of social anxiety and social phobia. *Clinical Psychology Review* **9**, 19–35.

Trower, P., Bryant, B. & Argyle, M. (1978). *Social skills and mental health.* London: Methuen.

Trower, P., Casey, A. & Dryden, W. (1988). *Cognitive behavioural counselling in action.* London: Sage.

Trower, P., Gilbert, P. & Sherling, G. (1990). Social anxiety, evolution, and self-presentation. In M. Leitenberg (Ed.) *Handbook of evaluation anxiety.* New York: Plenum Press.

Uno, H., Eisele, S., Sakai, A., Shelton, S., Baker, E., DeJesus, O. & Holden, J. (1994). Neurotoxicity of glucocorticoids in the primate brain. *Hormones and Behaviour* **28**, 336–348.

Van Deurzen, E. (1998). *Passion and paradox in psychotherapy: an existential approach to therapy and counselling.* London: Sage.

Vaughn, C.E. & Leff, J.P. (1976). The influence of family and social factors on the course of psychiatric illness: a comparison of schizophrenic and depressed neurotic patients. *British Journal of Psychiatry* **129**, 125–137.

Verdoux, H., Maurice-Tison, S., Gay, B., VanOs, J., Salamon, R. & Bourgeois, M. (1998). A survey of delusional ideation in primary care patients. *Psychological Medicine* **28**, 127–134.

Watzlawick, P. (1990). *Munchhausen's Pigtail. Psychotherapy and 'reality': essays and lectures.* New York: Norton & Company.

Wearden, A.J., Tarrier, N., Barrowclough, C., Zastowny, T.R. & Rahill, A.A. (2000). A review of expressed emotion research in health care. *Clinical Psychology Review* **20**, 633–666.

Weinberger, D.R. (1987). Implications of normal brain development for the pathogenesis of schizophrenia. *Archives of General Psychiatry* **44**, 660–669.

Weinberger, D.R., DeLisi, L.E., Perman, G.P., Targum, S., Wyatt, R.J. (1982). Computed tomography in schizophreniform disorder and other acute psychiatric disorders. *Archives of General Psychiatry* **39**, 778–783.

Wells, A. (2000). *Emotional disorders and metacognition: Innovative cognitive therapy.* Chichester: Wiley.

Wing, J.K., Cooper, J.E. & Sartorius, N. (1974). *The measurement and classification of psychiatric syndromes.* Cambridge: Cambridge University Press.

Winnicott, D.W. (1960). Ego distortion in terms of true and false self. In *The Maturational processes and the facilitating environment.* London: Hogarth.

World Health Organization (1992). *The ICD-10 Classification of Mental and Behavioural Disorders: Clinical descriptions and diagnostic guidelines.* Geneva: World Health Organization.

Wynne, L. & Singer, M. (1963). Thought disorder and family relations of schizophrenics: 1. A research strategy. *Archives of General Psychiatry* **9**, 191–198.

Yalom, I.D. (1980). *Existential psychotherapy.* New York: Basic Books.

AUTHOR INDEX

SUBJECT INDEX